T0374281

Mary Jo Hoffman was a Woman of Valor. Her life story, as told in *Life After*, should inspire faith and selflessness in all who read it.

Jim Witt
Pastor

Life After is a touching biography of faith and courage. Mary Jo's story is a love story – between a woman and God, between a woman and her husband, the author. *Life After* inspires with every turn of the page.

Wendy Wright
President, Concerned Women for America

You cannot read *Life After* and be unaffected. It brings tears and laughter not only to those of us who knew Mary Jo Hoffman, as I did, but for anyone who desires to live a life of character. Read *Life After* and be blessed.

Ta'Mara Hanscom
Author, The Caselli Family Series

As it has been said of Mary Jo Hoffman, "Her words were like thunder because her life was like lightning." She was a woman of great faith, and she left this world for the next with courage and grace. *Life After* tells her story beautifully.

Chuck Grassley
U.S. Senator

Life After

A Biography

A Life Story of Faith, Relationships
...and a Few Lesser Things

B.R. Hoffman

WestBow Press books may be ordered through booksellers or by contacting:

WestBow Press
A Division of Thomas Nelson
1663 Liberty Drive
Bloomington, IN 47403
www.westbowpress.com
1-(866) 928-1240

ISBN: 978-1-4497-6955-0 (sc)
ISBN: 978-1-4497-6957-4 (hc)
ISBN: 978-1-4497-6956-7 (e)

Library of Congress Control Number: 2012918554

Printed in the United States of America

WestBow Press rev. date: 10/26/2012

FOR SILAS AND LYDIA
In Memory of Your Mother

B.R. HOFFMAN

At Stonehill
Carmel-by-the-Sea, California
2012

Woman of Valor

Most often translated as "Woman of Valor," Chapter 31, Verses 10-31, in the Book of Proverbs describes the attributes of a virtuous, industrious woman. Written as an acrostic poem, the verses are recited in some Jewish homes on Friday night before the Shabbat dinner.

She is clothed with strength and dignity;
She can laugh at the days to come.
She speaks with wisdom,
and faithful instruction is on her tongue.
She watches over the affairs of her household
And does not eat the bread of idleness.
Her children arise and call her blessed;
Her husband also, and he praises her:
'Many women do noble things,
but you surpass them all.'
Charm is deceptive, and beauty is fleeting;
But a woman who fears the LORD is to be praised.
Give her the reward she has earned,
and let her works bring her praise
at the city gate.

Proverbs 31
Verses 25-31

Contents

"I'm often humbled to learn people are praying for my family and me, even when it's accompanied by "That's all I can do" or "It's the least I can do." But it is neither. It is, in fact, the very most you can do. I thank God for your prayers, and I love you."

Mary Jo A. Hoffman
August 2008

Acknowledgments

WHEN I WAS TWICE STATIONED at The Pentagon as an "Action Officer," my colleagues and I often begrudged the higher-ranking Generals who would review our reports. Returning to the office, we'd say "Well, he changed the word 'happy' to 'glad' this time" or some other such complaint.

With desk-jockeys editing our every page and sentence, we embraced a well-known retort: "Where were you when the page was blank?!" It was a sentiment at once understood by all writers who subject their work to the criticisms of friends, editors or other writers even as we acknowledge that criticism makes us better writers.[1]

For this work, the run-on sentences and unnecessary adjectives are entirely my own. Any errors in fact should be directed to the author and any praises should be directed to the family and friends who made it possible. It's truly been a labor of love to write of my late wife Mary Jo and share her story with friends or strangers.

The book couldn't have been written apart from the love and recollections of Mary Jo's mother Karen Stein. Mary Jo's sister Malinda also contributed

---

[1] This quote was immortalized by Maj. Gen. Perry Smith (Retired), a distinguished officer who served several tours in the Pentagon. Then-Captain Dick Poore and I had the honor to host him for a "Leadership Luncheon" for junior officers at the Pentagon in June, 1996. From *Assignment: Pentagon, The Insider's Guide to the Potomac Puzzle Palace* (New York: Brassey's, 1993), p. 73.

with love and grace. I also must thank my mother Kathleen Hoffmann and my sister Heather Soltero. They've shown their selfless love and support to my children and me daily, and I thank God for them.

Many of Mary Jo's friends contributed, including Paula Nofziger, Kathy Wise, Gill Abernathy, Sara Bridwell, Christina Severinghaus and JoLynn Handel. Carol Scott, Whitney Hanson and Lynn Zerschling were also very helpful, and I'm thankful for the fellowship they shared with Mary Jo.

I'd also like to thank John Donaker, Jim Witt and Gene Stockton. Each ministered to Mary Jo and was a great friend to her – and to me. I also appreciated Mark Disler's help with understanding Proverbs 31.

As I write the final words for this book, I'm especially grateful for my editors. Ta'Mara Hanscom, Barbara Grassley and Elizabeth Humphrey were friends to Mary Jo and patiently helped me to make *her* book better. They challenged and encouraged me throughout the writing process. Tom Kleen was a great help in formatting the final manuscript and the wonderful team at WestBow Press, especially Justin Swing and Gillian Lawson, lived up to their peerless reputation for professionalism.

Lastly, I must thank my children, Silas and Lydia. You influenced every page of the book and even chose the title and the photo for the cover. We wept and laughed together as we read the final manuscript, and I hope the book does justice to the extraordinary person who was your mother and my wife.

You've been so brave, and I'm so very proud to be your father. Though I expect you'll appreciate this book more when you're older, please know I wrote it simply because I love you, and I loved your mother. Now go outside and play – and don't come back inside until you're good and dirty.

Preface

WALKING THROUGH THE WELL-CARED CEMETERY in Indianola, Iowa, Mary Jo and I mourned the loss of her father DW. We glanced at the faded and weather-beaten headstones. "Here lies our son," read one. Another read "Father Leader Friend." Making conversation, I wondered aloud of the epitaphs engraved on granite. I wondered how to best describe a life in just a few short words in stone. Even at a time of mourning, Mary Jo was composed and reflective. She said:

"Someday even the headstones will be gone – and it will be only our faith and relationships that outlast us."

As is the policy for the stark-white modern markers, there is no epitaph for Mary Jo in Section 5, Grave 3895-5 at Arlington National Cemetery. Those who walk by her gravesite may not know she was an extraordinary person – perhaps best described by a reporter as "beautiful and brilliant, funny and kind."[2]

As her husband, she "made me want to be a better man," and she had a similar, inspiring influence on those around her – to be a better friend, a better mother, a better person. Her legacy is of a life well lived, and it

2 KCAU-TV, Jessica Cihacek, August 2nd, 2009.

continues to challenge and encourage others to live without regret or trepidation.[3]

As I shared in her eulogy, "Mary Jo's words were like thunder because her life was like lightning."[4]

Though Mary Jo was well known and admired, her life also gives testimony to what matters. Yes, she was admired for her talent and beauty, but she was beloved for her faith and kindness. I've written this biography both for those who knew and loved Mary Jo and those who desire to leave a lasting difference in their own lives. It was written for my children so that they may better understand the wonderful person who was their mother.

Perhaps selfishly, I also wrote it for myself. I hope to remember Mary Jo's selflessness and example while moving forward in joy and faith.

Life After is a tribute to Mary Jo, yet it's also a reminder to live and love selflessly. It's a reminder to leave a legacy grounded in faith and relationships.

We should remember our past and those we've loved and lost, but we should also move forward with joy to the promise of the future.

Mary Jo wouldn't have had it any other way.

Neither should you.

---

[3] Quote taken from "As Good as It Gets," TriStar Pictures (Jack Nicholson), 1997.

[4] Drawn from Pia Desideria, describing Phillip Jacob Spener, a 17th century preacher in Germany, considered the "father of Pietism."

Iowa Roots

> "The only thing we had in common was that she was from Iowa, and I had once heard of Iowa."
>
> Ray Kinsella
> *Field of Dreams*

PERCHED COMFORTABLY ON THE STEEL spring seat of his Farmall tractor, LaVern McMains first turned his steel blue eyes to the well-worn pasture and then the tall prairie of big bluestem and Indian grass. Dapper and disciplined, LaVern always wore a wool suit and tie to church, and even on the tractor, he wore a leather belt, with his linen shirt neatly tucked-in.

Known to many by his nickname of "Shorty Mac," LaVern was an affable and hard-working man. He wore a simple straw-woven hat to shade his eyes, and he surveyed his land with the thorough, experienced gaze of a farmer.

It was a look of contentment.

With seed money, literally, from his father – and a loan from Farmer's State Bank in nearby Bloomfield – LaVern and his new wife had purchased the three hundred acre farm with an eye to the future.

The purchase of the battleship-gray tractor with steel wheels stretched them further. Brand-new, it cost $595.00 and had the power of ten horses. This was decades before the Iowa landscape would be dotted with red and green tractors with multiple gears and air-conditioned cabs, and the young couple was rightly proud to have one of the few tractors in the area.[1]

Neither LaVern nor his wife doubted their ability to turn the tall prairie grass into a well-manicured field of Iowa corn.

LaVern often picked-up rocks on the prairie, a by-product of grinding glaciers that had at last retreated some 10,000 years ago. Walking the fields, he sometimes found sharp, hand-chiseled arrowheads and spearheads among the smooth, round glacial stones. He turned them over in his hand, admiring the craftsmanship of the American Indians who once roamed his land.

One tribe of American Indians – the "Ioway" – gave their name to the region. LaVern imagined the Ioway Indians revered the rolling hills and woodlands, teeming with buffalo and elk now long gone.

With lean, strong shoulders and hands that would never know a desk job, LaVern was well suited for the hardscrabble work of an Iowa farmer. He'd inherited an indefatigable work ethic from his father, learning and living the Midwest values of faith, family and work – in that order.

LaVern's faith in God guided his love of family and friends, even his work. He embraced the Bible as "God's Word" and heeded its warnings against idleness, committing the words of the Apostle Paul in Thessalonians to memory:

"If a man will not work, he shall not eat."[2]

This triad of beliefs – faith, family and work – fit LaVern like a pair of well-worn calfskin gloves – not that he ever wore any. He was an Iowan.

LaVern was an inquisitive, learned man, but it's doubtful he gave much thought to the history and geology of the area that shaped his upbringing.

In the country school he attended through the 8th grade, he learned the United States obtained control of the area in 1803 as part of the famed Louisiana Purchase. Settlers quickly converted much of the fertile territory to farmland, though there was continued fighting between settlers and Indians through the end of the century.

Iowa became a state in 1846, her borders set by the Mississippi River to the east and the Missouri and Big Sioux Rivers to the west. Rolling hills and prairie dominated the landscape, sprinkled with growing farms and separated by dense woodlands and river valleys. It was not as flat as outsiders expected, yet no one ever labeled Iowa as "mountainous."

The state's highest point – known as "Hawkeye Point" – was but 1,670 feet above sea level. Years later, a hog feed bunker would be placed on the high point, shaded by a corrugated tin roof. It was a spot often visited by tourists, the bunker adorned with license plates from all 50 states.

A grain silo stood nearby, stretching Iowa's highest point another 30 feet skyward.[3]

Farmers, though, aren't really interested in hills or mountains. They like dirt. Tillable. Fertile. Rock-free.

As it happened, Iowa was home to the richest and deepest topsoil in America, a product of the glacial melt from the Pleistocene Epoch and centuries of cyclical growth and decay of prairie grasses.

This nutrient-rich dirt attracts farmers like honeybees to pollen-rich violets, a fact Iowans acknowledged with pride and prejudice. For decades to come, Iowa farmers would lead the Nation in grain production and livestock, earning title as the "Food Capital of the World."[4]

This environment – this dirt – suited the farmer LaVern McMains quite well.

Up by 5:00 a.m. nearly every day of his life, he wasted little time in attending to the myriad needs of the farm near the small town of Mark, Iowa. With the help of friends and neighbors, LaVern planted nearly 80 acres of corn.

He circled the pasture nearest the farmhouse with a three-strand, barbed wire fence suitable to enclose his "herd" of pigs. He always called it a herd, though a well-read farmer once told him otherwise:

"Sounder," he said. "That's what you're supposed to call a group of pigs."

"Well, thank you Professor," replied LaVern.

The sounder numbered about 50. Eight milk cows also roamed the pasture, as did a small "brood" of chickens that had escaped from the makeshift henhouse.

"What do you call a bunch of chickens?" LaVern wondered aloud to Helen, standing by his side.

"About 12 dollars," she replied, grinning at her husband the farmer.

Helen was always by his side.

Like the man she would marry, Helen was an Iowan, born and raised. Her parents Lewis and Jeannette Kimball had likewise embraced faith, family and work as their mantra.

Lewis Kimball ran a chain of grocery stores in southeast Iowa and Helen would sometimes accompany him on routes, visiting other small towns like West Grove or Unionville. On occasion, they would venture north on the new U.S. 63 to the big city of Ottumwa, at the time a growing community of about 25,000 people.

She cherished time with her father and was devastated when Lewis Ross Kimball later succumbed to leukemia, in 1941. Helen was 27 years old. Her brother Harold had long been closer to their mother, who never remarried.

Like the McMains family, the life and times of the Kimballs were centered in Davis County.

Though named for distinguished U.S. Senator Garrett Davis, Davis County was borne of a dubious reputation. In its early days, the area was referred to as "Hairy Nation" due to the shaggy, unkempt appearance and rude manner of the men that resided in the area.[5]

This reputation did little to draw pioneers and entrepreneurs – or certainly, the attention of marriage-minded women.

Bloomfield was situated at the junction of U.S. 63 and IA 2. It was and is the largest city in Davis County and also served as the county seat.

Bloomfield was given its name when County Commissioners pulled a slip of paper out of a hat. In 1843, voters chose Bloomfield over Richmond as the "headquarters" for Davis County.

For Bloomfield, the reward was the design and construction of the Davis County Courthouse, a magnificent building that would serve as the city center for decades to come.

Designed by Thomas Nolan & Sons, the courthouse was completed in 1879. It was Second Empire architecture, as evidenced by its distinctive mansard roof, sandstone veneer and dormer windows. It also featured a Seth Thomas clock in the tower.

The Davis County Courthouse later put Bloomfield on the map for another reason.

In August of 1924, Henry "Dare-Devil" Roland came to town and attempted to climb the northwest corner of the courthouse. It was an event that captured the imagination and lived on in infamy.

Roland was a German born to self-promotion and also called himself "The Human Fly."

He began quickly on his ascent of the Davis County Courthouse but lost his grip around a cornice and fell 35 feet to the sidewalk below. The fall broke his hip – and his ego.

It's not known if Helen Kimball or LaVern McMains – then 8 and 11 respectively – witnessed the fall, but they were likely present for the well-publicized sequel.

In June of 1932, Henry Roland returned to Bloomfield. "The Human Fly" was focused and determined. It was reported that Roland was "determined to remove the blot from his record of successful climbs."[6]

This time – to the astonishment of onlookers – Roland scaled the courthouse walls like a spider monkey.

In just 11 minutes, Roland sat at the peak of the courthouse with a satisfied grin. In fact, he even climbed the bronze statue that was positioned on top and sat confidently atop the head of the blindfolded, bronze lady known as "Blind Justice." The statue stood about 123 feet above the courthouse grounds.

As recorded in *The Bloomfield Democrat*, Roland, a natural showman, even paused briefly for a death-defying handstand on a third-story ledge, delighted by the gasps of amazement from the large crowd gathered below.

In between these two events in Bloomfield's history, LaVern and Helen first met as teenagers.

One afternoon, Helen spotted LaVern walking on the town square. LaVern was well dressed and striding confidently, as always. Helen was smitten. It was 1929.

Helen was not shy and soon asked around about this dapper young man.

Eventually, she learned the young man's friends called him "Shorty Mac." She thought the name odd, given that he wasn't really short for the time. LaVern stood about 5 foot, 7 inches. McMains was also pronounced "Mick" and not "Mack."

It hardly mattered to Helen. His smooth, handsome face and twinkling eyes captivated her attention, and she boldly pronounced her intentions to her girlfriends. She said:

"Someday I'm going to marry that man. Really, I am."

She got her wish about two years later.

LaVern graduated from Bloomfield High School and began to court the pretty girl from Moulton. While the courtship began of attraction and affection, the relationship was founded on friendship and respect.

During their courtship, LaVern and Helen sometimes took a leisurely drive to Lake Wapello. Other times, they enjoyed a movie in Bloomfield or Ottumwa. Charlie Chaplin and Peter Lorre were two of their favorite actors.

It came as no surprise when LaVern mentioned marriage, but it was hardly a conventional proposal. In fact, it was delivered abruptly as LaVern jumped into the front seat of a friend's jalopy.

"I'm going into town to buy a new pair of shoes."

"Why now, what's the hurry?" said Helen, puzzled.

Struggling to be heard over the sputtering, 4-cylinder engine, LaVern shouted out the window: "We're getting married!"

"Well, it's the first I've heard of it!" Helen exclaimed.

LaVern drove off with a wink and a grin. It was a story Helen retold early and often to friends and family.

LaVern and Helen were married on November 25th, 1933.

The ceremony took place in the home of Helen's parents outside Moulton, Iowa. Only a few friends and family members were present.

By all accounts, it was a simple but elegant wedding, consistent with the persona of its two principals.

Helen was resplendent in a beautiful white dress her mother had made from an older wedding dress, complete with sparkling glass buttons. LaVern was as dapper as ever and wore his Sunday's best.

During the ceremony, LaVern pointed to the shiny new shoes he'd bought in town shortly after the proposal. The gesture earned a sweet, playful smile from his blushing bride.

The first year or so of marriage passed quickly and joyfully, yet it was not without its trials.

Hardscrabble and inauspicious perhaps best described the life of a young farming couple in 1930s Iowa, yet neither LaVern nor Helen was ever known to complain.

That first year, they lived in a small, four-room cement house on the outskirts of Mark. A single wood-fired stove provided nominal heat for an Iowa winter, and they would often awake with frost on the walls – and the blankets.

Saving money to buy a farmstead, LaVern delivered mail on horseback for the U.S. Post Office. He looped the dirt roads from Bloomfield to Monterey, Mark, Savannah and back. It was about 15 miles in all.

Trusted by all who knew him, LaVern also cashed checks or made small deliveries for the farmers in the area while earning $1.25 per day as a mailman.

With 10-12 families in Mark, the town became a gathering place for country folk. Mark was a draw because of its Baptist Church, gas station, grocery store and poultry house.

Though Mark would never number more than 100 people and would later disappear from the map entirely, it was well situated by U.S. Highway 63. It was just five miles North of the border with Missouri. Bloomfield was 11 miles to the northeast.[7]

Two of their neighbors in Mark were LaVern's parents – James Alva and Mertie Frances McMains.

James was known to most as "Alvie" though some called him "Shorty Mac" – a nickname he passed-on to his only son. Alvie and Mertie also had three girls: Wilma, Leone and Maxine.

As the baby boy, LaVern was often spoiled.

The McMains children grew up in the small two-bedroom home along the "Main Street" of Mark. The property included a few acres with a barn, a lovely little pond and a peach orchard.

The outhouse was relocated every few years or so.

It was not a farm in the traditional sense, but like many other area residents they tended to a few animals and crops for their daily sustenance.

Alvie McMains owned and operated the Shell gas station in Mark. It was situated across the street from the Baptist Church and just down the street from their home.

Though Alvie ran the two-pump station for many years, no one could recall that Alvie ever had an automobile of his own. He and Mertie only traveled to Bloomfield if someone took them.

Mertie was a skilled housewife. Gardening, cooking and canning were second nature and necessary, and Mark residents recalled Mertie delivered Alvie's lunch to the station each afternoon, always a well-prepared, hot meal, covered with a tea towel.

Like other residents, Mertie sold cream and eggs at the poultry house along Main Street. She used the money to purchase groceries across the street. It was a system that worked well.

As important as the grocery store and poultry were to Mark, however, they were not the heart and soul of the town. Nor was the Shell station – even to the McMains family.

Like most small towns, it was the local church that made Mark what it was.

The church was a place to celebrate birth, mourn death and honor marriage and family.

It was a place where even the legendary Iowa work ethic was affirmed. Parents often reminded children of the Book of Ecclesiastes, Chapter 9, Verse 10. It said:

"Whatever your hand finds to do, do it with your might."

Unlike the Amish and Mennonite sects nearby, the citizens of Mark did not desire to live apart from the rest of society but simply embraced faith and fellowship as guiding principles of community.

Prayer was an essential part of the community and as natural as breathing. It was not uncommon for a prayer service to stretch on for hours. Private, family prayer was practiced at dining tables, between husband and wife and parents and children.

After about a year in the tiny cement house, LaVern and Helen decided to take a leap of faith and buy the farm outside of Mark.

The farm included about 300 acres of prairie and woodlands. It was located about two miles south of Mark, adjoining North Fabius creek.

Combining their savings with loans from Alvie and the bank, LaVern and Helen became landowners.

They embraced the challenge of restoring the farmstead with great relish, with LaVern putting plow to dirt and Helen putting paint to the faded clapboard of the two-story A-frame farmhouse.

Helen's father Lewis built the kitchen cabinets by hand. The cabinets were of exquisite quarter-sawn oak and graced a small sunlit kitchen on the east side of the house.

Central to the kitchen was a much-used Hoosier cabinet. It included milk glass inserts, an enamel-covered metal countertop and a tin flour bin.

The farm outside Mark had become a home for LaVern and Helen. It would be their home for the next 45 years.

With the house painted and field plowed, the young couple turned their attention to family plans.

Their first child was born in 1936.

Charles was an easy child with a quiet, reserved and obedient nature. Usually. Not long out of cloth diapers, Charles was working alongside his father.

Through middle and high school, he proved himself as a beloved son and invaluable farmhand.

At the age of five, Charles welcomed sister Mary Karen. Likewise, she was a content and happy child and a great help to her proud parents.

Her family called her by her middle name, and by the age of seven, little Karen had already taken over many of the household responsibilities, freeing Helen to help in the fields.

Using his well-honed carpentry skills, LaVern even made a little stepping stool for Karen so she could better manage pots and pans atop the cooking stove.

Though perched over a hot cast iron stove of crackling skillets, Karen was never known to burn a finger or tip a pot.

Charles and Karen were birthed at home with help from Mertie. However, their younger brother Phil was born at the hospital in Ottumwa.

The contrasts between the siblings would not end there.

Phil was an inquisitive, passionate boy. He would also test his parent's patience, yet they loved him dearly. Thankfully, Phil also proved to be a tireless worker. When Charles joined the Air Force, the responsibility for early morning chores fell to Phil.

Years later, Phil again followed his brother's footsteps and joined the military. Both boys saw the writing on the wall and volunteered before they were drafted.

While life seemed to revolve around work on the farm, LaVern and Helen's Christian faith gave purpose and meaning to their lives.

LaVern began each day with reading scripture. It was a daily habit he'd continue his entire life, as he modeled religious discipline to his children.

Without fail, LaVern led his family in prayer before every meal and neither farm work nor illness would keep LaVern and his family from worship services at Mark Baptist Church.

The family looked forward to Saturdays.

Sometimes they enjoyed a scenic drive east to Van Buren County and the Des Moines River. More often they drove into Bloomfield and took in a movie at the Iowa Theatre near the courthouse.

While in town, LaVern and Helen relished the opportunity to catch up with friends and neighbors. They were eager to learn news of World War II and later, the Korean War.

Returning home on Saturday night, Helen set out church clothes while Karen shined shoes.

With Charles about to return home from the Air Force, Karen graduated from Bloomfield High School. Like many kids, Karen was uncertain of her future.

Though a bright, sincere student, Karen had given little thought to career or college. A quiet girl who'd grown up in the sheltered environment of a small farm, she'd hardly known the world outside Davis County.

Karen quickly rejected the thought of attending college out-of-state, or even in Ames or Iowa City, and instead, ventured just 24 miles from home for a job in Centerville.[8]

Hired as a secretary by the General Manager of the Appanoose County Telephone Company, Karen proved studious and reliable. The hard work and discipline she'd learned on the farm served her and the telephone company well.

Karen was a very pretty young lady.

With short dark hair and a petite figure, she had lovely, smooth skin. She also had a beautiful smile and sparkling hazel eyes, though they were often hidden behind horn-rimmed glasses.

It was little surprise this attractive young lady would garner the attention of boys and men, yet DW Archibold was the first with the confidence to pursue her.

DW Archibold served as the supervisor of the telephone line crew. He had been hired by the telephone company after returning from a two-year tour in the U.S. Army.

His mother, Coyla, ran the telephone lines in their hometown of Tingley, so it gave DW a leg-up on employment, though he'd also learned the trade at DeFry Technical School in Chicago.

DW was older than Karen by five years. He was also slim, tall and handsome. He radiated confidence and charm.

Karen quickly caught DW's eye, and he began spending a lot more time around the telephone office.

Soon after, DW and Karen were dating. They could frequently be seen driving around the Centerville area in his 1956 Ford Fairlane Crown Victoria. DW had purchased the car new after returning from Korea, and it was his pride and joy.

Karen was not impressed with the car.

She was, however, impressed with DW. She enjoyed his wit and wisdom, romance blossomed, and there was talk of marriage in the air.

DW Archibold was the first-born of Harry and Coyla Archibold of Tingley, Iowa.

Coyla claimed she intended to name him Dean Willard, but the birth certificate simply read "DW." He'd sometimes joke of his two-initial name, later telling his future son-in-law that it stood for "Dim Wit – just ask my wife!"[9]

Harry and Coyla Archibold were enterprising and industrious.

While Coyla ran the Tingley phone switchboard, Harry ran the local gas station.

Though rare at the time, Coyla worked a full-time job while also serving as a very capable homemaker. She was very loving and nurturing with the children.

Harry and Coyla raised three boys and a girl in Tingley, Iowa.

DW's two brothers – Jim and Mike – looked up to the eldest brother and were much alike him in talent and interests.

Jim was the spitting image of his older brother, and like DW, he worked for the phone company and served in the military. Mike also followed his brothers into military service.

DW also had a sister in Jo Ellen.

While the boys were rowdy and fun loving, Jo was reserved, gracious and elegant. She was a good student. She was also well liked and popular, and the Archibold boys were rightly proud and protective of their sister.

The siblings would remain close through trials and triumphs.

Since LaVern had already given his blessing, no one was surprised when DW and Karen announced their engagement.

The location for the wedding was even less of a surprise. It was to be held at Mark Baptist Church.

With the Reverend William Logan officiating, DW and Karen were married in June of 1960.

Charles' wife Judy served as the matron of honor. DW's brother Jim served as the best man.

Unlike the bridal shower – held the previous month with 85 women and children – the wedding was a small one with mostly immediate family and a few long-time friends.

As reported in the *Dallas County Republican*, the bride wore a lovely ballerina gown of white silk organza, with a draped neckline and wrist length gloves.

LaVern was tearful and proud as he gave away his beloved daughter. He put a penny in her shoe for good luck. Karen later glued the 1953 wheat penny into her wedding album for posterity.

A honeymoon in Colorado followed the wedding ceremony. Much of the honeymoon was spent traveling in the Ford Fairlane or holed-up in hotels along the way. The newlyweds enjoyed a stopover in Dodge City and a visit to the infamous Hangman's Tree at Boot Hill Cemetery.

For Karen, the highlight was the Rocky Mountains, as she was awestruck from her first sight of the towering, snow-covered peaks. It was a far cry from the rolling hills of Davis County, and Karen took pictures at every scenic point and overlook.

Refreshed and happy, the young couple returned to their home near the intersection of S. 18th Street and E. Prairie Street in Centerville.

With the new demands of home and marriage, the next few years would pass quickly. Since married couples were prohibited from working together at the telephone company, Karen took a job with a local agricultural office.

After about two years, they bought a 3-bedroom mobile home located on a private lot (#13) in Centerville.

DW and Karen spent most of their leisure time at home or with extended family, though DW sometimes enjoyed hunting and fishing with his brothers.

As with many marriages, conflict would come later, but for now, they were happy and looking to the future.

Down on the Farm

> "If enough people think of a thing and work hard enough at it, I guess it's pretty nearly bound to happen, wind and weather permitting."
>
> Laura Ingalls Wilder
> *On the Shores of Silver Lake*

DW AND KAREN'S BEAUTIFUL BABY girl was born at St. Joseph Mercy Hospital in Centerville, Iowa on April 5th, 1965.

The proud parents named her Mary Jo after Mary Karen, and DW's sister, Jo Ellen.

The extended family was overjoyed at the arrival of the little girl. Mary Jo's Great Grandmother Pearl Rosengrant wrote:

"Whenever a little child is born, all night a soft wind rocks the corn, one more buttercup wakes to the morn."

The new mother was overjoyed and showed the attention to detail of a micro-surgeon in recording nearly every detail of her baby girl's development.

Like other new mothers, she noted the baby's weight (6 lbs., 5 ozs.) and length (20") as well as the names of the attending doctor (E.A. Larsen) and nurse (Eileen Stounk).

However, she also saved the measuring tape and pink hospital bracelet ("ID 71889"). In the baby book, she even drew a diagram of the upper and lower jaw, with the date and number of each tooth dutifully recorded. For example: "#9, Upper Left, 7-15-66."

It was a labor of love.

Karen had no intention of returning to work at the telephone company, content as a stay-at-home mother and tending to every need of her little family.

By all accounts, Mary Jo was an easy baby just as Karen had been 25 years prior and slept all night from the time DW and Karen brought her home from the hospital.

Beginning at about one month, little Mary Jo smiled easily and often, though she cried nonstop through her first haircut. Karen saved the hair, of course.

Mary Jo was a beautiful baby with lots of dark hair. Her mother and Aunt Jo enjoyed curling her small head of hair, topping it off with a ribbon.

In the ever-expanding and highly detailed baby book, Karen recorded that Mary Jo "loved gravy."

DW's itinerant employment with the phone company soon took them 85 miles east to Columbus Junction – a small town of about 2,000 not far from the Mississippi River.

At first, they lived in the mobile home they'd relocated but soon "moved into a real house," as Karen put it. They purchased the house for $13,000.

The house had 2 bedrooms, an enclosed breezeway and an attached garage. Little Mary Jo loved the backyard, which included a swing-set. It was a light aluminum model with tent-link anchors to hold it down. She could swing for hours.

Mary Jo quickly made friends with other neighborhood toddlers and learned habits both good and bad. When she saw a little girl across the street have a tantrum, Mary Jo resolved to try one of her own. She lay down on the kitchen floor kicking and screaming.

Her mother was both horrified and bemused, yet responded calmly by swatting Mary Jo's bottom with a ruler. It was Mary Jo's first and last tantrum.

On another occasion, Mary Jo entered the house abruptly, slammed the door and made an announcement. She said:

"It's so windy I can't get the damn garage door closed!"

Karen immediately rebuked little Mary Jo for the curse word and raised her eyebrows towards DW, suggesting "I wonder where she learned that?!"

Grandma and Grandpa Archibold were visiting at the time and did their best to suppress snickers. Mary Jo escaped without a swat.

The year was 1968.

It was a year remembered as one of turmoil and strife, but the change was largely unnoticed by most Iowans.

To an Iowan, a hippie was as foreign as an Australian Aborigine. Likewise, "Flower Power" and Malcolm X never really became part of the lexicon of small-town Iowa.

However, Iowans were aware of the racial strife and its affect upon the country. They also followed the Vietnam War closely.

The war affected families directly and some small-town boys were never to return from it. Young men like James Cohron, Dennis Craver and Richard Earle – all of Centerville.

Talk of war became all too personal when Karen's brother Phil went to Vietnam. Karen wrote:

"It was a great worry to all of us to have Uncle Phil over there."

Vietnam was a formative experience of Phil's life, yet he seldom spoke of it when he returned or even years later. While in Vietnam, Phil sent home a postcard with a five-cent stamp marked "Pray for Peace."

DW, Karen and Mary Jo called Columbus Junction home for only a year before they made a move across the state to the small northwest Iowa town of Lake View.

Lake View was situated along the western banks of Blackhawk Lake in Sac County.

Little Mary Jo was now three. She adored her mother but neighbor Sandy Johnson also remembered Mary Jo enjoyed following her dad around. Sandy said:

"She followed him around like a little shadow when he was working on the yard."

For a time, Mary Jo called her father "Dee" and loved to sit on his lap. She got so excited when he came home for lunch.

Years later, the relationship between Mary Jo and her father would change – and not for the better – but for now the little dark-haired angel seemed to be a Daddy's Girl.

DW celebrated his 34th birthday at home with his little family. Mary Jo proudly helped Karen make a birthday cake and they endeavored to surprise DW after dinner. Returning home from work, DW had barely turned the knob when Mary Jo came running to the door. She exclaimed:

"Daddy, we baked you a cake!"

Not long after moving to the big, drafty house in Lake View, they welcomed another child into their little family.

Malinda Dee Archibold was born at the hospital in Sac City, and Mary Jo could hardly contain her joy as she waited to welcome her home. Karen remembered:

"I will never forget the sweet little expression on Mary Jo's face when she saw her sister for the first time."

Posing for pictures, Mary Jo was all too happy to cuddle her little sister and eagerly helped her mom to feed and clothe little Malinda. As the sisters grew older, they would diverge in interests and aptitudes, but a strong bond developed between them that would last a lifetime. Years later, Malinda wrote:

I remember walking through the gutters after a summer rain or going out at night with flashlights to get worms to use fishing. Mary Jo caught lightning bugs, picked dandelions to smear on my face and spent countless hours at the softball field, basketball court, in the swimming pool, even at band lessons, just to be with me.

The early years in Lake View were a happy time.

Birthdays were extra special, as Grandma Helen frequently whipped-up an angel food cake for the occasion. The recipe called for 13 egg whites.

The cake was as smooth and white as linen yet as dense as a kiln-fired brick. Today's store-bought angel food cakes are but a fluffy shadow of this legendary, homemade ancestor.

For Mary Jo's fifth birthday, she and eight little girlfriends gathered around Helen's centerpiece cake screaming and giggling with appetite and excitement.

The previous day, DW took Mary Jo to Sac City, where she picked out a green bike from a store window. Mary Jo was so excited she nearly came out of her shoes.

Christmas was also a joyous, exciting time in the Archibold household.

As the blessed holiday drew nearer, Mary Jo and Malinda were giddy with excitement, popping out of bed each morning to exclaim, "Is today the day?!" Karen shared whispers, giggles and kisses with Mary Jo as she put her to bed on Christmas Eve. Karen wrote:

"Mary Jo clutched me around the neck, pulled me in close and whispered 'When will it be morning?'"

On Christmas Day, Mary Jo and Malinda read the note from Santa with jaw-dropping wonder. Santa had written:

"Thanks for the cookies and milk, sorry I don't have more time."

Though Mary Jo was a naturally gifted student, the early years of school did not compare favorably to cake or Christmas.

Kindergarten began as a cry fest for both mother and daughter. Mary Jo hated naps and hot lunch, but she adjusted.

When Mary Jo began first grade, Karen expected it would go much better. It didn't. Karen wrote:

"Mary Jo cried every night that first week of school."

The young parents were puzzled by Mary Jo's behavior. It was thirty years later when Mary Jo finally revealed why she hated first grade in Lake View. She said:

Some older girls on the bus told me how cute I was. They said they were going to take me away from my mom and dad, and I'd never see them again. When I was older, I thought about telling my parents but I didn't want them to feel sad or guilty.

I also fantasized about punching those girls in the face – but then we moved to Chariton!

The Archibold family moved to Chariton in 1971.

Advancing in position and seniority, DW had more latitude with assignments, and he knew Chariton as a good place to raise a family. Finally, the Archibold family put down roots.

Their new home was a comfortable three-bedroom ranch on a corner lot.

Columbus Elementary School sat between S. 12th and S. 13 Streets just off Linden Avenue. It was about four blocks from the new Archibold family home.

Mary Jo and Malinda loved Columbus Elementary School.

It was a safe neighborhood school with great teachers and involved parents. Teachers challenged kids to learn, honored faith and traditions and promoted patriotism, beginning each day with the Pledge of Allegiance.

First grade in Lake View was quickly forgotten.

Though roughly twice its size, Chariton was not unlike Bloomfield in character and friendliness.

With a town square and a courthouse, Chariton was the county seat for Lucas County. It was also the largest town in the area, with about 5,000 residents.

The Lucas County Courthouse stood at the center of Chariton. It was not as grand or renowned as the courthouse in Bloomfield, but it was functional.

The move to Chariton also marked a return to family roots in southeast Iowa. Centerville was about 35 miles southeast of Chariton. Bloomfield was just another 25 miles east on State Highway 2.

Before the 20th century, Chariton was known as a center for high quality watch making. In more recent years, however, it had become better known as the headquarters for Hy-Vee, Inc. – a well-known regional grocery store chain.[10]

Chariton was also known for the Hotel Chariton as well as the stately home at 217 N. 17th Street.

The Hotel Charitone was a large brick-faced building that sat on the northeast corner of the town square. Sadly, it would later fall into disrepair. The magnificent house on 17th Street would later become the Lucas County Historical Museum.

Chariton's culture and character were decidedly Iowan. It was a town of faith and family. Neighbors gathered on porches to chat over a cup of coffee or watch the annual July 4th parade.

The Archibold girls were always proud to call it their hometown.

Mary Jo's affection for her little sister began to wane as Malinda grew up and started getting into her things.

She preferred to play with her cousin Kim, the daughter of Ken and Jo Ellen Johnson. Kim was also six years older and had always longed for a girl cousin to play with.

Mary Jo enjoyed playing with Kim and was awed by her impressive collection of Barbie dolls. Mary Jo pleaded with her mother for her own Barbie doll collection. She begged:

"Please mom, please – I really, really want a suitcase of Barbie dolls like Kim has!"

Mary Jo's wish was granted that Christmas with a Barbie Townhouse from Santa.

Many years later, she would pass it on to her own daughter in perfect condition with the box included. Mary Jo always kept her Barbies and all other toys in neat order and took good care of them. She did not like her sister getting into her things.

As a child, Mary Jo was plagued with health problems beyond the common cold or influenza, resulting in frequent trips to the doctor.

She often suffered through ear infections and tonsillitis. Later, she had her tonsils removed.

One year she had her right ear punctured and took penicillin.

When Mary Jo was just a few months old, DW and Karen noticed their little girl's foot turned-in. They took her to a podiatrist in Ottumwa who mandated braces on both feet.

Mary Jo wore the braces for about two months. After the braces, the podiatrist directed her to wear opposite shoes on feet for a time. It worked.

When she turned nine, Mary Jo was diagnosed with a more serious and life-changing condition: asthma.

DW and Karen had noticed Mary Jo was often out of breath or panting so they took her to an allergist in Des Moines. The allergist recorded:

"Patient is allergic to dust, pollen, mold, grasses, trees, feathers and cold air."

The underlying asthma proved manageable, but any person with asthma understands it can be a frightening or frustrating experience.

Thankfully, the doctor started Mary Jo on weekly shots and an inhaler. She continued to use the inhaler through high school and college.

Karen noted that Mary Jo improved greatly after the shots, but the first visit to the doctor for shots was not a pleasant one and Mary Jo nearly cried in anticipation. Karen said:

"Mary Jo, you are going to get allergy shots twice a week for a very long time, so you are going to have to be tough."

Karen observed that little Mary Jo never shed a tear.

Mary Jo rarely complained about her health problems and used the experience with asthma to educate herself and others on the condition.

In high school, she created an informational display about asthma ("Asthma: Greek for Panting"). She earned an award for the display and her usual grade of "A."

Even with medications, her asthma was sometimes so bad she could hardly breathe, and she often had to stay indoors during the summer season.

Mary Jo, however, was not frustrated that she had to remain indoors due to her asthma. As she often did in life, she turned obstacle to opportunity and setback to success.

Mary Jo developed a love for books. She even loved to read encyclopedias and nurtured a lifelong, unquenchable thirst for learning. It suited her stoic, studious nature and as a result, she blossomed in the academic environment.

From a very early age, Mary Jo loved lying in bed or sitting on her mother's lap as she read bedtime stories like *The Little Red Hen* or *A Fly Went By.* Later, she'd read anything she could get her hands on. She relished every page, character and story.

She read classics like *Anne of Green Gables, My Friend Flicka*, *Call of the Wild* and *Swiss Family Robinson.* She loved them all.

When Karen took the girls to the store, Mary Jo always used her allowance to buy a book. In contrast, her sister Malinda chose candy or gum.

For Christmas, Grandma Archibold gave Mary Jo a complete set of *Little House on the Prairie* books. From *Little House in the Big Woods* to *West from Home*, Mary Jo embraced the stories of Laura Ingalls like a long-lost sister. She was captivated with every turn of the page of the beloved series.[11]

Mary Jo felt a special connection to the *Little House* series.

The books were set in the rural Midwest of the late 1800s, and though classified as fiction, most of the books were autobiographical in nature. They told the story of Laura Ingalls and her family. It was a well-told story of the struggles and triumphs of life on the farm.

Mary Jo and Laura also shared a love of prairie fields and rolling plains – of farms, animals and farmers.

Surely the imagery and characters inspired Mary Jo and she soon begged her parents to let her visit Grandma and Grandpa McMains on the farm outside Mark.

Mary Jo's experience down on the farm would be the formative one of her childhood – a time of joy, wonder and beloved memories.

Among relatives, Mary Jo was likely viewed as the favorite of Grandma and Grandpa McMains, yet no one seemed to harbor any jealousy or resentment. Certainly Helen and LaVern didn't show any less love for their other grandchildren.

From before she could even walk, Mary Jo adored LaVern and Helen, and they enjoyed spoiling her with treats and toys. Karen wrote:

"Dad first gave Mary Jo ice cream on August 12th, 1965."

Mary Jo liked the ice cream, but she loved Grandma and Grandpa McMains for reasons other than treats and toys.

She loved the farm. Even at the age of two, Mary Jo enjoyed seeing all of the animals. She loved feeding the lambs or watching her grandfather slop pigs in the barn lot.

One evening while LaVern was doing chores, he realized little Mary Jo was no longer by his side.

Panic-stricken, LaVern's eyes quickly searched the feedlot for a sign of the little girl but found none. He dropped the bucket and hurried off to check the buildings.

Thankfully, the search didn't take long, as he soon discovered Mary Jo in a barn stall, sitting on an overturned slop bucket and feeding the little pigs out of her hand.

The little farm girl also enjoyed collecting rocks. She gathered quartz, river stones and the occasional geode and placed them in a metal can by the farmhouse.

She and Helen once marveled over a pristine arrowhead they found on the prairie, speculating it was much like the one LaVern had discovered decades earlier.

On a later visit, Mary Jo found two spearheads, and she and her grandparents examined them excitedly with a magnifying glass.

When it was time for harvest, Helen joined LaVern in the fields. Whether baling hay or pulling weeds from the endless rows of soybeans, Mary Jo was right beside them working.

Out of necessity, Mary Jo's first experience of going to the bathroom in the great outdoors occurred at the farm. For a little boy, it was a natural rite of passage and point of pride. But like many girls, Mary Jo found it awkward and difficult.

Grandma Helen's solution was to prop Mary Jo up on the V-shaped tongue of the manure wagon. Both were pleased by how well it seemed to work. Helen noted:

"Why, I believe this poop wagon is perfectly suited for the task, Mary Jo."

By the age of seven or eight, Mary Jo started going to the farm more often and DW and Karen also let her stay longer.

Mary Jo's favorite farm animals were the little lambs.

The lambs were born in the spring and sometimes the mother had twins or triplets so the mother didn't have enough milk for all her babies.

LaVern's solution was to fill a soda bottle with cow's milk. He put a big black nipple on the bottle and handed it to Mary Jo.

Mary Jo was thrilled to feed the baby lambs.

They greeted her arrival with eager, expectant bleating and followed her around and nudged her. Mary Jo giggled, jogged and then ran to the embrace of her grandparents.

Frequently, Mary Jo gave names to these lambs. She also gave names to the cows as well as many of the pigs on the farm.

However, the little farm girl understood the business end of the farm, well aware the farm animals were not akin to cats and dogs.

On one visit, Mary Jo and LaVern were feeding the cattle when she inquired "Where is Bosco?" Bosco was the name she'd given to a familiar brown and white heifer.

LaVern hardly hesitated before he responded "Well, we had him for supper last night!"

Responding with the wit and wisdom of a farm girl, Mary Jo didn't miss a beat. "Oh, he tasted pretty good!" she replied.

Grandma Helen was delighted to hear of the exchange.

More laughter and some debate followed with the story of Mary Jo learning to drive on the farm. LaVern and Helen seemed to disagree as to how old Mary Jo was when LaVern first let her drive the tractor and pickup.

Most likely, Karen was correct in her estimation that Mary Jo was 10 or 11 when she first drove the pick-up through the fields and down the gravel road to get the mail. LaVern sat close by her side on the bench seat.

LaVern thought perhaps Mary Jo was younger than 10 or 11. Reminiscing years later, he suggested "I think Mary Jo may have been eight or nine when she first drove."

Helen lowered the bar even further. She wondered:

"Maybe, just maybe, Mary Jo was in third grade at the time. I think she might have been as young as seven when she first drove that old pickup."

Mary Jo grew younger with each retelling of the story.

Maybe Mary Jo first took the wheel as a toddler. Perhaps she stood up on the bench seat of the Ford F-100 pickup with her arms reaching out for the steering wheel. Maybe her tiny hand stretched toward the shift handle – called a "three on the tree" – mounted on the steering column.

Such a young driver was sure to have problems – and she did, as LaVern admitted.

One day, he and Mary Jo returned from a project in the fields with an extended ladder sticking up and out the back of the truck.

With Mary Jo behind the wheel (whether 2 or 12, we don't know), LaVern directed her to drive into the metal storage building, forgetting about the jutting ladder behind them.

LaVern and Mary Jo shuddered as the big ladder crashed into the building, shaking the truck and leaving a permanent dent above the door. After the initial shock, LaVern wasn't all that upset. He quickly examined the evidence like a forensic scientist and swore Mary Jo to secrecy. Playfully, he said:

"Let's not tell Grandma Helen – it will be our little secret."

However, LaVern could never put anything past his wife. She quickly noticed the dent. At dinner, Helen inquired:

"Is anyone planning to tell me about the big dent in the shed?!"

Mary Jo joined her grandparents in laughter. For years to come, a glance at the big dent brought a smirk of memory.

She stayed down on the farm for four or five weeks that summer, and she would remember it as a time of idyllic wonder.

Whether throwing rocks down the steep slope beyond the pasture or sitting with Helen at the kitchen table, she cherished every small hour.

Like many of life's best moments, it was only later in life that she'd truly appreciate the priceless rarity of the memories made at the farm.

The love was nurtured and returned, for her grandparents relished each moment and made no apologies for spoiling their grandchild. They would reflect upon it many times in later years. Helen wrote:

"How we did enjoy you. You are so dear to us. We are interested in every phase of your life."

Mary Jo was not the only grandchild. That summer, her cousins Cree and Jennifer joined her at the farm.[12]

Writing often, Mary Jo told her family about their activities. She wrote:

"Cree wants me to tell you he fond a dead bird. Jenny is wining and crying today." [sic]

On the back of the letter, Cree drew a cow and a tractor. Jenny drew a three-story house.

All of the kids enjoyed the farm, and they also learned skills in addition to driving.

LaVern showed them how to wield a hammer and nails. He showed the children how to adjust a pipe wrench to loosen a sticky pump valve. Helen taught them how to make pancakes, cut rhubarb for a strawberry-rhubarb pie and mend LaVern's overalls with a big-eyed needle.

Two summers later, Mary Jo even learned how to kiss from her cousin Dennis. It gave new meaning to the term "kissing cousin." The cousins never spoke of it again, not for fear of their parent's reaction but of relentless teasing from classmates and cousins.[13]

Memories of the farm were always special to Mary Jo.

As a little girl, she was awestruck by the simple day-to-day sights and sounds of the farm. She listened for the first sounds of a baby calf or the baffle of an accelerating John Deere tractor with wide-eyed wonder.

But mostly, she appreciated each and every moment with LaVern and Helen – a loving relationship that would last a lifetime. In later years, they frequently exchanged letters and Grandma Helen reminisced about the farm. Helen wrote:

"I remember you feeding the pigs – putting water in a hole for them – training the cats – driving pickup, helping in the field – at least being with us in the field."

Almost always, Helen would end her letters "With Love and Affection." Sometimes she would close with a funny story or salacious rumor. In one letter, Helen wrote:

"Couple across the street has separated – he left her for a younger woman and has lost his mind!"

Much as Laura Ingalls had a century prior, Mary Jo sometimes spoke or wrote of her memories of Iowa and the farm outside Mark. Years later, she would live in Washington D.C. and share her observations with a reporter. Mary Jo said:

I miss my family, obviously and I miss sort of knowing lots of people and what's going on. I miss weird things—I miss a clear horizon. You don't realize that until you get out here. And there's something really cool about driving through Iowa in the summer and seeing all the corn. That sounds really corny, but it's true. You miss things like friendly people at stores. And we long every once in a while for Anderson-Ericson (AE) products; give me some AE sour cream or ice cream! I also miss Piper's candies. And I always bring back frozen meat from Iowa, especially Iowa chops – I always call my Iowa friends when I bring some back, and I say, 'Hey, come on over, I've got a little taste of Iowa.[14]

In 1979, LaVern and Helen sold the farm and moved to Bloomfield.

They were ready to retire from daily farm chores, so they purchased a small ranch house in Bloomfield that would be their home for the next 25 years. They maintained it in near-perfect condition and planted a raised, black-dirt garden that was the envy of the neighborhood.

Unfortunately, the family who'd purchased the farm outside Mark did not show such care and the old farm quickly fell into disrepair. As the years passed by, paint peeled from the farmhouse and weeds grew with impunity. The once pristine farm became littered with rusting barrels and discarded farm equipment.

LaVern and Helen only drove past the old farm a few times to take a look, and each visit brought only sadness. LaVern, Helen and Mary Jo had left the farm behind, and with it, they left a little piece of themselves.

That summer was the first Mary Jo didn't stay at least two weeks with her grandparents but it was just as well.

Little Mary Jo was growing up and moving on.

At the age of 12, she was already taller than her mother. She wrote:

"I'd always hoped I'd be taller, but it gave me kind of a funny feeling when it actually happened."

Though her childhood was imperfect, Mary Jo was always grateful for her own. She was thankful for the warm, sweet memories of life down on the farm and the Iowa values she would carry through high school and beyond.

She was grateful for faith, family and work.

Looking forward to new challenges and opportunities, she remembered the words of Laura Ingalls Wilder:

"It is the sweet, simple things of life which are the real ones after all."

Small Town

"A small town is a place where there's no place to go where you shouldn't."

Burt Bacharach

TEENAGERS SELDOM APPRECIATE THE BEAUTY, peace and pace of life in a small town.

Time may seem to move as slowly as a glacier pushing uphill, and growing up just seems to take forever. In addition, it's really, like boring. In the words of the teenage battle cry, "There's nothing to do around here!"

Seen through the eyes of adolescent angst, the streets of a small town loom like the walls of a prison. The walls are impossibly high, solid and impenetrable. Atop the walls, searchlights scan every alley and backseat as they probe the shadows.

The searchlights are manned by parents who are in turn aided and abetted by teachers or neighbors. The adults conspire like prison guards and are ever vigilant to report the slightest indiscretion.

Teens sense the only thing missing is the ball and chain – a big, heavy one shackled to the ankle. Tightly.

Like much of life, with time comes perspective.

Many teenagers who can't wait to leave the small town find themselves just as eager to return when it comes time to raise their own children.

It's a cycle repeated across generations, to the amusement of parents who once learned the lesson themselves.

Seen through older and wiser eyes, a small town seems tolerable and perhaps even inviting. Perhaps, just maybe, it's not a bad place to grow up after all.

Mary Jo Archibold thought so. Though she'd live in places as varied as Greece, Japan and Washington D.C., she'd always call Chariton her "hometown."

Chariton was a good place to raise a family and this was especially true in the 1970s and 1980s. Town folk were friendly and welcoming. Out-of-state visitors were often greeted by the "Iowa Wave" as they passed through Chariton.

Iowa drivers have long employed the Iowa Wave. It involved quickly raising the index finger above the steering wheel when passing an opposing vehicle. Whether a friend or stranger, it didn't matter. Iowans were and are a friendly lot.

Strange as it may sound to someone from the East or West Coast, neighbors actually knew each other's names in Chariton.

They also knew the names of their neighbor's children, making it that much easier to report indiscretions from atop the prison walls.

Chariton townsfolk were rightly proud to have earned the title of "1st Place for Youth Involvement, State of Iowa, Community Betterment Contest." It was a distinction they'd earned for the 5th straight year. Shop awnings and parade bunting proclaimed:

"Best Kids in the State!"

Though no one would mistake it for a bustling metropolis or a National park, it wasn't quite true to say, "There's nothing to do around Chariton."

With Courthouse Square as its epicenter, the small town offered parks, playgrounds, shops, dinner and a movie.

On Friday and Saturday night, kids and adults gathered at the Ritz Theater – an elegant, pale-brick movie house built in 1927.

The single two-story screen featured the biggest box-office movies of the day. An imposing, triangular marquee hung precariously over the sidewalk, supported by steel cables.

In large black letters, the marquee advertised *Jaws*, *Star Wars*, *Grease* and *Raiders of the Lost Ark,* among others. The marquee invited moviegoers to see "E.T. the Extra-Terrestrial. See it again – and again!" And they did.

Chariton was a friendly, tight-knit town. It was also quiet. Controversy was rare and crime almost non-existent, though there were a few well-publicized exceptions.

Chariton residents still remember when nice-girl Lisa Cline of the Class of 1983 married bad-boy Ray Chandler of the Class of 1982.

Early one morning, Ray said he returned from work to find Lisa dead. Authorities had a different take on it. As reported in *The Chariton Leader*, "Ray Chandler strangled his wife on their water bed with a thin cord, probably the cord on a curling iron later found in a ditch." Ray was promptly charged with murder but committed suicide while being held at the Lucas County Jail.

Of the tragic story, it would be understandable to think Chariton residents dubbed it "The Curling Iron Incident" or something similarly clever, but instead Ray Chandler would be remembered as "The Time Clock Killer."

As the story goes, Ray got his nickname when he broke a time clock at work. He was a forklift driver at the Hy-Vee warehouse.

While adults discussed this and other news, teens gathered at the popular pizza joint known as Gus and Nick's to play Paper Football. They slid a folded paper triangle across the table and raised their fingers as goal posts.

At Chicken George's, a small group of teens could also be found sitting around and talking or passing around a Rubik's Cube.

The most popular hangout was the Dairy Queen. With its red roof and teardrop "DQ" sign, teens could enjoy a blue coconut Slushie, a paper tray of crinkle cut French fries and a Dilly Bar.

Sadly for the teens of the era, it would be a few years before the Medd Brothers of Bettendorf would first combine ice cream with candy or cookies.

The legendary Blizzard was invented in 1985.

This was also the Golden Age of video games.

Space Invaders first piqued the interest of teenagers, even as it gave way to more complex and challenging games. Chicken George's offered Donkey Kong. The new Kum & Go convenience store offered Pac-Man. It was an addictive, maddening game that would go on to become the highest-grossing video game of all time.

Teenage boys were giddy with excitement when a sit-down model of Pac-Man was introduced at Gus and Nick's.

Students frequented the video arcade on the southeast corner of Courthouse Square and attempted to master Missile Command, Asteroids and Galaga. A student could earn free video games by showing good grades on his or her report card.[15]

Teens also enjoyed road trips to the Southridge Mall in Des Moines or the Hi-Vue Drive-Inn movie theater in Knoxville.

Many preferred to cruise around the streets of Chariton, though they didn't call it "cruising." To Chariton teens, it was to "Scoop the Loop."

Teens would pilot their Mustang or Monte Carlo – with Krager wheels and a glass-packed muffler – around Courthouse Square, then down Court Avenue and past the Dairy Queen. The turn-around was at the car wash just before the Pamida store.

It was a rite of passage repeated in small towns throughout America.

So yeah, it wasn't totally boring in the small town of Chariton and ironically, Mary Jo and her peers wouldn't remember most of the activities and things to do anyway.

Instead, she and her peers would have lasting memories of small town Chariton that were personal and relational. They would remember time spent together, a sporting event, an embarrassing moment, a trial or a triumph.

One event remembered by many of the late 1970s was when the 5th and 6th graders performed the song *Beth* for friends and family.

Some parents thought it an odd choice for elementary school children, since the song was made famous by KISS – a heavy metal band known for garish, otherworldly costumes and face paint. The highlight of a KISS concert was when lead singer Gene Simmons introduced the pyrotechnics by breathing fire. Sometimes he would spit blood.

Beth, however, was unlike any of the other hard rock songs in the KISS repertoire. In fact, it was a touching love ballad. Mary Jo and her classmates loved the song and enjoyed singing it for friends at family at Columbus Elementary School. Their only regret was they didn't get to perform in black/white face paint and 12 inch platform shoes.[16]

Another lasting memory of the era was of the famed Chariton Catalinas – a synchronized swim team of schoolgirls.

Synchronized swimming – a routine of elaborate moves in the water – captured the girl's imagination when it was popularized as an Olympic sport in the 1970s.

Whitney Johnson was one of the Catalinas, and she remembered the girls wore garish yellow body suits and orange flippers. After a performance, they posed on the diving board at the Chariton Municipal pool with oversized sunglasses and a smile.

In addition to Whitney, eager participants included Karen Ranshaw, Sherri Hull, Cristi Hawk, Katie Fisher, Lisa Hawkins and Julie Hawkins.

The Chariton Catalinas had no illusions of competing in the Olympics. None.

Lacking both skill and direction, they performed for family and friends looking something like a disoriented school of angelfish – beached, flopping about and gasping for air. Whitney said:

"We were horrible. I mean, really bad. But we had a great time doing it."

There were also memorable moments from high school. Most didn't come from a textbook or lesson – like the time Patty Daniel fainted during science class.

While watching a film about open-heart surgery, the graphic details proved too much for Patty, and she slumped to the floor like a sack of potatoes. Mr. Clark was the science teacher, and he reacted with characteristic coolness, propping Patty's head on a pillow and elevating her feet on a chair. "Just let her be," Mr. Clark told the class.

Patty's classmates snickered through the rest of the film. There were rumors she awoke with a curled black moustache courtesy of a classmate with a magic marker.

In the small towns of Iowa, the local high school was central to its identity and Chariton was no exception.

Chariton High School was formed in 1878 and had a first graduating class of six students.

In 1956, a new school was built near the center of town. Located along Grand Street between Osage and Orchard Avenues, it sat about eight blocks from the Courthouse Square.

Neither noteworthy nor plain, the imposing, brick building stood three stories tall and doubled as a community storm shelter, with portions of the limestone entrance pockmarked and discolored by age and weather. In later years, the school added an auditorium and parking lot to the west thanks to a generous gift from Hy-Vee and Russel and Vera Johnson.

Some older photos of Chariton High School students showed uniforms trimmed in silver, but the team colors had been red and white for as long as anyone could remember.

For a nickname and mascot, the school chose "Chargers." Sticking with that theme, "The Charger" was the title of the school yearbook.

As with any school, it was not the buildings or uniforms that made it what it was. It was the students that gave it a spark of personality – that made it come alive.

Drawing from Chariton and the surrounding towns of Russel, Derby, Williamson and Lucas, the CHS Chargers were like every other student, like some other students and yet like no other student.[17]

The students were small town, country, short, tall, shy and loud – yet they were also remarkably homogenous. Diversity came slowly to small town Iowa, and it was rare to have a person "of color" in a classroom. In fact, most Chariton residents could remember only one man of color in the community – a well-liked black man known as "Buster."

The staff also brought discipline and character to the school. Principal Daniel Redmond was a large man with white hair and big round glasses. He frequently roamed the hallways in a tweed jacket and dark tie.

Among the teachers, personalities ranged from the pretty and perky Jan Berg – who taught Home Economics – to the stoic and stern William Shumaker, Assistant Principal and Athletic Director.

Known lovingly as "Uncle Larry," Mr. Clark was the favorite teacher of many students. He was fun, funny, quirky and gregarious. Students were thankful Mr. Clark had decided to become a teacher instead of a mortician.

The story goes that Larry Clark changed his major from Mortuary Science to Education after the dead bodies and embalming fluid made him sick.

Around town, Mr. Clark was also well known as the owner of Clark's Greenhouse in Chariton. The running joke was he missed his calling as a mortician, but he still got to supply the funeral homes with flowers and greenery.

Though not as colorful as Uncle Larry, there were many other teachers who left an indelible impression on the students. Among them were Helen Krutsinger, Anne Koth, Bob Mittman and Steve Carman. Each was beloved for their warmth and viewed teaching as a "calling" rather than a job. The students loved them for it.

Of the 119 students in the Class of '83, Mary Jo Archibold was both ordinary and extraordinary.

In "The Charger," she was pictured between Tom Amos and Karen Bauer. She wore a golden cross and her hair was long, dark and straight. A full smile hinted at her playful and precocious personality.

As was the custom, the yearbook also listed the activities she was involved in beside her senior photo:

"Band, Basketball Manager, Concert Choir, Honor Society, Math Contest, AFS, Junior Science Club, SES Secretary, Music Contest, Marching Band, Pep Band, Softball Statistician, All State Auditions, Student Tutor."

As for most students, the activities painted an incomplete portrait that hardly resembled the person. Mary Jo Archibold was remembered not for what she did but for who she was.

The teenage years were an anxious transition for Mary Jo but not for the usual reasons. Precocious and mature, her mother once described her as "13 going on 30." She appeared bored by most adolescent pursuits and ignored most teen rites of passage both good and bad.

Mary Jo had no interest in video games and would rather read John Irving or the *Des Moines Register* than hang out on the Courthouse Square. She was bored with scooping the loop after just one U-turn at the car wash.

To the chagrin of parents, Well's Pond was a popular gathering place for Chariton teens. It was the place to go to hide from the searchlights and teenagers sometimes gathered there to sneak a smoke or a beer. Mary Jo was never among them.

Perhaps for those reasons, Mary Jo was not as popular as friends such as Karen Ranshaw. Karen was pretty, fun, sociable and athletic. Which is not to say Mary Jo was unpopular. She simply had no interest in it.

Mary Jo did have other interests.

She first took an interest in music and proved to be gifted. Like many young girls, she first took piano lessons at her mother's insistence but gave it up, a decision she'd regret in later years.

After the piano, Mary Jo tried other instruments. In the fifth grade, she began singing and playing the flute. She became very skilled with the flute and scored highly in many competitions.

It was her voice that proved to be her most skilled "instrument." She had a magnificent voice that carried high and clear, and she enjoyed singing in church and at school.

Mary Jo also enjoyed the sights and sounds of the marching band. She loved the camaraderie, the discipline, the rhythm, the marching, the way it looked and felt, and through it, she made new friends like Penne Probasco and Tracy Chaldy.

Encouraged by her mother, Mary Jo also took an interest in the Girl Scouts. Advancing as a Brownie and then as a Girl Scout, she earned many badges and led the troop in cookie sales. Karen served as the troop leader for a time and meticulously sewed and pinned the badges on Mary Jo's lime-green sash.

DW also got in on the act and helped Mary Jo earn a "Field Cooking" badge by demonstrating how to cook an egg over a campfire. With two eggs in a tin soup can, they scrambled eggs over a fire, stirring it with a stick. The mixture included small flecks of bark and ash but they ate it anyway. DW helped Mary Jo set up camp within sight of Red Hawk Lake, just outside Chariton.

These activities, however, were the exception. Mary Jo wasn't that interested in extra-curricular activities.

Odd as it may sound, she enjoyed school for the education rather than the activities, sports and hobbies. She'd inherited a lifelong love of learning and academics suited her abilities and temperament.

Surely Mary Jo had a brilliant mind, yet that was not what made her an extraordinary student – many brilliant students are easily bored or lack the motivation to achieve. It was Mary Jo's maturity and desire to excel that set her apart.

She was a little shy yet ironically, was also driven by a yearning to achieve or be noticed. Yes, she was humble and reserved, but she was also competitive.

In a high school term paper, she wrote:

"I have always been a 'fierce' competitor – not necessarily with people, but with the standard I set for myself. I have never been forced into achieving good grades. I 'compete' with my standard not only to achieve a high academic standard, but to prove to myself that I can excel in something."

The end result of this competitiveness was report cards (Karen saved them all) filled with A or A+ grades throughout high school, with two glaring exceptions.

The first grade that wasn't an A came her freshman year, second quarter. Mary Jo got a startling C+ in Physical Education from Mr. Swanson – her asthma undoubtedly limiting her ability to participate.

That same year, she also got a B+ from Mr. Salle in Algebra 1. The "bad mark" only made her more determined, and it was the last B she ever received through high school and beyond.

Despite the B+ in Algebra 1 or maybe *because of* it, she had great respect for Mr. Salle. Mr. Salle had been a mathematics instructor at Chariton since 1962 and students and faculty were saddened when he died unexpectedly of a heart attack at the age of 48.

In her senior year, Mary Jo was honored with the *Herman Salle Memorial Award* for math achievement.

Mr. Salle would've been pleased.

Along with a few other talented classmates, Mary Jo also enjoyed helping other students. Lisa Hawkins, Leslie Shipp and Mary Jo were called "the eggheads" and served as student tutors. Sometimes they even helped upperclassmen.

Whitney Johnson was a good student, but she was one of many helped by Mary Jo. Whitney wrote:

"I was in trigonometry, thinking this is going to be so hard, but it was a relief to know Mary Jo was in class, and that she would be willing to help you."

Dave Poli of the Class of '82 wrote:

"I hope you do good in trigonometry even though I am not there to do all of your work for you (ha ha)."

Mary Jo didn't excel at sports, at least partly because of her struggle with asthma. She lived in fear of asthma and felt it lurking like a boa constrictor, once writing of an attack:

"My hands started shaking, my pulse began to increase, and I could hardly breathe. This isn't happening, I thought, it's just a bad dream."

Because of it, Mary Jo always kept an inhaler close at hand, clutching it like an old friend or a well-worn life preserver. She was eager to avoid any physical activity that could set off her condition.

But like most things in her life, it's doubtful this thorn in the side would've dissuaded her from athletics if she truly felt called to participate in sports.

The reality is she didn't really enjoy sports because she wasn't any good at it. As she put it:

"I didn't have an athletic bone in my body."

She admired friends like Spencer Klaasen and Leslie Shipp, both superb athletes at Chariton High School. But Mary Jo couldn't run, jump, throw or catch to save herself. To say she "threw like a girl" would be an insult to other girls.

This lack of athleticism didn't really bother her and unsurprisingly, she used it as motivation to excel in other areas. In an English paper, she wrote:

"I am not athletically inclined, nor do I desire to be so. By achieving academically I feel that I 'make up' for this inadequacy."

Surprisingly, Mary Jo's interest in sports piqued when she accepted Mr. Carman's invitation to keep statistics for the softball team. "Yes, I'd be happy to do that," she said.

With a rational mind intrigued by numbers and positions, Mary Jo was a natural fit for the roles of statistician and team manager. Eventually she was given a team uniform and felt more a part of the team. She even came to enjoy the game.

More important, the softball players and athletes became her friends.

When the winter season came along, Mary Jo also served as team manager for the basketball team and with that position came more friendships.

During softball season, Margie Evans often gave Mary Jo a ride home. Margie was a "big girl" and served as the cleanup batter, but she also had an outgoing and infectious personality.

Mary Jo the non-athlete was grateful for Margie's friendship. She wrote:

"Margie became a very good friend of mine – we had common interests, but I could always be myself and she accepted me. With her acceptance came the acceptance of the rest of the team, and I will always be grateful to Margie for that."

Margie also felt great affection for Mary Jo. She wrote:

"Thank you for all the advice on things and listening to dumb things. Promise me you'll never change the way you are and the way you think about things."

Mary Jo also developed several close friendships during basketball season. Leslie Shipp and Lisa Hawkins became two of her best friends.

Like Mary Jo, Leslie and Lisa were precocious, smart and excelled in academics. They were members of the "Egghead Club." However, Leslie and Lisa were also outstanding athletes and very well rounded.

Leslie was the best player on the basketball team and earned all-state honors in volleyball. Lisa was a great friend and described herself as Mary Jo's "lifelong locker partner." She also wrote:

"Thanks for always being my friend. Good luck always and stay your cute, sweet self."

Lisa Crawford also became a best friend to Mary Jo.

Attractive, athletic and talented, Lisa was the "she's all that" of Chariton High School in the language of the day. She led the marching band as the majorette and was pretty and popular, but she was also smart and accomplished.

Mary Jo admired Lisa greatly, and it was a mutual admiration club of best friends. Lisa quipped:

"Someday I'll be able to say, 'Yes, I've known Doctor Mary Jo for a long time, she's one of my very best friends."

Mary Jo had many other good friends, including Joyce Allen and Whitney Johnson. She even had a pen pal in Pleasantville. Her name was Freda, and she and Mary Jo wrote for many years.

Given her maturity, Mary Jo was a model student who set a good example for both peers and underclassmen. It could be said she connected more closely with the teachers than with her fellow students.

Teachers were pleased to have her in class and knew this was not a teenager who launched spitballs and attempted armpit farts, but an adult in a teenager's body.

Mary Jo was smart, studious and determined, and she appreciated her teachers for who they were and what they did.

In fact, most of the teachers thought Mary Jo would become a teacher herself someday – and they were right.

Even Dale Wiley – stern and difficult to please – was impressed with Mary Jo Archibold. He wrote:

"Mary Jo's performance and her attitude are a pleasure to me."

Paul Cooper was a popular teacher who was especially well liked for his homemade tacos. He made them with fresh fried tortillas and sometimes made a batch for the students.

Called "The Taco King," Mr. Cooper was also impressed with Mary Jo. He wrote:

"It has been so enjoyable having you for a student the past two years. Your attitude, personality, cooperation, and academic ability will make you a success as you go through life."

She seemed to appreciate all of her teachers, but there were a few who were very special to Mary Jo's heart.

Helen Krutsinger was one of Mary Jo's favorites. As the Humanities/ Spanish teacher, the students called her "Mrs. K." She was a large, affable lady who wore her hair beehive-high. Students said Mrs. K reminded them of Aunt Bee from the *Andy Griffith Show*.

Mrs. Krutsinger was revered for her engaging questions and offbeat personality. She also had great respect for Mary Jo's academic talents. She wrote:

"Mary Jo is one of our brightest students, with a fine, inquiring mind."

The relationship between Mrs. Krutsinger and Mary Jo Archibold was deeper than teacher to student. It was a very special friendship. In Mary Jo's Senior Book, Mrs. K wrote:

"I admire you so much and if I had been blessed with a daughter, she would have been just like you! You really are a beautiful young woman and I am glad you are as beautiful inside as you are on the outside. You're a real winner and I love you."

Anne Koth was another liberal arts teacher who had a similar, lasting influence on this remarkable student. Mrs. Koth was popular among students, and she challenged them with classical works and writing assignments.

Mrs. Koth held great admiration for Mary Jo and said she was "A special gal, with many talents."

Though she adored Mrs. Krutsinger and Mrs. Koth, neither was closer to Mary Jo than Bob Mittman.

Bob Mittman was a math teacher at Chariton High School. He had filled the intimidating shoes of Herman Salle, and he became a lifelong friend to Mary Jo.

While Mary Jo's math skills and discipline made her a teacher's favorite, it was her personal character that so impressed Bob Mittman. In a note to her parents, he wrote:

"Mary Jo is one of the finest students and persons I have ever known."

Likewise, Mary Jo felt great affection for Bob Mittman that extended well beyond the classroom.

When it came time for the faculty to vote for the students who best exemplified the ideals of the National Honor Society, Mary Jo Archibold was an obvious choice to serve as President.

Both teachers and students felt pride for her to represent the Senior Class, and she did it with grace and professionalism. Her good friend Leslie Shipp served as Vice President.

When Mary Jo's high school academic record came to a close, her transcript showed a cumulative grade point of 3.966, stained only by those two grades from freshman year.

Of the Chariton High School Class of '83, five students were named State of Iowa Scholars and received state scholarships: Mary Jo, Leslie, Lisa Hawkins, Sheila Schmitt and Coleen McCullough.

Lisa was honored as the class valedictorian and Mary Jo was honored as the salutatorian. Mary Jo was also presented with the *All-American Girl Achievement Award.*

At graduation, Mary Jo was pictured between her dear friends, Lisa and Leslie, who had inspired her throughout high school. She was genuinely pleased that Lisa had earned top academic honors.

Many years later, Lisa shared the details of their class standing – her words humble, gracious and resonating with respect for her friend Mary Jo. Lisa wrote:

Going into our senior year, we were dead even in our GPAs and were both at the top of our class. I opted not to take physics that year because it was known as a GPA-killer. Mary Jo took the class and got an A- so I ended up with the title of valedictorian and she, salutatorian. But I have always known that the honor was really hers, and I told her that right after our picture was taken.

For graduation, the Class of '83 went with a conventional motto the students thought was serious and profound. It said:

"Today is the beginning of all our tomorrows."

It was a safe bet for a motto and used by countless other seniors in other schools, with variations such as "Yesterday, today; today, tomorrow."

In retrospect, class mottos usually sound trite or jaded anyway but hey, it's just high school.

Some students lamented they didn't stick to their guns and adopt the informal class motto. It said:

"We are sexy, we are free – we are the Class of '83."

At the graduation ceremony, Mary Jo shared hugs with her dearest friends and enjoyed every moment. Exchanging a few last photos and inscriptions, she and Mrs. Krutsinger shed tears despite their pledge not to cry.

In typical fashion, Mary Jo saved the photos, tassels and even the napkins from the reception held at First Baptist Church.

She also saved her letter sweater and preserved it perfectly in a sealed plastic bag. The sweater was linen white with a big red "C" and was adorned with an assortment of band medals as well as letter pins for basketball and softball.

The letter sweater reminded Mary Jo of the one worn by Sandra Dee in *Grease.* Mary Jo thought maybe, just maybe, she'd pass it on to her daughter someday.

Other than tears with Mrs. Krutsinger and her mother, Mary Jo smiled and laughed through much of the festivities at graduation. She'd enjoyed most of high school, yet she was eager to move on and forward.

Perhaps Mary Jo would've echoed the words of another class valedictorian from another time and place. Her name was Sonia Sterrett, and she wrote:

"High school was full of good times, but you couldn't pay me to go through it again."[18]

Yeah, that's about right.

Students, teachers and parents praised Mary Jo and thanked her for being a friend or positive example. There was a sense this girl was going places – she had big things ahead in her future.

But Mary Jo didn't seem to really have a sense of it. Though precocious and accomplished, she was as uncertain of her future of any teenager and wondered what lay ahead. Years later, she put it to words in an interview with *The Chariton Leader*. She said:

I don't think I ever really thought I'd get out of Iowa. When I went to my 10-year class reunion and saw everybody, several people said "Oh, we always knew you'd do something exciting." But I never thought of myself like that and when I go back, I always wonder – what if I had stayed?

Like most seniors, Mary Jo bought a copy of *The Charger* and like most people, she kept her yearbook for many years – though most don't keep theirs in mint condition, double-sealed in a Ziploc bag with a pack of dessicant to absorb moisture.

Yearbooks are remarkably similar – whether named *Hawk* or *Raider* or red or black – in that they tell a story of adolescence. The yearbook tells of activities and academics and of inside jokes and embarrassing moments.

The yearbook reminds you of a nickname, a favorite food or the boy or girl who broke your heart. In it, students share inscriptions or a funny story. If you're lucky, they might write something that speaks from the heart.

Mary Jo's yearbook was like that.

Other than the motto, there's nothing profound but the signatures were real and lasting and reflected genuine affection. Sheryl wrote:

"I've heard these annuals will last forever, just like our friendship."

Everyone leaves some regrets from adolescence. If Mary Jo had any, it was that she didn't always share her heart – her affection and admiration – with those she knew and loved.

When you walk across that graduation stage, it's hard to look over the sea of caps and gowns and realize you'll never see some of these people again – like Margie Evans, Mary Jo's softball buddy who died in 2007 at the age of 43.

If Mary Jo were to go back in time, maybe she'd hug her teachers again and tell them "I love you." Maybe she'd wish she could tell her friends they were special or "Thanks for the laughs and memories."

Twenty-five years after graduation, Mary Jo attended another Chariton High School reunion – this time in the company of her husband. Like most reunions, it was sparsely attended and included beer and bar food as a main course.

It was fun, though – kind of like high school but without the adolescent angst. Partying into the evening, the former classmates reminisced about Senior Skip Day and Happy Joe's restaurant while *Styx* and *REO Speedwagon* played on cassette tapes.

Mary Jo was no longer the studious girl with long dark hair and dimples. She'd grown into a beautiful, accomplished woman and many of her classmates were anxious to talk with her at the reunion. The classmates shared stories and pictures of their children. It was a nice night.

One last time, Mary Jo enjoyed the company of her classmates and they, hers.

They would never see each other again.

Broken Home

"An adolescent is somebody who is in between things."

Andrew Greeley
An American Clergyman

Like most teens, Mary Jo wouldn't remember most of the time spent in the classroom, as even then, she understood most learning doesn't occur in school anyway.

That's often how it is with growing up, as it comes in fits and starts, more often prodded along by the school of gentle nudges or hard knocks.

As Mary Jo matured through adolescence, her beauty began to emerge, but this was a decade or so before men would notice she was "beautiful," when she was most often labeled as "pretty" or "cute."

She was self-conscious of the small cleft in her chin, but perhaps in the way a teen notices a blemish or Cindy Crawford knows she has a mole. With smooth, natural skin and slight dimples, Mary Jo was blessed with a natural beauty. She had fine long hair and a radiant smile.

Her eyes were captivating, and it was somewhat puzzling to define the color. Specks of green and gold danced below the surface of the iris and the color seemed to change in light or laughter. For the record, she always listed "blue" on a driver's license or a passport, but it hardly described her eye color.

Mary Jo's hair was light brown or chestnut, but her hair color also seemed to change with the light or season. She liked to keep her hair long and straight, though there were a few experiments with feathering or curls she saw on a TV show. *Charlie's Angels* influenced more than a few schoolgirls of the era.

Through junior high and much of high school, her hair draped to the bottom of her back. When she eventually cut it, her classmates hardly recognized her in the hallways.

Mary Jo's mother Karen topped-out at 5 feet, 1 ½ inches – always insisting on that half-inch as the vertically challenged sometimes do – so it wasn't much of a feat when Mary Jo first surpassed her in height. By her junior year, Mary Jo reached 5 feet, 6 inches or "5 feet, 6 and a half" as her mother would say. She would stay at that height through adulthood.

With help from an orthodontist, Mary Jo had beautiful, straight teeth, a near-perfect smile and a personality to match it. In pictures, she smiles easily, and friends remarked she "never took a bad picture."

Photogenic and friendly, her eyes sparkled playfully, and it made for a magical combination. Many years later, a friend would describe her smile perfectly:

"They had a smile that could light up a room' is an overused adage, and in as much as it's a nice compliment, it would scarcely do justice to describe Mary Jo. She had a smile that lit up hearts."

Mary Jo dressed conservatively and often wore a simple, off-white blouse and a dark blue skirt. She loved shoes but often chose functional, clunky models because they worked better with corrective shoe inserts.

When designer jeans like Jordache and Girbaud became trendy, only a few students at Chariton High School attempted the look. This was long before rips, cuts and patches became fashionable and strangely, made the jeans even more expensive.

Since it was Iowa, leg warmers, spandex and the parachute pants of M.C. Hammer never quite caught on. God be praised.

At Chariton High School, a few boys did go for the *Miami Vice* look with pastel Polo shirts and Ray-Bans but it never quite caught on. After all, this was Levi and Wrangler country and new fashions were promoted at your own risk. Teenagers can also have long memories for clothing and hairstyles.

Classmates still remember when Shawn Garton first wore Calvin Klein jeans to school. Greeted with yells of "Hollywood!" and "Hey, Brooke Shields," poor Shawn will probably still hear about it at the 50-year class reunion. It was tough to be a fashionister in Chariton, Iowa.

"Conservative" was a word used to describe Mary Jo's personality as well as her clothing and political persuasion. Though universally liked, she chose friends carefully or even cautiously. She preferred a smaller group of deeper, more meaningful relationships to the wider circle of popularity.

Just as with adults, she connected well with upperclassmen. The general opinion amongst students was that Mary Jo was smart and likeable. Whitney Johnson said:

"Mary Jo was sincere, kind and smart – a class act."

"Sweet" was probably the word used most often by classmates to describe Mary Jo.

In the yearbook, Rachel and Tammy described her as "sweet" while Ken added "sweet and cute." "Nice" and "mature" were two other adjectives commonly used to describe her personality.[19]

Despite her sweet, likeable personality, Mary Jo was never among the popular "royalty" at Chariton High School. She was neither popular nor unpopular.

She was sweet, but she was not the spring Sweetheart Queen. She was nice, but she was not the Homecoming Queen – a title that went to her friend, Janice Rankin.

That is not to suggest Mary Jo wasn't well liked. She was. But it's fair to say some thought she was too perfect, too Christian or too "Goody Two-Shoes." It's likely partying or scooping the loop would've widened her circle of friends.

But Mary Jo wasn't drawn to the latest teenage rites of passage. When her peers hung out at Well's Pond or Red Hawke Lake, Mary Jo was usually studying. When the softball team planned a party, they knew Mary Jo would not be among them. Margie Evans said:

"If we're going to party, I'd better take Mary Jo home first."

Though Mary Jo had the attention of some boys, she was unsurprisingly cautious and particular about dating. She was her mother's daughter, to be sure. Boys seemed to sense her lack of interest and focused on those who were more attainable or perhaps less intimidating.

A friend speculated she was "the kind of girl you marry, but not date."

Though Mary Jo didn't seem to have much interest in boys, Spencer Klaasen was an exception. It appeared Mary Jo had a crush on him, at least for a time.

Perhaps she was intrigued that this handsome, athletic boy was also smart, sincere and likeable. Spencer was the "he's all that" of his class. Mary Jo thought he was really special, but there was no love connection between them.

Other friends thought Mary Jo might like John Kridelbaugh, but it was only a rumor. John was a good-looking jock, but he was always goofing around and Mary Jo didn't really care for him. Like other girls, Mary Jo also thought Scott Moon was handsome but like other boys, he only had eyes for Karen Ranshaw.

When Mary Jo did date, it was usually older boys – which made sense. During her junior year, she went to the Sweetheart Banquet with Randy Offenburger from the Class of '81. Randy was an all-around nice guy and probably best known as the only boy who could grow a full beard while still in high school.

Randy thought of himself as a cowboy and even signed his name "Tex." It was a nickname he kept into adulthood. Friends said both Randy and his brother Andy were crazy about Mary Jo, but she looked at them only as friends.

After the Sweetheart Banquet, a friend relayed that Randy had hoped to kiss Mary Jo but his odds were better to land a starring role as a bearded cowboy on *Gunsmoke* – and that show ended in 1975. "Tex" later achieved other dreams and moved to Oklahoma, where he worked on a ranch and earned his nickname.

That same year, as a junior, Mary Jo went to the prom with John Koth, the son of Anne and Gene Koth.

John and Mary Jo enjoyed the decorations and the prom theme of *Fantasy Island*. After dancing at the prom, they watched *The Warriors* – a forgettable movie about a gang of leather-clad toughs who fight their way across New York City.

As before, there was no love connection between John and Mary Jo. John later married Sheri Hull – another classmate and an alumnus of the famed Chariton Catalinas. John and Sheri moved to Idaho.

For the senior prom, the theme was *Romance in the Orient*. Mary Jo looked lovely in a ruffled pink dress and wore a corsage of white and pink carnations. This time, her date was Adam Bahr. Adam was nice, sincere and tall, with auburn hair and a ruddy complexion. He and Mary Jo enjoyed a classic Iowa meal of chicken and rice with baked potato and buttered corn.

But alas, no sparks were revealed. The details of the decorations, date and dinner were remembered only because Mary Jo kept the program.

Mary Jo never seemed bothered by her lack of a high school sweetheart, despite her temporary crush on Spencer Klaasen. Like her precocious girlfriends, it wasn't central to her self-esteem and she just didn't seem to have time for it.

But it doesn't mean she didn't think of love and romance or even struggle with her place in the world.

Mary Jo radiated charm and confidence, but she had the doubts and questions many teenagers held in their heart. She could be both shy and gregarious. She appeared poised and professional, yet was also sensitive and easily embarrassed.

Her personal journal and school papers were filled with introspective wanderings that told of a girl in search of herself.

Mary Jo showed an early gift for the written word. At about the age of eight, she first began writing "Mary Jo's Book of Poetry" and published a poem titled "Raindrops." She wrote:

"I like it when they fall, all over the place, best of all, when they fall on your face!"

Her first creative writing sample was published in the local newspaper. It was the story of *Patrick O'Leary* – a cantankerous leprechaun with an appetite for 24-carat gold and jelly doughnuts.

Later, Mary Jo wrote of more personal and profound topics.

She wrote of her hopes and dreams. She wrote of triumphs, but also of disappointments and even loneliness.

Her diary contains the soulful ramblings of a teenage girl – that most sensitive of human beings – and her long-ago words make you want to reach out with a hug.

It makes you want to reach back in time and tell her she's special, gifted and loved. You want to tell her that adolescence is a time of induced apprehension – but it will pass.

Through this period of *between things*, the one constant in Mary Jo's life was faith. It was a faith imparted through family, especially the example of her mother and grandparents.

It was a faith that would give her life purpose and meaning while guiding a lifetime of choices.

Mary Jo heard the Gospel of Jesus Christ early and often while attending First Baptist Church at the southwest corner of Grand and Linden in Chariton. One day, she said:

"I just chose to dedicate my life to Christ."

Mary Jo was nine years old when she made the transformational decision. The following Sunday, she was baptized by the Reverend Edward Quick.

Even her dad came to church that day.

Reverend Quick was an old school preacher of the fire and brimstone seminary. He was a stoic, white-haired man, and his clothing was similar to his message – plain, stark, black and white. Mary Jo would develop a greater appreciation for him as an adult. She said:

"I guess Reverend Quick scared me a little with a message of hell and damnation, but he also got my attention. I felt God used him for His purposes."

Ron Stein was the other pastor at First Baptist Church of Chariton, and he could not have been more different from the senior pastor. Reverend Stein was affable, witty and admired as much for his humor as his leadership of the church softball team.

The young people of the church especially looked up to Reverend Stein. It helped that he was a superb athlete who had been drafted by the Boston Red Sox in 1961.

Mary Jo loved Reverend Stein, and he would later have an impact on her life in ways she couldn't imagine.

As a Christian, Mary Jo centered her life on the disciplines of faith – of worship, prayer and Sunday school. She also sang in the church choir. But her faith was deeper, more personal and lasting than sitting in a pew. Her mother Karen said:

"Mary Jo would go into her room, close the door, pray and have devotions before she went to school each morning."

Even as a child, she gave 10% of her earnings and allowance to the church. She was a mature, faithful child. As Karen noted:

"Mary Jo once returned from a Youth Leadership Camp and was so excited to tell everyone about how the Holy Spirit works in our lives. Her peers looked at her like she was speaking a foreign language – she was spiritually so much more mature."

Most kids probably didn't notice the faithful example and maturity of this young lady, but some did. Leann was a friend from high school, and she wrote:

"Mary Jo, you are a super example of a Christian young person, and that is so much needed in Chariton."

Adults certainly noticed Mary Jo's faithful witness. Adults like David and Nancy Dunfee would become as dear to Mary Jo as her own family. David and Nancy served as youth leaders at the First Baptist Church in Chariton, and they were a kind, encouraging couple. Nancy wrote:

"Even as a teen, Mary Jo possessed an empathy for others that usually is seen only as one matures. And her radiant smile printed an indelible image on our hearts. She always gave from her heart."

Dick and Lucille Young also developed an abiding relationship with Mary Jo. She first got to know Dick and Lucille as Sunday school teachers and later helped them to mentor other teens.

Dick and Lucille had experienced devastating heartache with the loss of their son and as only the strong and faithful are able, they used it as an opportunity for ministry. They loved Mary Jo like a daughter. Lucille remembered:

"Mary Jo always seemed older than her age – and she certainly left a lasting impression on all of us who knew and loved her. The maturity level in all areas was incomparable to anyone we have ever known."

Around Chariton, it was common for teens to work part-time to earn money for gas and gifts. Tammy Comstock, Shawn Steinbach, Phil Hobt, and Mark Adcock worked at the Hy-Vee store. Amy Stapp fit shoes at the Family Shoe Store. A few lucky teens got to work at Piper's Candies – famed for its English toffee and handmade Easter eggs.

Mary Jo first began working as the "Saturday Teen" at Young's Inc., which was owned by Dick and Lucille Young. Young's Inc. was a paint and wallpaper store located on the Courthouse Square in Chariton.

Mary Jo was 14 and impressed her bosses with her work ethic. Lucille said:

"As with everything else she did, Mary Jo gave 110 percent."

Mary Jo was grateful for the work experience, as she recounted in an English paper for Mrs. Koth. She wrote:

"I dust, wait on customers, mix paint, inventory, order things, stock shelves and write up the tickets. Occasionally, when I have nothing else to do, I watch people."

While working at Young's Inc., Mary Jo developed what she called "shaker phobia." In a paper for English class, she wrote:

"I have been afraid of that paint shaking machine ever since that fateful day when a gallon of Dutch Boy latex wall paint became a puddle at my feet."

Mary Jo was red-faced with embarrassment and ran into the bathroom in tears. When she emerged, her boss Dick put his arm around her and said, "It's okay, it's alright," and cleaned up the mess himself.

On the home front, Mary Jo described things as a "mixed bag," with more than the usual teenage adjustments. She grew ever closer to her mother, choosing to emulate her in dress, character and religious discipline. Karen and Mary Jo were best friends and shared a strong, unbreakable bond as mother and daughter.

Mary Jo also shared a genuine friendship with Malinda. The rare argument between siblings was usually based on sharing a small bathroom.

Malinda wasn't an exceptional student like her big sister, but she had other talents and interests. She was a skilled athlete, and she and Mary Jo often spent time together on the softball fields.

The sisters were different in other ways. Mary Jo was precocious, independent and enjoyed time spent alone. Malinda was sociable, playful and easily bored. Mary Jo enjoyed books and band but Malinda enjoyed jungle gyms and television. Mary Jo wore a skirt and blouse while Malinda wore jeans and a sweatshirt.

Named after Mary Karen, it could be said Mary Jo was a reflection of their mother while Malinda Dee, in contrast, was a reflection of their father, DW. Malinda said:

"I always felt maybe I was the boy my father never had."

As differences often do, it led to some conflict between Mary Jo and Malinda, but the relationship was grounded in love and faith and came full circle in adulthood. Malinda wrote:

As we got older, people commented more on our similarities, from our looks to our voices and mannerisms. Mary Jo personified Christ in every example of her life. She was my sister, my dearest friend, my mentor, and probably my biggest critic. She was the one person that I looked up to, strived to be like, and one of the people that my goal was to please.

While the sisters drew closer through their differences, the same could not be said of father and daughter. No doubt, they loved one another but somehow, at some point, Mary Jo was no longer a Daddy's Girl. As she put it, the "relationship became strained."

The first signs of strain came in adolescence, and with the wisdom of hindsight, Mary Jo would admit she was partly to blame.

She was strong-willed, questioning and maybe a little bit of a know-it-all. Karen observed:

"Mary Jo and DW would argue, then she would just get up and go to her room."

DW was critical of Mary Jo and not very sensitive to the self-esteem of young girls. Malinda put it another way:

"Dad could be a real asshole."

No, life was not all sunshine and roses in the house at 1503 Armory Street in Chariton.

DW's smoking was also a point of contention. It could be said he was a "chain smoker," and it was a continuous source of friction between DW and Karen, especially in view of Mary Jo's asthma.

Mary Jo remembered a few arguments about it, and she said even DW's mother and siblings weighed-in. According to Mary Jo, Grandma Coyla Archibold said, "A man's home is his castle."

Karen was not amused.

As with a lot of marriages, DW and Karen might've admitted they could've or would've handled it differently, but it's fair to say that neither DW nor Karen was especially good at giving or receiving criticism.

Unfortunately, a weakness for Marlboro cigarettes was but one of DW's vices, for it was alcohol that eventually doomed the marriage.

DW wasn't the first Archibold to struggle with alcohol.

Some family and friends say his grandfather was an alcoholic. DW's father Harry was reserved and hard working, but he also had a problem with alcohol. He could be loud and angry when drunk.

Once DW returned home to find his father in a drunken stupor and raging at Coyla.

According to DW, he heaved a big black boot at his father and the heavy heel hit its mark, knocking Harry out cold at the top of the stairs. When Harry came to with a headache and a bump, the family just pretended it never happened.

DW said his father never drank again.

In the military, DW enjoyed drinking with his brothers in arms, but he was never loud or violent like his father when drunk. Later, when Jim returned from the military, the two brothers spent time hunting and fishing – and they also shared a few drinks.

To his credit, Jim later quit cold turkey – both smoking and drinking – but DW continued a long, unhealthy struggle with the bottle. Their younger brother Mike was also an alcoholic, and it led to an early death.

Alcoholism wasn't something they spoke of in the Archibold family, but the girls knew their father DW had a problem. Mary Jo even chose to write a term paper on the subject. Titled "Abstinence – An Aid to Safety," she wrote:

Excessive drinking interferes with one's job, family life, and relation to society. A person sometimes turns to alcohol because of problems in life, or succumbs to social or group pressure and begins journeying down the long, expensive, dangerous road of alcoholic indulgence. My life is just beginning and I want to keep my mind keen, my body healthy and myself free from enslavement to habit-forming drugs like alcohol.

It's unknown if Mary Jo ever showed the term paper to her father. Probably not.

Thankfully, unlike his father, DW was not a violent drunk, though he showed anger on occasion. During one heated argument with Karen, he ripped the phone off the wall in a rage and frightened Mary Jo and Malinda. Embarrassed, DW the telephone repairman replaced it the next day.

The incident the girls remembered most was when DW took Malinda to the Drake Relays in Des Moines. According to Karen and Mary Jo, DW left Malinda with a friend and then spent the day at a bar downtown. Karen was furious. DW made excuses, but trust was broken and the Archibold girls had a long memory.

DW moved out of the house in 1981. Though it was traumatic for the girls, they sensed it was coming. Mary Jo was 15 and Malinda was 11.

For a time, DW lived with his mother. Malinda visited on some weekends, but Mary Jo seldom chose to visit. She was busy with high school, yet she also harbored some bitterness toward her father.

There may have been some hope of reconciliation in the marriage, and Karen prayed early and often for discernment. But in the end, she said:

"I told DW to choose his family or the booze, and he chose the latter."

No doubt, DW saw it through different eyes. He may have felt Karen was impatient, nagging and judgmental. Karen acknowledged she was not without fault or sin.

It takes two to make a marriage, and unfortunately, sometimes the vows of love are buried in bitterness and disappointment.

It happens.

The divorce was finalized a year after DW moved out. It would take time for Mary Jo's relationship with her father to heal and grow. She learned a house was not always a home, and she learned responsibility and forgiveness.

After the divorce, Karen worked three part-time jobs, including one at the Hy-Vee corporate office. Mary Jo was very helpful to her mother and took care of the home and her sister.

Slowly but surely, Mary Jo reconciled with her father DW. Karen wrote:

"Mary Jo struggled all her life to make peace with her dad, finally realizing she didn't have to honor anything he said or did, but by scripture she had to honor the fact he was her father."

Understandably, Mary Jo's relationship with DW influenced her view of other men. Perhaps subconsciously, she compared other men she came to know to her own father.

She greatly admired the faith and character of men such as Dick Young, Bob Mittman, Ron Stein and David Dunfee, and she probably saw how her own father fell short in his choices and character.

Still, Mary Jo loved her father – and he loved her. Mary Jo's Aunt Jo later said:

"DW was always quite proud of Mary Jo and loved her dearly."

His affection and admiration only increased in later years, as she grew into a beautiful, accomplished woman.

Mary Jo welcomed the coming end of adolescence. She was not anxious to put childhood regrets behind or rush blindly into adult hood, but she was ready for the future. This bright, attractive young lady had learned the lessons of adolescence and was eager for a bright, new future.

Mary Jo had felt both love and heartache. And sometimes, she thought, "They feel like the very same thing."

Alma Mater

> "Here is the world. Beautiful and terrible things will happen. Don't be afraid."
>
> Frederick Buechner
> *Beyond Words*

A LOT OF 18-YEAR OLDS DON'T have a plan after high school. Some might have plans to join the military, go to college or work in the local meatpacking plant – but a lot don't and fewer still are ready for the world awaiting.

Mary Jo was not one of those kids. She had a plan – written on two pages, single-spaced.

Since she was already viewed as an adult, the transition to official adulthood went largely unnoticed, except by her mother. On her 18th birthday, Karen wrote:

"So you are officially an adult! You have brought so much joy to my life, and I am so very proud of you."

Though few of her relatives attended college (Aunt Jo and Uncle Mike were exceptions), it was assumed Mary Jo would go to college given her stellar academic record, maturity and discipline.

Even in middle school, Mary Jo told her mother of her plans and was determined to go to college. The only question was where – and with more than 50 fine colleges in Iowa, it was not an easy choice.

She considered Simpson College – named after Matthew Simpson, a Methodist minister who spoke the last words at the memorial service for Abraham Lincoln.

Simpson College was a private liberal arts school in Indianola, and it was also the alma mater of Aunt Jo and her husband, Ken.

However, Mary Jo quickly narrowed it down to three other alternatives. It would be one of the three public universities where she could use her state scholarship: The University of Iowa, Iowa State University or the University of Northern Iowa (UNI).

She chose the latter.

Mary Jo was impressed by the academic rigor of UNI and had heard good things about it from Penny Probasco – an upperclassman from Chariton and a friend from marching band.

Several classmates from Chariton's Class of '83 also decided upon UNI, though it wasn't clear if it influenced Mary Jo's choice of college.

Among the UNI-bound classmates were Patty Daniel and John Kridelbaugh. Kurt Wallace also joined them and became a good friend to Mary Jo.

Last but not least, Spencer Klaasen also opted for UNI. When a friend suggested Mary Jo chose UNI to follow Spencer, she laughed – and blushed.

The UNI campus sat in the city of Cedar Falls in northeastern Iowa. The sister city to Waterloo, Cedar Falls was a straight shot up Highway 63 from Bloomfield – or what Iowans called "two or three hours, give or take."

William Sturgis was the first permanent white settler in Black Hawk County, and he plotted the town in 1845. He first named it "Sturgis Falls" after himself but the name didn't hold as the town expanded.

Sturgis was a fascinating figure, with roots dating back to the Revolutionary War – his grandfather served as a captain under George Washington. William Sturgis was an "entrepreneur" before the word existed. He founded a trading post, sawmill, cattle ranch and a silver mine in Montana.

In between, he outlived two wives and fathered nine children.[20]

As it grew, the city took its name from the Cedar River and its gentle, sloping falls. It was an obvious location for a mill. Later growth was steady, owing to agriculture, meatpacking, manufacturing and the legendary tractor company, John Deere. By 1983, the population of Cedar Falls had grown to about 36,000.

Still, Cedar Falls was dwarfed by its sister city of Waterloo, with a population of about 75,000. The comparison was not lost on the residents of Cedar Falls.

Legend from a past century has it that Cedar Falls was first picked as the county seat but Waterloo residents attempted to steal the county records from Mullarky's General Store. In 1855, Waterloo leaders forced a referendum through the state legislature and proved victorious because of their larger population.

Some say Cedar Falls residents still haven't forgotten.

The UNI campus dominated the west side of Cedar Falls, intersected by Hudson Road running north and south. The campus covered about 900 acres. It was also the largest employer in a town with streets aptly named "College" and "University."

Buildings on campus included an eclectic mix of the new and old. The Honor's Cottage – formerly the President's home – was built in 1890 of Gladstone brick in the Victorian style.

Across campus on the northwest side, the UNI (pronounced "You-Nee") Dome stood out as a modern marvel of Cedar Falls, seating up to 22,000 people.

Students remembered the air-supported roof collapsed often until replaced by a metal one in 1995.

The most recognizable symbol on campus was the Campanile (Italian for "Bell Tower"). The Campanile stood 100 feet tall at the near-center of campus. It was built and dedicated for the school's fiftieth anniversary.

The title of tallest building belonged not to the Campanile or the UNI Dome but to the two largest dormitories: Bender Hall and Dancer Hall. Known as the Tower Complex, each building was 11 stories tall and housed up to 595 men and women.

The Maucker Student Union was also a well-known hangout on campus. It was a place students gathered to have a snack, workout or simply escape the bitter cold of winter.

The Union had a Hardee's Restaurant and Mary Jo frequently enjoyed sitting with friends at Hardee's, enjoying the cheap coffee. This was back when coffee was just a quarter, when only Italians spoke words like "latte" and "macchiato."

Instead of the Towers, Mary Jo learned she would live in Hagemann Hall of the Regents Complex. Hagemann Hall – a large, nondescript brick building – was built the year of Mary Jo's birth, and it sat just east of the dome.

In addition to Hagemann Hall, the complex included three other dormitories – Rider Hall, Noehren Hall and Shull Hall – but students rarely called it the Regents Complex or even knew the name. To the students, it would always be "The Quad."

In the center of the quad, the Redeker Center served as a dining hall and meeting place. When Mary Jo arrived in 1983, it had been newly outfitted with carpet, lighting and paint.

In Hagemann Hall, Mary Jo was assigned to the fourth floor – called "Lannie House." The move-in proved both exhausting and emotional. Karen wrote:

"I remember taking her to UNI and unloading all her things. We had to carry stuff up four flights of stairs, and I could hardly stand to leave her there."

For Karen, it was a lonely, 150-mile trip back to Chariton. "I cried all the way home," she said.

Mary Jo lived at Lannie House for two years. As always, the academics came easy but dorm life was an adjustment, and she was miserable for much of the first year.

That's because the quads were known as the "party dorms." In the round-hole, party atmosphere of Lannie House, Mary Jo stood out like a square peg. In contrast, her roommate fit in perfectly, and Mary Jo often returned to her room to find bottles, boys or both.

Before long, Mary Jo made some good friends, just as in high school. One of those friends would become her best friend forever.

Her name was Paula Rippentrop, and she met Mary Jo on the first day of college. "I also met her mother," Paula said, "because she was cleaning out the cabinets in Mary Jo's dorm room."

Paula was an attractive and spunky co-ed with a quick wit. She was athletic, loved the outdoors and was a self-described "tomboy." Though she and Mary Jo had different aptitudes or interests, they shared a contagious laugh, and it was heard often in the hallways of Lannie House.

Paula was from Titonka – a small town about 120 miles northwest of Cedar Falls. The daughter of Roger and Yvonne Rippentrop, she chose UNI because one of her favorite teachers from high school went to UNI.

Their friendship was a life-changing one, and Mary Jo and Paula were nearly inseparable during the college years. They spent hours talking and laughing about school, boys and the future.

They talked about life, really.

Sometimes Mary Jo and Paula joined a group of friends on College Street – a two-block area of shops, bars and restaurants adjoining the campus. It was known to most as "The Hill."

The Malt Shoppe was one of their favorite places, where you could play the old-school pinball machine or add M & M's to your malt or milkshake.

It was almost as good as a Blizzard at Dairy Queen. The Malt Shoppe was later replaced by Sub City.

They also enjoyed the Other Place – known simply as "The OP" to most students. Mary Kay's was another favorite restaurant, revered for their French fries covered in chili and cheese.

The most common gathering place for Mary Jo, Paula and their group of friends was not a store or restaurant. More often, they sat on the floor of the Lannie House hallway or sipped coffee at the Student Union. They enjoyed the coffee from Hardee's while discussing President Reagan, the Olympics or why their friend Sara should dump her boyfriend.

In later years, the locations changed and the best friends enjoyed Highlander Grog or Cinnamon Swirl at Cup O' Joe – a cute, trendy coffee shop on Main Street.

The issues were also different, yet the conversation was largely the same – easy, fun and encouraging.

Mary Jo never forgot she went to college to get an education.

Much as in high school, she excelled in academics. During her freshman year, she was inducted into *Phi Eta Sigma* – the Freshman Honor Society.

She also made the Dean's List that first semester – and every semester through graduation.

Mary Jo's professors were impressed with her discipline and academic performance. She rarely missed class and was never late with a paper or assignment.

Dr. Clem Cartelos was one of her professors, and he was influential in her decision to major in psychology. Later, she would wryly call it "a real practical degree," but she was intrigued by the topic and worked hard to earn high marks.

Paula observed that Mary Jo was a great student and beloved by the professors. Paula said:

"Mary Jo always worked hard, was nice to everyone, and I don't think she procrastinated a day in her life."

During the first year, Mary Jo also got involved in Campus Bible Fellowship (CBF). CBF was created to encourage Bible study amongst college students, but it also offered social activities and partnered with local churches.

CBF was an international ministry that began in Iowa Falls, with its first college chapter at Ellsworth Junior College in 1966. The UNI chapter in Cedar Falls was the second chapter.

The CBF members met at a house across from the Towers on Campus Street. It was a two-story house with a large porch and lime-green asbestos siding, and they called it "The Greenhouse."

It had garish, red and black shag carpet and dark wood paneling, but for many of the Christian students on campus it was like a second home.

The students played football and Frisbee in the backyard and took turns at the barbecue grill. "It was kind of like a Christian fraternity," one student said.

Tom Hammond and his wife June led this fraternity while also serving as the long-time pastoral team at Cedar Heights Baptist Church. Jeff Dodge and his wife, Theresa, were the co-leaders.

On nearly any day, students visited the Hammond household to share lunch or even do their laundry. More important, students spoke with Tom or June about college, faith and relationships.

Tom and June Hammond loved the young men and women and left a legacy of faith in their hearts. Tom was a gracious, compassionate man and always had time for the students. "He loved people," said his son Chad.[21]

Mary Jo made many new friends at The Greenhouse, including Steve Elmore, Steve Hanson, Elizabeth Humphrey, Mark Hoffman, Scott Young, Tammi Mether, Mark Peterson, Jay Grassley and Joe Schreck. Mary Jo adored them all and especially remembered Steve Elmore's sense of humor. She joked, "Steve and Jay were the brothers I never wanted."

Mary Jo and friends spent a lot of time together at The Greenhouse, solidifying friendships and making memories. On Tuesday nights, the tradition was to watch *Moonlighting* and then do "Share and Prayer." As Elizabeth Humphrey described it:

"They were some of the best years of my life – the depth of relationships, sharing and living. And we had a blast too."

At Spring Break, the CBF group went on trips together – to destinations like Tulsa rather than Daytona Beach. They bumped along in a converted school bus, playing cards and games, making up new nicknames and memories.

Pastor Hammond also served as chaplain for the UNI team, and in that role, he brought new members and a new dynamic to the CBF, with players like Andre Simms.

Andre was a big, black guy from Chicago. He was also popular, gregarious and a natural preacher. He was soon elected President of the CBF and encouraged other players to join.

Players like Hank "The Tank" Terrell – another big guy, but fun and easy-going – and Stephn McNeal – handsome, fun loving and lightning-quick on the field.

During her time at UNI, Mary Jo attended Cedar Heights Baptist Church just east of the UNI campus on Neola Street. Unless home in Chariton, Mary Jo was there every Sunday, enjoying Pastor Hammond's preaching and the Godly influence of those around her.

Surprisingly, Mary Jo never considered herself "religious" in the traditional sense. Sure, she attended church, read the Bible and prayed, but her faith was not based on rules of liturgy or an order of worship.

It was not positional, but relational – and she lived it.

Mary Jo's easy confidence of faith was attractive to others, especially Paula.

Mary Jo and Paula often had discussions about faith, yet Paula was hesitant to embrace a life of faith. She was also a self-described "party girl."

Like us all, Paula had questions and doubts.

As Paula told it, there were other Christians who "witnessed" to Paula – sort of. A "crazy chick" named Caroline once told Paula "You are going to hell in a hand basket."

Mary Jo was different, and she nurtured Paula's soul and character. It was Mary Jo's Christ-like witness, not her words, that spoke to Paula, and the two girls eventually prayed together in the hallway at Lannie House, each with a cup of hot chocolate in-hand. Paula said:

"Like anyone, I knew of Jesus Christ, and I'd heard the beautiful language of the Bible. But when I finally became a Christian, it was not because of what I read, but because of what I saw. I first saw Jesus in Mary Jo – in the way she lived and loved me."

It was a transforming moment for them both. Mary Jo and Paula would remember it for the rest of their lives.

On the dating scene, it was much of the same as in high school for Mary Jo. Even one of the characters was the same, as she still had a crush on Spencer Klaasen for a time. But Spencer never seemed to have any interest in her and so it went nowhere.

So Mary Jo never participated in that old, revered UNI tradition of *campaniling.* Legend held that female students became "true coeds" when kissed at midnight at the Campanile.

Like a lot of girls, perhaps Mary Jo didn't date much because she was simply too busy. She was focused on her studies. She was dedicated to her faith. She often worked on weekends.

Mary Jo also spent many weekends at home in Chariton. When she didn't return home, she called her mother and sister at least once a week, without fail. Malinda said:

"There was never a conversation that we didn't know how much she loved us and that she put us before her needs."

Mary Jo also worked to restore the relationship with her father DW and visited him often in Indianola.

Shortly after Mary Jo began college, DW's Aunt Margaret had moved in – not with DW, but with Karen and Malinda.

Karen, Malinda and Mary Jo enjoyed Aunt Margaret's company, as she was fun and full of life even though she'd been widowed twice. Karen said:

"Aunt Margaret laughed easily – and with no children, felt affection for Mary Jo and Malinda as if they were her own daughters."

Before long, DW found love again.

Though he had developed emphysema and other health struggles, DW met Sandi Allen, and together, they seemed to find some peace and happiness. Sandi and DW were married in September of 1983 – just over a year after he and Karen were divorced.

Mary Jo and Malinda were happy for DW – and so was Karen.

By the end of her sophomore year, Mary Jo was more than ready for a change from the party-like atmosphere of Lannie House, and she moved off-campus with her friend, Suzanne.

The move was likely precipitated by Paula's move off campus.

Paula had moved way off campus – to Boston. She ventured eastward to serve as a nanny, and she would be gone for a year.

Mary Jo and Suzanne's place off campus was a quadplex. It sat on Olive Street and had two apartments downstairs and two apartments upstairs. The apartment was just a stone's throw from campus and she and Suzanne – also a psychology major – made it "cute and homey," as one friend described it.

Mary Jo missed her best friend terribly, but the year passed quickly. When Paula returned, she also moved to Olive Street – just two doors down from Mary Jo and Suzanne.

Given her finances, it was a stretch for Mary Jo to live off-campus, but she budgeted her money to the dime. Ever frugal, she still drove the silver Chevy Chevette she bought when she was 16.

She'd paid for the car herself and never had an accident. In fact, she never got a ticket. Ever.

Karen gave Mary Jo a credit card for emergencies, but she never used it.

Pastor Ron also gave her a $50 bill and said, "Tuck it away and don't use unless it's a real emergency." From time to time, Mary Jo loaned Ron's $50 bill to friends for gas or groceries, but Mary Jo still had an emergency $50 bill when she graduated.

Mary Jo was able to attend college mostly due to scholarships, money she earned working and the support of her family.

The State of Iowa scholarship was $600 dollars but was only good through her sophomore year. Other grants and financial aid included a small stipend from the Mid-American Baptist Women's Student Aid Fund.

Mary Jo never took a loan for college and she graduated without debt, but it was never easy.

To earn spending money, she worked at Seiferts – a women's clothing store at Crossroads Mall. She admitted some of her earnings were spent on fashionable clothes and cute shoes, but she budgeted carefully.

After her junior year, Mary Jo went through her finances, prepared a budget and realized she would be about $2,000 dollars short for her final year of college.

Since the divorce decree specified her father would pay half her tuition, Mary Jo had hoped he would honor it and went to visit DW and Sandi in Indianola.

She arrived at the home in Indianola with some trepidation, but soon summoned the courage to ask DW for help with college.

According to Mary Jo, he responded by sitting down at the kitchen table, where he spent about 30 minutes looking through his checkbook and account statements while pecking away at a calculator.

Finally, he looked up and announced:

"Well, I've gone through everything, and it looks like all I owe is $100 dollars."

Despite simmering emotions that felt like a hot flash, Mary Jo calmly took the $100 check with a curt, "Thanks, Dad," and a hug, said "Good Night" to Sandi and headed out the door. But by the time she settled-in behind the wheel of her car, her stoic demeanor cracked behind tears of disappointment, and she drove home to Chariton with a heavy, angry heart.

When she arrived home, Mary Jo was ashamed to even tell her mother about the visit with DW, but she soon broke down in tears and told Karen all about it.

Karen was angry, but quick to dry the tears and find a solution for her beloved daughter. Always practical and sacrificial, Karen sold off her life insurance policy the next day for exactly $1,900 dollars.

She handed the check to Mary Jo with a $100 bill.

It was not a story Mary Jo was eager to share with anyone, yet she did tell a few of her best friends. Years later, she told her husband. Each time she told the story, she ended it the same way. She said:

"And so I resolved to never ask my father for anything again. And I didn't."

Returning to UNI for her senior year, Mary Jo continued to excel in academics even though she was uncertain of the future and her choice of major. It seemed to go quicker than previous years, and she was delighted Paula had returned.

Mary Jo graduated cum laude and was offered an appointment as a graduate assistant in the Department of Psychology with a tuition scholarship and a stipend of $4,400 dollars.

Mary Jo, however, felt she'd been called to social work and turned down the graduate scholarship.

Through college, Mary Jo was intrigued by psychology and sociology, writing papers such as *Creating a More Effective Juvenile Justice System*.

She was interested in social work, but she wasn't quite sure what to do about it.

Encouraged by prayer and words of encouragement from Tom Hammond, Mary Jo decided to pursue a position as a social worker with The Lighthouse in Kansas City. She was offered the job and headed there shortly after graduation.

The Lighthouse was a home for un-wed mothers that had just formed two years prior to Mary Jo's arrival. Its purpose was to "Provide Christ-centered care to young ladies facing unplanned pregnancies in the Kansas City area."[22]

At The Lighthouse, Mary Jo was given the title "counselor" but was uncertain of the role. On "Day 1," she wrote:

"As I sit here I don't really know where to begin – so much has happened. They all stare at me."

The girls looked scared and so Mary Jo did what she did best. She encouraged, hugged and loved those poor, scared girls.

Eventually, Mary Jo realized that was her role – to encourage and support the girls. She made a difference by praying with the girls, providing advice or resources and even holding their hands in the delivery room.

And she prayed:

"God please give me the words to say to these girls. Give me a girl who I can make an impact with for you. Let them see Christ living in me. Help me to learn, retain, remember and perform my duties well."

To say the least, living in the inner city was an adjustment for the small town girl from Chariton, Iowa. At one point, she wrote:

"After the police & helicopters and the reports of stabbings and such, I'm not really sure I feel safe in this neighborhood. I wonder if the hubcaps are still on the car? Is the car still there?"

After just a few months on the job, Mary Jo jumped at the opportunity for a mission trip that would take her overseas to Japan.

Sponsored by the Campus Bible Fellowship, Mary Jo stayed in Japan for a month. Friends Barrett, Cyndi, Marcia and Sheila joined her on the adventure.

The girls stayed with missionaries in Himedji City in the Kansai regions of Japan, teaching English and sharing the Bible with Japanese school children.

The camp was conducted primarily in Japanese and Mary Jo observed, "It was quite the humbling experience."

The team of young adults enjoyed the cultural experience. They sipped green tea and relished the batter-fried tempura and exquisite, colorful sushi. Mary Jo and her friends even performed a skit called "American Restaurant" for the amusement of their Japanese hosts.

Returning home, Mary Jo excitedly shared her tale of Japanese adventure with family and friends. She also showered them with gifts: A colorful scarf and a tiny, purple cup for her best friend, Paula; and a teapot and ornate fan for Karen. For herself, she purchased a gray ceramic tea set with a bright fish pattern.

Mary Jo also did some soul-searching while in Japan, and when she returned to Kansas City, she gently told the staff she would be leaving by the end of the year.

After praying about the decision, she wrote:

"LORD, may it never be my job, but may it always be my ministry."

Mary Jo headed home to Chariton for Christmas eager to see family and with gifts in hand.

Unfortunately, Great Aunt Margaret fell sick and passed away two days after Christmas.

Mary Jo and Malinda were distraught. Even DW cried when he learned Margaret had passed. Pastor Ron helped with arrangements for the funeral and was a great comfort to the family.

Mary Jo didn't stay long after the funeral. Embracing her mother and sister, she encouraged Karen and Malinda to join her for a short walk to Dairy Queen, just like old times.

Enjoying their dipped ice cream cones, Karen, Mary Jo and Malinda talked about Aunt Margaret. They talked about DW. They talked about the dog, Ginger. They talked about the future.

As Mary Jo prepared to leave, Karen hugged her daughter tightly and put some money in her hand.

Mary Jo was going to the big city.

Capital City

> "Enjoy your time in public service. It may well be one of the most interesting and challenging times of your life."
>
> Donald Rumsfeld

"WELL, WE'RE NOT IN IOWA anymore," Mary Jo thought, gazing admiringly at the towering limestone facades and Corinthian columns of America's grand, capital city.

Encouraged by Jay Grassley – a good friend from The Greenhouse – the small-town girl from Chariton first visited Washington D.C. on what she called a "field trip" during her junior year at the University of Northern Iowa (UNI).

Jay Grassley was a native Iowan, but he was much more familiar with the spectacular, historic sights of Washington D.C., owing to his father's service as a U.S. Senator.

Mary Jo was awed by the majesty of the big city.

Joined by her best friend Paula, Mary Jo loaded up the Chevy Chevette with enough clothing, diet coke and granola bars for the 16-hour drive and a three-day stay.

The girls also talked Kurt Wallace into going with them. They shoehorned Kurt into the back seat and jokingly referred to him as their "chaperone" for the journey.

By all accounts, the trip was a laugh fest and the miles went quickly.

Jay's mother Barbara, always gracious and welcoming, insisted the college kids should stay with them at their home in Alexandria, Virginia, a suburb just across the Potomac River.

Short on cash, they gratefully accepted the invitation and made plans for a whirlwind tour.

Mary Jo, Paula and Kurt loved the sights and sounds of the National Capital region. They were impressed by the spectacle of the National Mall and little things like a doorjamb inside the White House that was still blackened from the War of 1812.

They spent an entire day at the Smithsonian Museum yet saw only a small fraction of its offerings. When they returned home, they excitedly told friends about the fragment of moon rock from the Air and Space Museum. The small fragment was worn smooth and concave by the touch of millions.

On the second day of the visit, they joined Senator Chuck Grassley for lunch in the Senate Dining Room. The dining room was resplendent in ornate Schumacher wallpaper, century-old oil paintings and a magnificent window dedicated to George Washington.

Enjoying the famous white bean soup – a senate staple for nearly a century – the college kids glanced around at politicians they recognized from television.

The conversation soon turned to public service and politics, and Senator Grassley suggested Mary Jo should come to work for him – or "Come to work for Iowa," as he put it.

It was the second time he'd made the offer and Mary Jo was flattered, but she kindly declined. She said:

"I'm not interested in politics and want to be involved in ministry."

In time Mary Jo reconsidered, but not because of a growing interest in politics or government. It was because she developed a deep respect and admiration for Chuck and Barbara Grassley.

She'd also changed her mind about social work based on her experience at The Lighthouse in Kansas City. As her mother said, "She got burned out very quickly."

So the next time Senator Grassley asked Mary Jo about coming to work in Washington D.C. – prodded by Barbara and Jay – Mary Jo simply said "Yes, I'd like that."

In January 1988, Mary Jo moved to Washington D.C. and brought Paula along for the ride. After helping to unpack, Paula returned to Cedar Falls for her final year of college.

Mark Rittgers was the first to greet Mary Jo. A big and friendly young man, Mark had become friends with Mary Jo at UNI through mutual friend Kent Bailey.

Mark was also a Grassley staffer, and he and Mary Jo would develop a lasting friendship. Mary Jo said:

"Mark was the only person I knew besides the Grassleys when I moved to D.C. – and he became a dear friend."

On the first day in the Grassley office on Capitol Hill, Mary Jo also hit it off with Stephanie Rodemeyer. They were coworkers and decided to become roommates.

They quickly set out apartment hunting and eventually settled on a small apartment just off Columbia Pike in Arlington, Virginia. The apartment was in a high-rise building and had a pool on top.

Mary Jo and Stephanie were roommates for about a year – until Stephanie got engaged. Later, Stephanie moved on from the Grassley office and took a position in the White House.

Before she even settled into the apartment, Mary Jo began searching for a church home in the area.

She prayed, checked the yellow pages, asked around at the office, and not long after, sat in a carved oak pew in the expansive sanctuary of the First Baptist Church of Alexandria.

It was a grand, impressive church building that dominated the landscape along King Street – one of the most famous streets in America, weaving down through Old Town to the Potomac River.

Founded by Pastor Jeremiah Moore in 1803, First Baptist Church of Alexandria had a storied and fascinating history. Pastor Moore was a fearless preacher who was once jailed for "preaching doctrine that was not in accordance with the Church of England."

Historians report Pastor Moore was set free thanks to the spirited defense of his lawyer. That lawyer was Patrick Henry, best known for his "Give me liberty or give me death" speech in 1775. Pastor Moore was also instrumental in the adoption of the First Amendment to the U.S. Constitution.[23]

Mary Jo quickly embraced First Baptist Church of Alexandria as her church home. It would become the epicenter of life-changing relationships over the next decade.

She was delighted when her friend Mark Rittgers joined her in worship – and even more pleased when he met and married a girl named Sarah soon after.

Mary Jo began work on Capitol Hill by reporting to her cubicle in the Hart Senate Office Building, Room 135. She was eager and full of promise.

In contrast to its neo-classical neighbors, the Hart Building was a contemporary nine-story structure of cement and glass. It had a marble façade and a towering atrium.

The Hart Building was the largest of the senate office buildings. Located on Constitution Avenue between First and Second Streets, it was also the farthest from the U.S. Capitol. Unknown to most of the public, a subway connected the two buildings.

Mary Jo's first role on staff was that of staff assistant. It was a catch all title with duties that included answering constituent questions or complaints, taking messages, sorting mail and serving as office gopher.

She did it with professionalism and a smile and was always eager to help a coworker or a constituent.

Within a few months, Mary Jo's title changed to receptionist. The role and responsibilities were largely the same. After a time, her title changed yet again to legislative correspondent.

As a legislative correspondent, Mary Jo had more contact with the professional committee staffs and also got to know Ken Cunningham.

Ken had worked for Congressman Tom Tauke (R-IA) before Senator Grassley hired him as Chief of Staff. Amongst the staff, Ken had a reputation as a serious guy with a serious moustache, but Mary Jo helped to loosen him up by trading barbs and sarcastic witticisms.

Soon after, Mary Jo interviewed for a new position and was promoted to scheduler. Something akin to an executive assistant, the role of scheduler required organizational and people skills par excellence. It was a role she'd make her own for seven years.

On a typical day, Mary Jo fielded 50-75 phone calls, sorted through mail, invitations and an average of 15-20 requests for appointments with Senator Grassley.

She once summarized her duties in an interview with a reporter and friend, Pam Parry. Mary Jo said:

"My job is to tell him what he's supposed to do and when he's supposed to do it."

Senator Grassley didn't disagree. He said:

"I think she has the toughest job in the office."[24]

Grassley was not what the public viewed as a typical senator. In contrast to many of the capacious egos on the Hill, Senator Grassley was humble, kind and eminently likeable.

His awe-shucks manner belied a brilliant, inquisitive mind, and it was that rare mix of intellect and personality that made him a formidable politician, routinely reelected with 70% of the vote.

In time, Mary Jo became one of his closest advisors and a genuine friend. She also developed what coworkers called a "fierce loyalty" to Senator and Mrs. Grassley.

To the point, it was once reported that during a routine committee meeting another senator wagged his finger and cursed at Senator Grassley. It was the kind of thing that happened from time to time in the passion of politics, and Senator Grassley was barely offended. In fact, he responded in his usual unflappable style and forgave his colleague before they left the room.

Mary Jo, however, was a bit slower to forgive and forget the indiscretion. In fact, she was furious when she heard of it and marched into Senator Grassley's office to make sure she'd heard it right. From then forward, whenever the name of the cursing senator was mentioned she said, "Oh, you mean the Honorable Senator F-Word from the Great State of Arizona!"

The Hill could be an exciting and even intoxicating place to work, and Mary Jo relished the opportunity to influence issues or simply discuss them with her colleagues in the Grassley office.

Issues were as diverse as the use of biotechnology in agriculture, wind energy farms and the North American Free Trade Agreement. Staffers also confronted intriguing people and political issues like Newt Gingrich, the government shutdown and the Clinton-Lewinsky scandal.

"It was a very exciting time," she recalled. "I knew what happened before it hit the newspapers."

But like most offices, it was not the issues she looked back on and remembered with fondness. In later years, most people can't recall the point papers, briefs and Powerpoint presentations that once seemed so important anyway.

It's hard to remember the work you did, but easy to remember the people you worked with.

You remember their personality and influence. Maybe you remember a funny story or an office party. Sometimes that thing military leaders call *esprit de corps* develops and coworkers become more like friends.

If you're lucky, the people you work with may even become like your family.

In the Grassley office, Caran McKee quickly became such a friend to Mary Jo.

Caran was an attractive blonde with a warm, professional presence and a captivating smile. She and Mary Jo shared a quick wit and organized most office parties. They also shared frequent cups of coffee and an unflinching loyalty to Senator Grassley.

In later years, the two women would draw even closer and look to one another as sisters. Caran wrote:

"I'm grateful for your loving, fun and steadfast friendship. You've been a great influence on my life."

Mary Jo also became close to several other ladies in the office, including Penne Sienknecht. Penne was hard working, loyal and trustworthy. She and Mary Jo encouraged one another daily, sharing laughter and mentoring interns.

Jill Kozeny also became a good friend. Jill was the long-time communications director for Senator Grassley. Shannon Royce was a good friend as well and "coworker" hardly described the relationship between them.

Due to his role and personality, it took some time to draw closer to Ken Cunningham, but in time, Mary Jo got to know his warmth, kindness and love for his family.

Mary Jo greatly admired Ken's wife Sherry. Sherry was a kind and loving woman of great faith. She also had the patience of a saint, which came in handy while homeschooling four bright, energetic boys.

Around the Grassley office, Mary Jo was regarded as nice, cheerful and understanding, but she could also be tough-as-nails and decidedly partisan.

One of the favorite stories in the Grassley office was "The James Carville Encounter," as told by a coworker who once ferried Mary Jo across town for an appointment.

As they were driving down Pennsylvania Avenue in afternoon traffic, Mary Jo's coworker slowed cautiously near an intersection known for distracted tourists and busy staffers.

Suddenly, she was forced to brake hard and fast as a bicyclist darted out in front of the car.

But even as her foot touched the brake, Mary Jo had recognized the bicyclist as James Carville – the hyper-partisan Democratic operative. According to her coworker, Mary Jo yelled out "No! Don't stop, run him down!"

They laughed all the way back to the office, eager to share their Carville encounter with friends in the Grassley office.

Acquaintances were often surprised to learn this sweet girl from Chariton had a steel backbone and little patience for dishonesty, meanness or Democrats. Perhaps it was also a reflection of the pace and lifestyle of the big city.

Mary Jo grew up a small-town girl and was accustomed to people who would greet you with a smile and "How are ya?" or the Iowa Wave – that flick of the index finger above the steering wheel.

Washington D.C. was something different.

Despite its charming restaurants and spectacular sights, most of the populace was too busy to notice other people and had little patience for smiles or greetings.

For instance, the D.C. Wave utilized a different finger and was never accompanied with a smile but with an expletive. Whether on a metro train or a bustling sidewalk, eye contact was generally shunned and busyness was exalted.

Maybe that's painting with too broad a brushstroke, but it's clear Mary Jo never truly embraced the hectic pace and shark-like lifestyle of Washington D.C. She was not enamored with the culture of the big city. Dave Bowman observed:

"Mary Jo didn't let D.C. mold her and was a woman of great character. She didn't let Capitol Hill get to her head and even though the life of a staffer got hectic, she was always smiling."

Though she never embraced the frenetic pace, Mary Jo still held great affection for the sights and sounds of the big city. In an interview with *The Chariton Leader*, she said:

This is a wonderful place to live – there's just so much to do and so much to see that I don't know if you could ever do it all. Living here has given me a real appreciation for history that I never had living in Iowa; you run into (history) here. You can go into a restaurant in Old Town where George Washington used to hang out. Those sort of daily encounters with history have given me a real appreciation for it.

One of Mary Jo's favorite duties in the Grassley office was to serve as tour guide for visiting Iowans. She'd interpret maps, pass out tickets and send them out on the town with a smile.

Of the constituents, she said "You are Grassley to them," and she represented the senator with grace and professionalism. It was more than a job. She said:

"The best thing about working in this office is that in a lot of ways, it's like you never left home because you have so much contact with Iowans. I talk to Iowans all day long, and it's just a lot of fun. It's like a little piece of home here."

Back home in Iowa, there was a big, big change on the horizon for Mary Jo's mother, and it would be a frequent topic of conversation between mother and daughter.

With Mary Jo and Malinda out of the house, Karen decided to move to Mason City and take a position as the human resource manager at the Hy-Vee store on the east side of town.

As it happened, Pastor Ron Stein had moved to Mason City the year prior and served as the senior pastor at the First Baptist Church on East State Street.

And well…Karen and Ron began dating.

Dating isn't quite the right word, though. It was more like a courtship.

Ron and Karen spent a lot of time together in Bible study and then started going out for coffee.

Given their past, Ron and Karen were wary of a relationship, yet it grew slowly out of a genuine friendship. As Karen said, "It just kind of snuck up on us."

Ron and Karen were married in September of 1991. Mary Jo and Malinda would grow to love Ron Stein, and he would become like a second father to them.

The family was very proud of Mary Jo. They took turns visiting her in Washington D.C. and were very pleased to meet Senator Grassley and his staff.

Followed by a tour, of course. Ron had the bean soup.

Grandma and Grandpa McMains also visited the Grassley office and were treated more like royalty than constituents. When Grandma Helen returned home, she wrote a letter to Mary Jo and thanked her for the tour. She wrote:

"I'm so happy you like your life and work, and I thank God every day you have such a wonderful Christian man as your boss."

Over the years, Mary Jo's responsibilities and influence grew in the Grassley office. Ken often sent her in to give the senator bad news or ask if the staff could leave early ahead of a snowstorm.

It was hard to say "No" to Mary Jo. In an interview with *The Chariton Leader*, Senator Grassley said:

Mary Jo is probably the person on the staff that I have the most day-to-day contact with. Whether it's political, legislative or personal, you have to coordinate everything through her. She does a top-notch job. She has a good personality. A friendly person with a smile and a healthy attitude towards work is absolutely essential.

Mary Jo helped people with flags, passports, grants and a myriad of other questions

She even handled the occasional crackpots with grace and kindness. When a "scientist" called with his ideas on magnetic levitation, she listened patiently though she knew he'd call again with an even more ludicrous idea.

The actor Don DeFore called once in a while with feedback on the latest bill in Congress or just to chat with Mary Jo and Senator Grassley. He was bright, engaging and always interested in politics.

Mr. DeFore was from Cedar Rapids and campaigned for President Reagan, but he was best known as "Thorny" on *The Adventures of Ozzie and Harriett.* He had also been a friend to the late and legendary Marilyn Monroe.

Among the many other things she did in the Grassley office, Mary Jo pushed papers through the arduous process for citizenship and made a friend in Julio Motta. Julio was from Columbia and proudly became an American citizen.

Mary Jo also coordinated the Ambassador's Tour of Iowa, charming dignitaries and their staffs and making new friends from Sioux City, Iowa to Jakarta, Indonesia.

Michael Wyganowska was serving as the Second Secretary of Poland at the time and became a good friend to Mary Jo. He was delighted to introduce her to his wife Dorota, and later their daughter Julia. A few years later, Mary Jo also helped the Wyganowska family become American citizens.

When Mary Jo learned a friend had applied for a job in the office of Elizabeth Dole, she marched confidently into Senator Grassley's office with papers in hand.

Mrs. Dole had been newly appointed as the director of the Red Cross and was in need of an executive assistant. Mary Jo also knew Senator Grassley was close to Senator and Mrs. Dole. She said:

"My friend's resume is stuck on a desk somewhere at the Red Cross. I'd like you to call Senator and Mrs. Dole and tell them my friend Carol Maltman would be perfect for the job."

Senator Grassley had little choice but to call and sure enough, Mrs. Dole called Carol the next morning. It turned out Carol was perfect for the job, and she took it the following afternoon.

It was something Mary Jo did a hundred times for constituents, friends and friends of friends. As Senator Grassley said:

"Mary Jo is always busy helping other people."

In later years, Mary Jo's position and responsibilities changed to consulting and fund-raising, but her calling to help never wavered, and she gained new friends and admirers at every turn.

John Flannery and his wife Suzie became good friends through their mutual friendship with Senator Grassley.

John was another strong father figure for Mary Jo. Blessed with a sharp and engaging mind, he looked to Mary Jo as his own daughter and jealously screened boyfriends, ready to pounce on potential shortcomings.

Mark Disler was a respected lobbyist and became a good friend to Mary Jo as well. He was also a "rock" for Mary Jo in later health struggles. Mark greatly admired Mary Jo. He wrote:

"Mary Jo did a wonderful job for Senator Grassley. But much more than that, she was a wonderful person and friend."

Tad Davis was also a lobbyist and an all-around great guy. He echoed Mark Disler's sentiments and was delighted when Mary Jo joined him for an office party atop the Willard Hotel. The star of the party was a magnificent view of the Fourth of July fireworks over the Washington Monument.

Mary Jo frequently shared a working lunch with John, Mark, Tad or Layna McConkey – a health consultant and another good friend. Layna was a dynamo of energy and enthusiasm, and she gave hugs like a Kodiac bear despite her petite frame.

Though these relationships were special to Mary Jo, it was her relationship with Senator and Mrs. Grassley that was the formative one during this period in her life.

She described Chuck and Barbara as "like second parents" and loved them dearly. They were so close that "Senator Grassley has to remind me occasionally that I'm not his mother," Mary Jo joked, with a grin. She also said:

That's the difference between Senator Grassley and a lot of folks – he cares about what happens to people and he cares about his staff. He's very much like a parent. He meets the men I date. He won't say outright if he disapproves, but you can tell.[25]

No doubt, the relationship between Chuck Grassley and Mary Jo Archibold was deeper than that of U.S. Senator to scheduler. As with others, Mary Jo noted the senator's positive, healthy interest in the personal lives of his staff.

As the story goes, the senator even seemed to view himself as an accomplished matchmaker from time to time.

In truth, it was Ken Cunningham – not Senator Grassley – who first introduced Congressman Tom Tauke to Beverly Hubble, but that's not how many on Capitol Hill remember it. Beverly was a bright, attractive lady who handled media relations for Senator Grassley, and he thought very highly of her.

Though Ken introduced the pair on a blind date, Chuck "Cupid" Grassley took a great interest. It was said he shadowed Beverly like a Cold War spy, tiptoeing down hallways, peeking around corners and scanning documents for classified information.

While Tom and Beverly did their best to keep the relationship under the radar, Senator Grassley was even more determined to learn of it. As Beverly said, "Senator Grassley knew I was seeing someone and kept pestering me to find out who it was."

Under the threat of near-constant surveillance, Tom and Beverly suspected it was only a matter of time before their courtship would be discovered – and it was. Tom wrote:

"During a dinner in the House Dining Room, Beverly and I looked over and there on the other side of the room was Senator Grassley, grinning like a Cheshire cat."

Like a good politician and with a self-assured smile, Grassley "claimed full credit" for the marriage, to the great amusement of his staff.

It was not his first attempt at matchmaker – and it would not be his last.

Pickett House

> "No love, no friendship, can cross the path of our destiny without leaving some mark on it forever."
>
> Francois Mocuriac

Mary Jo enjoyed working on Capitol Hill, and she loved her colleagues for their wit, wisdom and lasting influence.

However, Mary Jo was not career-minded, nor were the politics of Washington D.C. the center of her universe.

Just as in high school and college, it was her faith and the relationships based upon it that centered her soul, passion and priorities.

To a person, the people she worked with understood that fact, including Senator Grassley. He said:

"Mary Jo is a very good witness for her faith. Her faith is very central in her life."

Though Mary Jo understood faith transcended religion and church buildings, it was First Baptist Church of Alexandria that served as her pivot point.

The church building stood out as an impressive, stately brick edifice along King Street. Its white steeple towered over even the oaks and cottonwoods in the neighborhood. A revolutionary-era surveyor's stone sat in the expansive parking lot, protected by a wrought-iron fence.

Some said the church grounds were surveyed by none-other than George Washington. But then, the same has been said of Blessed Sacrament Elementary School and perhaps even the nearest McDonald's at Bradlee Shopping Center.

Area pastors referred to First Baptist Church of Alexandria as a "mega church" due to its large and diverse membership, and like other large churches, most of the Sunday schools and activities were divided by demographics. This organizational structure of various groups was as imperfect as its members, but it worked.

The "Singles Group" was one of those groups.

The group was further separated into three sections, grouped loosely by age and labeled "Singles 1, 2 and 3." Sometimes this proved awkward and they changed the numbers around to keep people guessing but again, it worked.

Singles 1 was made up of forty-somethings, yet it was a dynamic, fun-loving group. Britt Grouby, Gary Morris and Linda Ramsey took turns at the helm, often combining Bible study with food and games, replete with laughter.

More than once, the "Young Married" group at the end of the hall had to ask them to "Keep it down, please."

Singles 3 was better known as the "College and Career" group. It was comprised of twenty-somethings and led by Dave Crittendon or Richard Richie. It was also an enthusiastic group, though with a high turnover rate. Some "leakage" also occurred from older groups, and sometimes a thirty-something visited.

Which is okay, but it's true a fifty-something man once pushed the boundaries. "Hey, I was just looking," he deadpanned when the singles pastor politely suggested another group.

Lastly, there were the thirty-somethings of Singles 2. It was the largest group, broken into two sub-groups titled "2A" and "2B."

Of the two divisions, the latter was better known because it featured a band named…wait for it: "The 2B Band."

The 2B Band led the group in praise and worship, often with contemporary numbers by Rich Mullins, Michael W. Smith or Dennis Jernigan, and they weren't bad. Seriously.

Kathy Wise and Robin Reichenbach shared vocals while John Elliott and/or Glenn Pruitt played guitar. Sometimes on a good day, a keyboardist joined in.

Turnover was frequent in Singles 2, though not because of age and an accompanying "promotion" to Singles 1. It was because of career moves or more often, marriage.

Singles 2 was a fun-loving group. In fact, it proved so popular at First Baptist Church of Alexandria that rumors circulated of newly married couples who had asked to stick around. "Sorry, but that's just kind of awkward," they were told.

Some of the Singles 2 leaders of the time were Kathy Wise, Alice Turner, Sara Simko, Linda Revilla, and later, Mary Jo. For a while, Glenn Collier led the Bible study. Other leaders included Mike Yokitis, Charlie Niemeier and Trevor Friend.

Overseeing this ever-changing, complex group of single adults was the Minister of Singles and Missions.

His name was Jim Witt, and he was a Texan, born and raised. Easy-going and patient, Jim had earned his seminary degree from Southwestern Baptist Theological Seminary in Fort Worth, Texas. After graduation, he accepted a ministry position nearby at Sagimore Baptist Church.

Jim had only been at Sagimore for about a year when Jay Wolf, then Senior Pastor of First Baptist Church, called and asked him to come to Alexandria, Virginia. But Jim said, "No." Twice.

Jay Wolf was undeterred. A charismatic and bold leader, Pastor Wolf oversaw a dramatic period of growth for the church, and he had a persevering spirit. He called a third time and Jim finally consented to pray about it.

"If I feel the Holy Spirit calls me, I'll consider it," Jim said.

The following week, Jim was awoken by a phone call. Picking up the receiver, he heard a powerful, resonate voice. It said:

"Jim, this is the Holy Spirit. Come to Alexandria."

"Hi Jay," Jim responded.

"How did you know it was me?" Jay said, disappointed.

"The Holy Spirit never calls me before 9 a.m.," Jim deadpanned.

Thanks to his baritone voice and sense of humor, Pastor Wolf finally had his man. Pastor Jim Witt reported to Alexandria in 1987, and it proved to be a life-changing calling.

Pastor Witt was delighted to shepherd, encourage, challenge, cajole and love the single adults of First Baptist Church for nine memorable years.

The singles were a remarkable group with a colorful cast of characters.

Chuck Hull was tall, dark and handsome, and he had steel-like eyes and a handshake to match it. Chuck never talked about his work, but a friend once noticed Chuck's badge and gun. The gun was a semi-automatic Sig Sauer, Model P229.

"That gun looks like standard issue of the Secret Service," the friend said. Still, Chuck said nothing.

David Bowman was popular, fun and engaging. Some said he was a professional photographer but others whispered, "I heard Dave works for the CIA." Like Chuck, Dave said nothing.

There were rumors Jim Boggess worked for the CIA too, but when pressed Jim also said nothing. It only increased the mystery. Perhaps it was a ploy to attract girls, God only knows.

Many of the other single adults also worked for the government, whether on Capitol Hill or at White House or some other well-known, three-letter organization.

Linda Gibson was a flight attendant for American Airlines. She was not the frumpy, unfriendly kind you sometimes encounter today but elegant, professional, stylish, and yes, attractive.

Lisa Elek was also attractive and gregarious. Of Lisa, Mary Jo once said, "She's the most vivacious person I've ever known." No doubt, Lisa was never boring.

At a 1970s dance party, Lisa once wowed guests as a dead-on look-alike for Farrah Fawcett. At least two guys asked her out that night. They were disappointed when she later married Rex Jordan.

Rex was a military officer assigned to Air Force One.

Richard Stead was another intriguing person in Singles 2. He was a seismologist and had a doctorate degree from CalTech. Richard had a full beard and a robust laugh. On weekends, he dominated opponents in Trivial Pursuit and ran marathons.

Into this mix of Christian singles, Mary Jo felt at home and among family, and she made friends quickly and easily.

She attended worship services and Bible study faithfully. She also joined the singles group, sometimes singing with the 2B Band. Mary Jo helped out by making coffee and flyers. Even while a newcomer herself, she was peerless at making others feel welcome.

Pastor Witt appreciated her can-do attitude and it wasn't long before Mary Jo became one of the group leaders. She was always helping and serving. Pastor Witt said:

"Mary Jo is one of those go-to people because she does everything well. There's a real consistency to Mary Jo's life that shines through in the way she lives."

Within the first months of attending First Baptist Church of Alexandria, Mary Jo also developed a friendship with Glenn Collier. Then it became something more.

Glenn was a nice guy and a faithful Christian. Though about the same height as Mary Jo, he was stocky and moved like the athlete he once was.

Glenn had been a college-level gymnast and could do a handstand as easily as to walk upright.

Before long, Glenn and Mary Jo were spending a lot of time together, and it was apparent Mary Jo liked this fellow a lot more than the guys she knew in high school and college.

When Mary Jo told Glenn her living situation was less than ideal, he was understanding and helpful. Glenn promptly called Kathy Wise because he knew Kathy had just lost a roommate from her house in Alexandria.

Glenn was eager to help – but Kathy, not so much.

Though it's true a roommate had moved out, Kathy and her remaining roommate Cristy Rice were happy with things as they were. So Kathy told Glenn, "No thank you, we don't want another roommate right now."

Later, Kathy reconsidered. "I kept praying about it, and I felt I should at least sit down and talk with Mary Jo," she said. With her roommate Cristy about to marry Mark Hissong, Kathy also thought she might take another roommate after all.

Both Kathy and Mary Jo recalled the meeting as cordial, yet business-like. Their time together gave little hint of the deep, abiding friendship that would develop between them.

Both would remember and laugh about Kathy's rules for roommates. Kathy called these rules her "Three Absolutes."

1. No wild parties.
2. No overnight boyfriends.
3. No alcohol.

That Kathy even felt the need to explain these rules to Mary Jo showed how little she knew of her new roommate.

Kathy Wise was sweet, loving, generous and understanding.

She had auburn hair and a southern drawl from deep in Texas. Kathy had known Pastor Witt's sister back in Texas and was delighted when Jim was "called" to come to Virginia.

Kathy had moved to Washington D.C. in 1981 after graduating from her beloved Baylor University in Waco, Texas. When she decided to move to the Washington area, she was guided by three other principles. She wrote:

"I had three goals: First, to get out of the Bible belt; second, to live east of the Mississippi; and third, to go where I knew at least one person."

As it happened, the one person Kathy knew was Carol Davis, the pastor's daughter at First Baptist Church of Alexandria.

Kathy and Mary Jo shared a home in what they called "The Pickett House."

The Pickett House was placed at an angle on a corner lot at 497 North Pickett Street, at the intersection of North Pickett Street and Taney Avenue. Patrick Henry Elementary School was nearby and so was the I-395 superhighway, just eight blocks in the other direction.

The house was of the Cape Cod style, with an open floor plan, a carport and a full basement. Half of the basement was finished.

Upstairs there were two bedrooms and one bathroom. The bathroom was a throwback to the 1950s, with alternating pink and black tiles.

The ground floor had the same layout, but the girls converted the extra bedrooms into what they called "sitting rooms," which was, of course, girl speak for what a man would call a TV room.

Mary Jo loved the simple house, especially the screened-in porch and the easy layout of the kitchen.

She also enjoyed tending the flowerbeds along the fence line and could often be found with a bulb planter or garden spade in hand, her hair tied back by a bandana.

The homes in the neighborhood were remarkably similar, though some could be classified as ranch or split-level. There was a nice park at the end of the street at Holmes Run with a playground and a creek running through it.

It was peaceful, picturesque and felt like the other side of the world from Washington D.C., though it was only about five miles as the crow flies.

The neighborhood was also the location for the annual, Mile-long Yard Sale along Taney Avenue, and Kathy and Mary Jo looked forward to setting up their table and sipping hot chocolate every year.

They didn't really care to sell anything, really, and the neighbors weren't necessarily friendly, but it wasn't Southeast D.C. either. At least they don't shoot you in Virginia.

For the roommates, it took some time to warm to one another, perhaps because of the first impressions. Kathy and Mary Jo were friendly, but they were not friends.

The relationship changed after a visit from Mary Jo's best friend Paula, who was now living in California.

Mary Jo had been preparing dinner when she entered the screen porch and found Paula and Kathy in deep, heartfelt conversation. Kathy was in tears.

Later in the evening, Mary Jo wondered aloud, "I've been here a year and you never sat down and cried with me."

The relationship grew slowly but surely, and it wouldn't be long before Mary Jo had another best friend in Kathy Wise. It deepened into a life-changing fellowship in Christ.

Though Mary Jo admired and respected Glenn, their relationship went in a different direction. It was not deepening but weakening.

Not long after moving into the Pickett House, friends thought Mary Jo might be ready for marriage but Glenn didn't ask. He had some reservations and wasn't ready for marriage.

About six months later, Mary Jo sensed he was ready for marriage but then she wasn't – nor would she be. Mary Jo broke off the relationship and Glenn's heart with it.

Instead, it was Mary Jo's sister Malinda who got engaged.

Malinda accepted the proposal from her high school sweetheart, Jeff Greubel. She was thrilled to tell Mary Jo and excitedly asked her to come to Iowa and serve as her maid of honor.

Mary Jo arrived a few days in advance of the wedding and was delighted to accompany Karen, Malinda and Jeff to worship service. Malinda wrote:

For the wedding, I'd purchased and set-aside a very special pair of earrings to wear with my dress. Mary Jo was home from Washington D.C. and joined us for church. She was sitting in the third row of pews, and I was singing up front because it was my day for music. I looked down at Mary Jo and saw that she was grinning from ear to ear. She was wearing my new earrings!

Jeff and Malinda were to have three children: Casey, Chelsey and Carly. Mary Jo was present for the birth of each of them and even flew back home from overseas for the birth of the youngest, Carly. She loved her nephew and nieces as her own and frequently shared gifts, advice and a hug.

Back at the Pickett House, Kathy and Mary Jo had an open room so they welcomed a few other roommates into the house, but the roommates did not stay for long.

The new roommates were not ejected because they broke one of the three absolutes. They left because they got married.

Cheryl Wardrop was a friend from the singles group, and she was the first to move into the basement of the Pickett House.

Friendly and attractive, Cheryl quickly caught the eye of Jeff Ray while attending First Baptist Church of Alexandria. They were engaged and Kathy Wise soon gave the Pickett House a new nickname: "The Home for Not Yet Wed Women."

Jeff and Cheryl were married and moved first to North Carolina, then on to Texas.

Carol Maltman was the next to move in. A self-described "Air Force brat," Carol was working at the Red Cross for Elizabeth Dole. She was also a new Christian.

Carol enjoyed living with Kathy and Mary Jo and said, "Mary Jo was a good mentor to me." But Carol didn't stay long in what she called the "magical basement" at Pickett House.

Carol had met Timothy Scott through the singles group. Timothy was a patent attorney, and he fell in love with Carol and proposed marriage. He also learned Mrs. Dole was as protective of her staff as was Senator Grassley.

"I remember getting grilled by Mrs. Dole," Timothy said.

Kathy and Mary Jo's next roommate was Nina Blanco. Nina had been diagnosed with multiple sclerosis, but it seemed to have little affect on her positive attitude. Tod Shook noticed, and he proposed marriage. The basement was empty again.

Kathy and Mary Jo's next roommate was the one exception to the three absolutes.

His name was Phillip Hurst, and he was the only man to live at the Pickett House. A good friend from the singles group, Phillip was granted what Mary Jo called a "sympathy waiver" from the three absolutes because he was recovering from an emergency appendectomy.

An enlisted man in the U.S. Marines, Phillip later suffered a leg injury while in training at Officer Candidate School but went on to an even higher calling and became a pastor.

For a brief period, a few girlfriends thought there could be romantic sparks between Phillip and Mary Jo. It made sense, as both adults were confident, talented and attractive.

But Phillip and Mary Jo viewed their relationship as more like that of a brother and sister – though they did once test their friendship with a kiss under the mistletoe.

However, no sparks or fireworks accompanied the kiss. It was remembered as similar to the kiss shared by Luke the Jedi Knight and Princess Leia.

The Pickett House was a frequent location for parties, usually with friends from the singles group and without the booze, which disappointed a few.

The invitees were an intriguing, fun-loving group and included Linda Revilla, Shirley Sprinkle and Kim Tucker.

The three girls shared a house on Oronoco Street and were known at parties as "The Oronoco Sisters."

Gill Abernathy lived nearby on Terril Street, and she and her roommate Cindy Evans would be frequent guests at Pickett House parties. Gill would also become one of Mary Jo's best friends.

Phillip Hurst, Chris Camplejohn, Beth Beard, Carol Mills and Rebecca Bentley were a few of the many others who joined in the fun. When a guest received an invitation to a party at the Pickett House, they knew they were in for a memorable evening.

For a New Year's Eve party, Kathy and Mary Jo fashioned an elaborate, multi-tiered New York skyline out of cardboard from a refrigerator box. The cardboard buildings were adorned with hand-painted windows and twinkling Christmas lights.

The girls even managed to rig-up a bulb that served as the ceremonial light ball over Times Square. It was attached to a pulley and tethered to the ceiling with nylon string.

Guests applauded and some even kissed as Phillip carefully lowered the 100-watt light bulb over the cardboard skyline at the stroke of midnight.

Always a fashionista, Gill Abernathy showed up to the New York party dressed as the infamous hotel heiress Leona Helmsley. Adorned with a plumed velvet hat and fake mink shawl, Gill pulled it off with panache.

Mary Jo was not to be outdone, and she introduced herself as "Wanda, Toll Booth Operator." Mary Jo entertained (and insulted) the partygoers with her spot-on Jersey accent.

Greeting each guest at the door, "Wanda" demanded, "Where's your danged token?!"

When spring came, Kathy and Mary Jo hosted the entire singles department for a barbecue. Jim Witt, Alyson Essa, Nancy Thompson, Pam Parry, Victor Castillo and many others joined them for a party under the carport in the driveway.

Mary Jo impressed their guests with hors d'ourves and a killer dip of Rotella and Velveeta cheese.

Though not as talented in the kitchen as Mary Jo, Kathy was delightfully proud when she unveiled her Texas supreme nachos, fresh off the charcoal grill. Kathy grinned with satisfaction at the stack of nachos laden with ground beef, cheddar cheese and jalapeno peppers.

At the first bite, a guest observed "Hey, these chips taste like lighter fluid!"

Mary Jo always enjoyed the parties, visiting with friends, laughing and telling stories. She had the gift of hospitality, and people noticed. Rebecca Bentley Hall said:

"Mary Jo was compassionate and so very generous with affection for others. Her smile would light up a room. You didn't have to be 'best friends' with Mary Jo – she made you feel like a special friend no matter how close you were with her."

In addition to the Pickett House parties, Mary Jo attended many large, well-organized social outings with friends from the singles group. The group enjoyed a ski weekend at Wisp Resort in Maryland, a hike up Old Rag Mountain and white water rafting on the Cheat River in West Virginia.

Mary Jo enjoyed most of these outings with Glenn, though she remembered he was annoyed because her asthma kicked in during the hike up Old Rag Mountain. However, Whitney VanLandingham said:

"I just remember her laughing and smiling all the time! What a beautiful girl!! We all had so much fun together."

The annual highlight of the singles group activities was a weekend retreat to Bethany Beach in Delaware.

They stayed at The Addy Sea. It was a picturesque Victorian mansion with gingerbread latticework and cedar shingles. It was also an ideal setting for spiritual renewal and relaxation, with a large collection of rocking chairs on the expansive porch and a sweeping view of the Atlantic.

Mrs. Gravatt was the owner of The Addy Sea, and she enjoyed hosting the group. However, the elderly lady was understandably particular about her antique furnishings and well-kept grounds. She did not appreciate anyone who ventured off-trail and walked on the sand dune.

During one retreat at The Addy Sea, prankster Jeff Ray got up early in the morning to hammer a stake with a sign on the dune. The sign read, "Kathy Wise was here!" in large black letters.

Mrs. Gravatt was not amused.

At the beach retreat, the singles spent much more time together than they ordinarily would after a worship service, and they really got to know one another. Mary Jo also made two dear friends in Elaine Gilliam and Deborah Kay Hays during trips to the beach.

They played board games and cards until late in the night and Frisbee and football during the day. Most of the girls sat on the beach and read a novel or a magazine.

On Saturday night, it was the tradition to hold a talent show of sorts at The Addy Sea. The group was often entertained by the acting skills of "The Fabulous Oronoco sisters."

The singles enjoyed Bible study overlooking the ocean on the front porch and cherished the time of fellowship. The retreat grew so popular they even had to rent out a hotel nearby, but it didn't have the personality and memories of The Addy Sea.

Mary Jo loved the beach and frequently returned to Bethany Beach with other girlfriends. One of her favorite things to do was to ride along with Elaine in her convertible with the top-down and sun shining. They drove to Bethany Beach and back laughing all the way. On one trip, Elaine remembered:

> We drew close to a truck loaded with freshly picked corn and saw the cobs bouncing out of the bed and onto the side of the road. With the top down, Mary Jo suggested I pull up close, and she would stand up and snatch the corn as it was dropping from the truck! Since this would require some very precise driving and balance, I decided to stop at the next farm stand instead. Mary Jo kept reminding me, "Hey, we could've gotten our sweet corn for free!"[26]

When Mary Jo and Elaine returned from the beach, they frequently gathered with other friends at Atlantis restaurant. It was also a common gathering place after worship service on Sunday morning.

Atlantis was a nondescript Greek-American restaurant in the Bradlee Shopping Center just off King Street. Mary Jo described the waitresses at Atlantis as "snarky" but the food was pretty good, and she loved the large ceramic coffee mugs.

On many weekends, Mary Jo volunteered at a homeless shelter on North Henry Street in Alexandria. It was called the Carpenter Shelter, and Mary Jo often worked there with Russ Sullivan and other friends from church to clean, organize and serve meals.

She also began teaching English as a Second Language classes in the basement at First Baptist Church of Alexandria.

In addition, Mary Jo worked with the youth and taught first and second graders about the Bible. She also visited with the elderly at retirement homes and led a small group of single Christian women.

Mary Jo was always helping, serving and encouraging others. Friends like Nancy Thompson noticed her faithful witness and were generous with praise. Nancy wrote:

"Mary Jo was the best example of a true Christian woman that I've ever known."[27]

It was a high compliment that reflected the high regard her friends had for Mary Jo. They were impressed with the natural grace and kindness she showed to both friends and strangers.

Friends noted she often sought-out newcomers to worship services, even though she may have preferred to catch-up with friends she hadn't seen in a while. She wanted visitors to feel welcomed, encouraged and loved.

Caroline Tirona was a sweet, kind lady who worked as a nanny, and she remembered Mary Jo's hospitality with great affection. Caroline wrote:

"Mary Jo always, always made me feel welcome – just like what Jesus would do."

Sara Simko was another person who was first welcomed by Mary Jo, and it had a lasting impact on them both.

Sara was a lovely and confident woman, but she had only recently moved from Florida and admitted to a little anxiousness about making new friends. She was understandably nervous when she stood before about 500 strangers and was introduced as a new member at First Baptist Church of Alexandria. Sara said:

I was standing at the front of the church when this attractive, confident gal came forward and introduced herself. She was smiling and friendly, and her nametag read "Mary Jo." I'll never forget it – she just seemed so pleased to meet me and was so kind and encouraging. She asked me about myself and then told me about the singles group that met upstairs. Then, taking my hand, Mary Jo said, "And you will come with me."

Sara did go with her, and Mary Jo promptly introduced Sara to other new friends – people like Kathy Wise, Gill Abernathy and Linda Gibson. Sara also met Kevin Bridwell – a man who would become her husband.

In Sara, Mary Jo had another best friend, and they would remain dear friends for life.

Gill Abernathy often remarked on Mary Jo's God-given ability to put people at ease. She made them feel important, no matter who they were or where they were from.

Gill came from a small town in North Carolina, and she moved to Alexandria not long after graduating from the University of North Carolina. She knew Cindy Francis from Chapel Hill, and it was Cindy who first invited her to First Baptist Church.

Gill was a charming, professional woman. Tall and elegant, she had a sugar sweet southern accent and an uncanny ability to match clothing and accessories. Whether wearing turquoise or lavender, Gill was always able to "accessorize" with a matching broche or tennis bracelet.

Gill was also extremely loyal and a great encourager. She would become a dear friend to Mary Jo. Mary Jo loved her dearly, and the feeling was shared. Gill wrote:

"I love you for just being the inimitable, the one and only Mary Jo."

Some thought it odd that Mary Jo had such lovely, accomplished girlfriends, yet seemed to have such poor luck with boyfriends – much as in high school and college.

Mary Jo's perspective on the subject was mature and insightful, and she once shared it in an interview for *Christian Single* magazine. She said:

"I don't think it matters if you are married or single. My philosophy is that you should live a life that is pleasing to God."

Jim Witt was Mary Jo's pastor, and he liked that answer.

Pastor Witt was married a bit later in life and would always be grateful to Kathy Wise for introducing him to Alyson Essa. Alyson was a cute, petite lady of Lebanese and Palestinian heritage, and she and Jim had met at First Baptist Church of Alexandria.

During her time with the singles group, Mary Jo had several conversations with Pastor Witt about boyfriends. She began to wonder if she would ever be married. "Am I doing something wrong?" she wondered. "Are my standards too high?" she thought.

As a pastor, Jim Witt understood his role was often to simply listen, and he was hesitant to offer advice. But he did sometimes sense a deeper desire or hurt, and he knew Mary Jo as well as any of her best friends. Jim wrote:

People saw Mary Jo as pretty, smart, tough and accomplished – and she was all that. For some men, I suppose this may have been intimidating, that perhaps they couldn't measure up. But ironically, if that's all you knew of her, you didn't really know her at all because she was also sweet, loving and vulnerable. Mary Jo was strong, but like all of us, she just needed to be loved.[28]

Mary Jo's relationship with Russ Sullivan was different from the one with Glenn, and it lasted nearly two years.

She felt great respect and admiration for Russ, as he was smart, disciplined and had a genuine heart for serving others. Russ was a frequent volunteer at city shelters and led an effort to bring diversity to the First Baptist Church of Alexandria.

However, the relationship between Russ and Mary Jo was an uneven one. It was based more on respect than love or affection.

As Mary Jo once put it, "We just never seemed to have a future together." Later, she'd joke, "It would've never worked out anyway because Russ was a Democrat!"

Still, Mary Jo was hurt when the relationship with Russ fell apart and not eager to begin another one.

Nonetheless, it wasn't long before a new visitor to the singles group asked Mary Jo out on a date. Jed was tall, athletic and a pilot in the Air Force.

However, Mary Jo's girlfriends didn't like this new boyfriend as much as Mary Jo did. One even remarked, "Jed was a scoundrel."

After about six months of dating, Mary Jo and Jed broke up and her loyal, protective friends were quick with comments like, "I never liked him anyway." Another said, "Just say the word, and I'll burn his house to the ground."[29]

The relationship also led to a rough patch with Kathy Wise, who said, "I didn't think Jed was the right person for Mary Jo." But as they had before, Mary Jo and Kathy worked through it and developed a friendship that was deeper and more meaningful.

It wouldn't be long before Mary Jo would face some changes, first with her career and then with her roommate.

Though Mary Jo loved working for Senator Grassley, she'd grown tired of the commute and lifestyle. The commute was a seven-mile grind that often took more than 45 minutes.

Shelley Dolf was an intern in the Grassley office and once had to drive herself home when Mary Jo had to work late. "I was utterly terrified by the six lanes of bumper-to-bumper traffic," Shelley said.

Mary Jo was tired. She was tired not just of the commute, but the politics and hustle and bustle of it all. She even talked about it in an interview with a reporter from *The Chariton Leader*. She said:

"I think I'm ready for a change. I love my job, but I've never liked politics."

While still on Capitol Hill, Mary Jo had started taking classes in linguistics at George Mason University in Fairfax, Virginia. Intrigued by the study of languages from her work with foreign students, she was awarded an M.A. with honors in May 1996.

Eventually, Mary Jo applied what she learned and began teaching English as a Second Language classes part-time at Northern Virginia Community College. The college was "NOVA" to locals, and it was there that she made two new friends in Kelly Mine and Daiva Miller. Both were fellow teachers.

Mary Jo's roommate Kathy Wise was also ready for a change.

Kathy had decided to move back to Waco, Texas to attend Truett Theological Seminary. It would bring Kathy back to Texas and her parents, whom she loved nearly as much as the Baylor Bears.

It was tough for Kathy to leave the Pickett House and as tough for Mary Jo to watch her go.

Mary Jo was anxious for the future. She was anxious for a career change or a new roommate and wondered what changes lay ahead. She was thankful for her family, friends and career, but she was ready for a change.

Mary Jo was also ready to move on from the Pickett House. She was to leave the "Home for Not Yet Wed Women" behind.

The Captain's Wife

"Someday, someone will walk into your life and make you realize why it never worked out with anyone else."

Anonymous

CHEMISTRY – THAT "SPARKY THING" that sometimes exists between a man and a woman – can't be forced nor easily defined.

Sometimes it grows slowly, and other times it comes on like a lightning bolt – perhaps even at first sight, as they say. You remember that first glance or the way her hair glows in the sun.

It's hard to define. You just know it when you see it.

For Mary Jo and I, chemistry developed quickly though not at first sight. It bubbled like liquid in a glass beaker, urged on by unseen flames as if a Bunsen burner.

The first time I saw Mary Jo, I was sitting in a rear church pew at First Baptist Church of Alexandria and listening contently to the church orchestra. Roger McGee was the Minister of Music and Worship, and he led the orchestra.

Looking down the aisle, I noticed the legs and then the very pretty face of a young lady playing the flute.

It wasn't until a few weeks later that I learned her name. She spoke first just outside a room on the second floor of that same church.

"Umm, you need some help with that, mister?" she said.

"No, not at all, I often spill coffee on myself," I replied.

"Sounds like you've got problems," she laughed.

"You don't know the half of it," I said, glancing first at her nametag, then at her legs, and she was gone.

A few months prior, I had been working in the high desert of southern California, sent there to fine-tune the weapons system for the B-2 bomber.

But as fate would have it, the Air Force selected fifty captains for a new fellowship program at the Pentagon and The George Washington University, and I was one of those captains.

I grew up Catholic and even served as an altar boy, so the First Baptist Church of Alexandria may have seemed an odd place for me to go to church. But I'd made some friends who were Baptists, read the Bible for myself and looked-up the stately church on King Street in the yellow pages.

Later, a friend informed me I was still Catholic because of my baptism and confirmation. "You're still a Catholic Brent," he said, "but like the rest of us, you're just not a very good one."

Admittedly, it was an adjustment to attend worship services. Sometimes I got distracted and made the sign of the cross or looked for a place to genuflect. But I did adjust and eventually ventured upstairs to where the singles met, prodded by a friendly pharmaceutical representative. His name was Chris Phillips.

Chris and I became friends and then roommates. We shared a home on Old Dominion Boulevard in Alexandria. It was a historic neighborhood of stately homes, mature trees and in the spring, impressive displays of azaleas.

We were both long-time bachelors, and friends were amused to learn Chris and I ate most meals on paper plates and had a 50-gallon trashcan in the kitchen. We thought it was a brilliant set-up, as neither of us liked to do dishes or take out the trash.

Unlike yours truly, Chris was entertaining, sociable and always on the lookout for a party. He'd heard about a party at Chuck Hull's house and dragged me along.

At the time, Chuck Hull spent days protecting Vice President Al Gore – or so we were told.

At his party, we met a friendly lady named Kathy Wise, and I heard she later told Mary Jo, "My goodness, you've got to meet this guy – he's killer handsome, charming as a prince and bright as a shining star."

Okay, I made that up. What Kathy said was:

"Mary Jo, I met this guy named Brent. He's also from Iowa. I think you'd like him."

As it turned out, Mary Jo and I had already met, and she remembered the spilled coffee. The following Sunday, we found ourselves seated next to each other at the Olive Garden on King Street with a large group of friends from the singles group.

When Mary Jo told me she was kind of dating someone, I leaned over and whispered, "Well, I guess I'll just have to be patient and wait for my chance."

In my mind, it was bold, smooth and romantic, but she laughed a little too loud and drew glances. I humbly retreated to my coffee and managed not to spill it.

About a week later, Mary Jo invited me to join her and some of her many friends on a tour of the Capitol Dome, accompanied by Senator Grassley.

Our group was excited, even giddy, as the Architect of the Capitol escorted us through the old capitol structure. He navigated up and down serpentine steps and paused to point at the based of the statue *Freedom* that sat atop the capitol dome.

Then we entered a small door and looked down on the rotunda of the capitol. Above us was the *The Apotheosis of Washington* – a magnificent fresco created by Constantino Brumidi in 1865. Just inches away, it was breathtaking.

Since the U.S. Senate was not in session, Senator Grassley graciously escorted us out onto the senate floor. He showed us the senate desks with names carved or written inside.

The desks dated to 1819 and included names like Daniel Webster and Andrew Jackson. Senator Grassley pointed out the Jefferson Davis desk, which had been punctured by a bayonet from the Civil War. A patch of light-colored wood putty stood out from the deep mahogany.

As a student of American history, I was so excited I could've done cartwheels on the senate floor, but they tend to frown upon that kind of thing. I was told you could probably get away with a cartwheel on the house side.

Not long after, Mary Jo arranged for my parents, Ray and Kathleen Hoffmann, to meet with Senator Grassley. We enjoyed the bean soup in the senate dining room, then bought cuff links and scarves in the gift shop.

As we were leaving, my father said to me, "How about that girl?" And the senator said to Mary Jo, "How about that guy?"

Finally, I called Mary Jo to ask her out on a date, but it turned out she would be busy that Friday. So we decided I'd accompany her to the farewell reception for the ambassador to Singapore. "What should I wear?" I asked. "Clothing," she said.

At the embassy, she introduced me to the ambassadors and their wives, we made small talk and I pretended like I went to these shindigs all the time. I also ate a plateful of satay and somehow, some way, managed not to spill the coffee.[30]

From then on, Mary Jo and I spent nearly every weekend together. We toured the Smithsonian Museums – all of them – and walked through the galleries of the National Gallery of Art while talking and laughing, then holding hands and looking for a quiet corner.

Dates included a concert at Wolf Trap in Vienna and *Les Miserables* at the Warner Theater in D.C. I fell asleep at both, but Mary Jo was forgiving and nestled into my shoulder.

We enjoyed dinner at Gadsby's Tavern in Old Town – a Revolutionary-era hangout for guys with names like John Adams. George Washington really did sleep there.

For Mary Jo and I, it could be said our relationship was built on friendship, but there were a few small bumps at the beginning. After the first date, Mary Jo told girlfriends "He's cute and charming – but he also talks a lot and can be kind of goofy."

Mary Jo's roommates, however, were solidly in my corner.

Deborah Kay or "Debbie" moved into the Pickett House not long after Kathy Wise moved out. Debbie was sweet and motherly and always encouraging to me.

"If it doesn't work out, I'm available, honey," she said, with a wink and an accent from deep in Tennessee.

Mary Jo was different from most other girls I'd dated – and in a good way. She was quick-witted and kept me on my toes. She was a godly woman and committed to purity before marriage. Her relationship with God was more important than any relationship with any man.

I had little understanding of Mary Jo's past relationships and even less interest in talking about them. But surely, she had some hurts, and it takes time for trust to catch up with chemistry.

Years later, Pastor Witt, a good friend to both Mary Jo and me, commented, "I can see how Mary Jo could fall in love quickly – but trust, that took some time."

It was an issue I brought up in our men's Bible study group since relationships with women were a frequent topic of conversation. The group included Ron Gallagher, Gerry Simard, Steve Smith, Chris Brady, Trevor Friend, Mike Yokitis, Richard Stead and Chris Phillips. We developed a strong bond of trust and fellowship.

We teased one another as men are known to do, but we also sharpened and challenged one another. Mike Yokitis was an especially loyal, encouraging friend and always available to listen.

Later, Mary Jo's former boyfriend Glenn Collier also joined our group. He harbored no bitterness towards her and like other men, had only positive comments about Mary Jo.

The relationship between Mary Jo and I was "interrupted" when I was sent on an unplanned deployment to Saudi Arabia. Sent there as a force protection officer after the horrific bombing at Khobar Towers, it was my first direct contact with the evil of Muslim terrorists. It would not be my last.

I was not impressed with Saudi Arabia and certainly didn't leave my heart behind, but I did leave my appendix. By the time the cigarette-puffing French surgeon examined me, I was searching for a knife to operate on myself. But that is another story.

While in recovery, I received a heartfelt letter from Caran McKee – Mary Jo's dear friend from the Grassley office.

In the letter, Caran wished me well and expressed her admiration for Mary Jo. I could also read between the lines. "Grab the brass ring and don't mess this up," she seemed to say.

When I returned, Mary Jo and I picked up where we left off, but the dates were different. There were no more checklists of things to see and do.

Instead, our dates were casual and comfortable. We went antique shopping and Mary Jo purchased an antique dresser. Together, we refinished it on the screen porch at the Pickett House and then had dinner with Debbie.

We went to a few movies, including *Jerry Maquire.* It was about a sports agent and starred Tom Cruise, yet it was a surprisingly deep, touching movie.

I was puzzled why Mary Jo didn't shed a tear, and I asked her about it:

"There was a lot of cursing, and I was never sure if it was a comedy, romance or drama," she said.

"Don't think so much," I responded. "It was all of those things – and those are the best kind."

In the spring, we enjoyed dinner at the Inn at Little Washington in the tiny town of Washington, Virginia. It was a magnificent, romantic restaurant that some people considered the best in America, if not the world.

When I made the reservation, I hadn't known it was "The Place" to propose. I stared nervously at my food as two young men proposed nearby, but nonetheless it was a delightful evening. As souvenirs, Mary Jo kept the embossed napkin, the engraved box of truffles and even the candy wrappers.

She kept everything except the bill, though I still remember the total because I nearly had to take out a loan. It was $425 dollars.

Slowly but surely, I felt a tug in the chest I hadn't felt in many years and knew that our "friendship had caught on fire." Given my own doubts and history, it took a while for me to realize Mary Jo was "The One," but I was determined not to let her get away. This wasn't high school, and I wanted to get it right.[31]

I often gave Mary Jo white or yellow roses, and the bouquets grew more elaborate as our romance blossomed. Each bouquet was larger and each card more romantic than the one before.

I resolved to ask her to marry me because she lived with joy, laughed easily and loved God, children and dogs. She was truly a woman at peace with herself and "made me want to be a better man," as I once heard it said in a movie.[32]

On March 13th of 1998, I sent a note to Mary Jo's office and told her we'd be doing "something special" the next day, Saturday.

The note was attached to a thick, fragrant display of red and white roses. In flower code, I'd learned the mix of red and white roses signified an engagement or impending marriage, but I rightly guessed Mary Jo wouldn't decipher the symbology.

I'd previously talked to Mary Jo's friend Caran about it on the phone, but when she and Mary Jo discussed the flowers and the accompanying note, Caran proved to be a skilled actress.

Caran wondered aloud if "something special" meant something different to a guy. "Maybe he's taking you to a monster truck show or something," Caran quipped.

Mary Jo would be delighted to share the story with family, friends and even strangers in the years to come. She wrote:

Saturday morning, I got up early but Debbie was already up, which was weird because she sleeps in on Saturdays. Brent took me to our favorite place, Alexandria Pastry Shop in Alexandria, and showed me an "itinerary" over breakfast.

The itinerary had scheduled times to be at specific places for tours: Washington National Cathedral's Bell Tower, the basement of the Lincoln Monument, etc.

Only later did I learn the itinerary was a fake.

As we left the pastry shop, a limo pulled up and I'm puzzled as Brent calmly opens the door and invites me inside where he tells me, "This is the surprise, we're going to tour D.C. by limo."

Of course I was surprised, but I was also suspicious. But I figured well, this is the kind of thing he'd do. He later said "my eyes got big," but again, he said something to make it seem like no big deal and was wary of my expectations.

We arrived at the cathedral early, where Brent tried the side door. He seemed puzzled it was locked, though he later told me he had called to make sure it would be locked. He turned and said, "I'm thinking they don't open until 9:00, shall we just walk around for a bit?"

So we walked out into this magnificent English garden filled with Hostas and azaleas, and then sat down on a sturdy teak bench, lightly shaded by a dogwood tree.

Then, I remember, he smiled and calmly asked me to close my eyes. I did, and he placed a diamond and tanzanite bracelet around my wrist.

When I opened my eyes, I was awestruck by the bracelet, and he was kneeling, and he asked me to marry him! I started to cry, and somewhere, through the tears, he asked, "Did I hear a yes in there somewhere?"

"Yes, yes, I said." And then I had some questions!

Oh boy, did she have questions. It was something I was used to given her meticulous, need-to-know nature, and it made surprises difficult. She was genuinely surprised, though, and the questions came fast and furious.

"My word, the bracelet is fantastic, but not a ring?" she first asked.

"Yes, yes, of course, but I'd like to help you pick out a ring, and we're going to New York to do just that." I said it with a smirk, pulling a new itinerary out of my inner pocket.

"New York? What? Wow, when?"

"Well, now, actually."

"Now? But I'm not ready, I don't even have a bag!" She was smiling, but there was some panic in her voice.

"Debbie packed your bag, it's in the limo, and the driver is waiting, right where he left us."

"Wow, I love it, you sneak, but he's driving us? Are we staying somewhere?"

"He'll take us to Union Station. We're taking the train. We're staying at the Plaza. Any more questions?"

"Oh, my. You are something else, I love you."

"I love you too," I said.

With a kiss, we were off for the train station.

On the train, Mary Jo caught her breath, smiled with delight and held my hand tightly. After she called her mother, she then called Nina Shook to cancel their lunch date. She said:

"I'm sorry I can't make it to lunch at Atlantis, but I have a good excuse. Brent asked me to marry him, and we're on our way to New York City!"

When we arrived at Grand Central Station, Kevin Bridwell and Sara Simko were there to greet us. Sara had moved to New York City the previous year and Kevin had followed. Kevin and Sara were also engaged, with the wedding planned for May.

Mary Jo was surprised to see them, and she and Sara were giddy with excitement as they discussed the proposal and plans for the weekend. Sara greeted Mary Jo with a tearful embrace and a gift bag full of bridal magazines.

In New York City, we stayed at the world-famous Plaza Hotel just off Fifth Avenue and Central Park. We were awed by its history, grandeur, and little touches like plush monogrammed towels and embossed chocolates. Mary Jo said, "I felt like a princess."

When we returned home, Mary Jo was thrilled to describe what she called "the most exciting day of my life" to her friends. They were almost as excited as she was. Almost.

I stood by patiently as Mary Jo told the tale again and again, feeling conflicting emotions of pride and embarrassment.

Speaking on behalf of many of my buddies, Mike Yokitis told me, "Thanks for nothing, pal – thanks for making it absolutely impossible for the rest of us."

Some years later, I discovered how much the engagement weekend had meant to Mary Jo, as she had written all of her memories in a special book that included a hidden cavity for souvenirs.

She had saved the train tickets, a brochure from Tiffany's, an embossed card from the Plaza Hotel (Room 241) and a picture from the Diamond District along West 47th Street.

Below the souvenirs, I discovered a brief, handwritten note on lined yellow paper. The handwriting was the familiar scrawl of Senator Chuck Grassley. He wrote:

"Young Staff – Now I've got Mary Jo engaged does anyone else need my help? CEG"

The location of the proposal would always be special to Mary Jo. After our wedding, I surprised her with a trip to the National Cathedral and we walked through the garden grounds. I'd purchased a small, commemorative brass plate and placed it on the back of our special bench. It read:

March 14th, 1998

On this day, before God, Brent Hoffman proposed marriage to Mary Jo Archibold. She accepted.

Mary Jo's focus quickly turned to the wedding, scheduled for Saturday, June 27th of 1998 at First Baptist Church in Alexandria.

Her first priority was a wedding dress, and she chose a satin and lace design with beautiful knitted flowers. The Alexandria Pastry Shop was an obvious choice for the wedding cake.

Mary Jo was delighted when my grandmother Johanna Hoffmann hand-crocheted a few smaller, matching flowers. We called her "Oma," and she expertly attached the flowers to a lovely veil of white lace and tulle.

My mother Kathleen insisted she would take care of all flowers – and she did. She lovingly created a bridal bouquet of forty roses with baby's breath and later preserved it in a shadow box as a treasured gift for Mary Jo.

The choice of pastor was an easy one. Our friend Jim Witt had performed many weddings – sometimes two on a Saturday – and was eager to officiate the wedding. He said:

"You do some with mixed feelings, then others you just feel this is right before God, and this will work."

But Jim also understood that a wedding doesn't make a marriage, and he promptly referred Mary Jo and I to Joyce Sibley for pre-marital counseling.

Mrs. Sibley was a Christian counselor. She was also likeable and encouraging, yet Mary Jo had some trepidation about the pre-marital counseling. This was because Joyce had recently counseled two mutual friends who decided to call off their own wedding.

During the sessions, we used *The Five Love Languages* by Dr. Gary Chapman and other resources, and we discussed communication, conflict resolution, finances and sex. It was not stressful but fun, and we figured that must be a good sign.

Mary Jo was determined to have a small wedding, as it would make it more intimate and the planning would be easier. She'd participated in the wedding of many friends and didn't want her own to be harried or stressful. She said:

"I just remember Sara (Bridwell) worked so hard on her wedding, then she didn't even have time to do her hair!"

Though we debated the subject, we also decided not to have multiple bridesmaids or groomsmen. On all issues of the wedding, in fact, I deferred to the bride. Mary Jo's sister Malinda was the maid (matron) of honor. My brother Eric was the best man.

Before the wedding, I wanted to put Mary Jo at ease and make her laugh, so I shared the story of the last time Eric had served as best man.

It was our cousin's wedding, and when we got to the part where the pastor asked for the ring, I noticed Eric reaching into his pocket very, very slowly. I also noticed he was white as snow – with perhaps a tinge of green – at about the same time I felt his body pressing against me next to him on the altar. As if in slow motion, Eric managed to reach forward and place the ring in the pastor's outstretched hand with one final, Herculean effort before he collapsed at the feet of the bride.

My father rushed out of the audience to help me drag Eric behind the altar while the ceremony continued behind us. We soon learned Eric had passed-out from the affects of the all-night bachelor party from the evening before. As his brother, my reaction typical – I teased him mercilessly.

Years later, that marriage ended in divorce, and Eric was quick to tell our cousin "Hey you can't say I didn't warn you. I sent you a *pretty strong signal* during the wedding!"

For our own wedding, Mary Jo's roommate Debbie served as her personal attendant.

Debbie looked vibrant despite wearing a cute wig to hide the effects of chemotherapy. As the guests were seated, she carried around a copy of the program and proudly noted she was the only person listed not as "Friend of the Bride (or Groom)" but as "Friend of the Couple."

The ceremony itself was brief, but memorable. Paula and Steven Nofziger read scripture. Two of my friends, Dan and Kim Jenkins, did the same.

DW walked Mary Jo down the aisle and described her as "a radiant bride – absolutely beautiful."

Kathy Wise, Caran McKee and Shirley Sprinkle sang, first removing their glasses so they could not make eye contact with Mary Jo. They did not want to cry.

Eric – the Best Man – was a rock.

And just like that, Mary Jo and I were married, almost two years to the day after our first date. Mary Jo said:

"It was the most joyous day of my life."

At the reception, Mary Jo visited with everyone, giving countless hugs and kisses. She shared farm tales and a loving laugh with her beloved grandfather LaVern. She was so engaged and busy she didn't even get a bite of the wonderful food.

Newlyweds Kevin and Sara Bridwell picked us up for the drive to the hotel in Washington D.C. Mary Jo was so hungry she ate reception leftovers in the car.

Mary Jo and I had several discussions about where to go for a honeymoon, torn between Alaska and Hawaii. The decision was complicated by my military orders to Greece – I was to report in November. Eventually, Mary Jo and I decided we'd go to Alaska and save Hawaii for a later anniversary.[33]

Arriving in Anchorage to twenty-three hours of daily sunlight, we managed to take a nap at the hotel only because of the blackout curtains and then boarded the glass-domed train for Talkeetna.

In Talkeetna, we went on the first of many adventures – a fishing trip on the Talkeetna River.

Wearing large rubber waders and a big smile, it took Mary Jo about forty minutes to land a 36-pound King Salmon. It was an exhilarating experience, though she said "I've got a bruise on my hip to show for it."

Mary Jo was exhausted but delighted, and we air mailed the salmon back to Debbie in Arlington, frozen in dry ice.

We enjoyed many other sights and day trips during the honeymoon, including a spectacular tour of Denali National Park, a mountain hike, a helicopter tour of Glacier Bay and a canoe trip through the Chilkat Bald Eagle Preserve.

Hiking in the Alaskan Range, we were awestruck by the rugged beauty of the peaks above tree line and the gentle crunch of tundra underfoot.

Floating down the Chilkat River, we watched transfixed as the eagles perched majestically along the shore and soared near our raft, moving effortlessly.

It was as if the eagles were posing for the camera.

Shortly after our return, we were off to Germany so I could complete training needed for the assignment to Greece. Mary Jo patiently read books and explored the military base while I was in training, then we spent every weekend traveling.

Belgium was one of Mary Jo's favorites. She described Bruges, Belgium as "A wonderful, beautiful city – lots to see & lots to eat!" Bruges was home to countless tourist attractions such as The Church of Holy Blood. The lower chapel of the church was built in 1129.

But in Bruges, Mary Jo and I best remembered the French fries. Prepared in animal lard and served with mayonnaise and a little plastic fork, they were a fantastic indulgence. We also enjoyed the vanilla custard ice cream, which looked a lot like butter.

Another weekend, we toured the Netherlands, meeting our newlywed friends Trevor and Catherine Friend in Haarlem. We toured the Corrie Ten Boom house made famous by *The Hiding Place* and then posed for pictures by a windmill. In the pictures, Mary Jo, Catherine, Trevor and I can be seen glancing warily at the powerful, fast-moving windmill vanes behind us.

After another weekend in London, we took a pause from the traveling and parted in Frankfurt, Germany. It was time for me to report to my assignment in Greece. Mary Jo was headed home, back to Alexandria. Later, she wrote:

"We have now been apart for almost one month and for some reason it seems to be getting more difficult rather than easier."

On December 1st of 1998, Mary Jo arrived in Greece. She wrote:

"Well, I'm finally in Greece! It's about what I expected. I think I'm going to survive hanging out in the hooch – it's cozy and as long as I have plenty to read, I'll be fine – I think!"

The "hooch" was one of seven tiny houses erected on the NATO base at Araxos Air Base for the American military officers.

It was 10 feet by 32 feet, with a tiny bathroom and a "one butt kitchen," as Mary Jo called it. But we had no complaints, as it was only a temporary home, and we spent most of our leisure time traveling anyway.[34]

The assignment at Araxos would prove to be the most challenging of my military career. The unit had the highest inspection failure rate of any in the Department of Defense, an archaic mission that was a relic of the Cold War and laughably lax security from the host nation.

During the assignment, I worked with and for two commanders – one an alcoholic and the other an incompetent. When my tour was over, I authored a report advocating for an end to the mission, but that is a story for another time and place.[35]

Our mission at Araxos was classified and Mary Jo knew about none of it, but nonetheless embraced the unofficial role of base morale officer. She baked and delivered cookies, always offering a smile and a word of encouragement.

It was quite a transition for Mary Jo from accomplished, professional career woman to "the lady who bakes cookies." Most knew her only as "The Captain's Wife," yet it was a role she enjoyed.

When I was working, Mary Jo often enjoyed the magnificent beaches of Greece, traveling with John Philibin and his girlfriend Becky Duke. Mary Jo and Becky spent a lot of time together and developed a lasting friendship.

Mary Jo made other friendships largely because of the Araxos Christian Fellowship. Founded and led by First Sergeant Dave Hess, Araxos Christian Fellowship was a fun-loving little church, and we met every Sunday for worship service in the recreation center on base.

Frank DeVillier, Ricky Higby, Barry Alcorn, Christine Gramlich, Sam Vines and Tom O'Brien were a few of the members of Araxos Christian Fellowship. A few of us took turns preaching and teaching. Dave led a weekly Bible study in his hooch.

After careers in the military, Dave and Barry were called to serve as pastors.

Living in the region of Achaia, our travels made the Bible come alive with frequent expeditions to Ancient Corinth, Thessaloniki and other famous archeological sites.

We followed the footsteps of the Apostle Paul, Timothy and Silas across Greece, standing on Mars Hills in Athens where Paul shared the gospel with the Areopagus. We crossed the Mediterranean channel to visit the legendary site of the oracle Delphi. Mary Jo wrote:

"There were olive trees as far as the eye could see."[36]

We also toured the amazing monasteries of Meteora, perched precariously on towering pillars of rock.

Of the monasteries, I was most fascinated by the Monastery of Holy Trinity built in 1475. It was made famous in *For Your Eyes Only*, with a memorable scene of James Bond scaling the cliffs while his team waits to be raised on a basket elevator.

Mary Jo was fascinated by the "rooms full of skulls and bones," as she wrote. We also watched transfixed as a monk blessed a Mercedes-Benz, waving a copper kettle of incense under the hood of the car.[37]

Despite the magnificent locations, Mary Jo's travel log was filled with more pedestrian observations. In Athens, she wrote:

"I got a nice leather purse at a great price – awed by Brent's bargaining skills."

Many of the entries in her travel log were about food. In Patras, she wrote:

"We enjoyed a wonderful meal of pasta and bean soup, cannelloni, roasted chicken, pork steak with mushrooms, potatoes, crème caramel and tiramisu."

For our first wedding anniversary, Mary Jo and I went to Italy. Somehow, it made our other travels feel like an unremarkable drive through an Iowa cornfield.

Mary Jo and I spent a week touring Rome, left speechless by the beauty of the Vatican, the magnificent frescoes of Michelangelo and incomparable works of Leonardo da Vinci and Raphael.

Mary Jo found Rome and Venice "truly breathtaking." After posing on the Spanish Steps, she wrote:

"Brent and I had a mid-day tea break at Babington's Tea House for their special blend and scones – very nice!"

"We toured Venice and got lost in its winding streets – and it was great!"

Excited to tell family and friends, she searched for the right adjectives but there were none. "Italy – oh my word!" she exclaimed.

Mary Jo corresponded with family and friends and was dismayed to hear roommate Debbie was again struggling with cancer. The breast cancer had metastasized and Debbie underwent a bone marrow transplant.

It was devastating news, and Mary Jo prayed daily for healing.

Grandma McMains also wrote often, usually about her adult children and their families.

She also enjoyed telling Mary Jo about the weather, the farm or church with snippets like "Just had 24 (in attendance at worship service) last night & that was counting the missionary."

Mary Jo's mother Karen was usually reluctant to travel, and so Mary Jo was delighted when Karen decided to come to Greece accompanied by her friend Lucille Young.

Mary Jo was thrilled to give Karen and Lucille what she called "The three-dollar tour."

Driving our old, reliable Mercedes diesel to the island of Zakynthos, they were nearly stranded by Mary Jo's limited skills with a manual transmission, incorrect maps and unkept roads. Mary Jo wrote:

"At one point, we were on a cow path road with a shepherd and his flock of goats."

After returning to the mainland, the ladies toured the traditional sites in Athens and ancient Corinth and then the Mega Spelion – an ancient, obscure monastery near Kalavryta. It was the oldest monastery in Greece, built in 395 A.D.

At the Mega Spelion, they were impressed by the sheer rock cliffs and well preserved frescoes. Karen, Lucille and Mary Jo were also respectful of the monks, who asked the women to put on long black skirts over their pants.

When Mary Jo asked about the bathroom ("*parakalo, tualetta*?"), a monk escorted the ladies to a small room with a centuries-old cement floor. Off to the side, the monk pointed to the *tualetta*. They saw he was pointing to three semi-round holes hacked out of the cement floor.

Karen, Lucille and Mary Jo left shortly thereafter, quickly depositing the black skirts in the basket outside and laughing all the way to the car.

Mary Jo's friends Kathy Wise, Gill Abernathy and Jill Johnson also visited her in Greece. She wrote:

"We enjoyed a "wonderful day in Nafplio – climbed all 999 stairs of the Palamide fortress. Built between 1711 and 1714."

They also took a tour of Olympia, but the barren, non-descript site of the Olympic flame was a disappointment. In fact, there was no flame.

The docent's description of the early Olympics, however, was far more entertaining. The girls listened intently to her colorful description of the athletes running, wrestling and fighting in the once-grand arena.

All of the athletes competed in the nude. Buck-naked.

The photo album grew quickly with pictures and mementos from our travels.

On a paper plate, Mary Jo's friend Michael Wyganowska had drawn a map of the best shops to buy amber in Warsaw, Poland. There was also a Babington's tea bag attached to a 1000 Lire note and a napkin from Caffe Florian, with a drawing of the Ponte dei Sospiri ("Bridge of Sighs") in Venice.[38]

Before leaving Greece, we took one last trip – a magical cruise of the Greek islands in the Aegean Sea.

Santorini was a picture-perfect island of black lava beaches, dotted with stark white buildings with blue roofs, yet Mary Jo's record of the visit included only one entry. She wrote:

"My donkey almost gave out."

Our last stop on the cruise was the island of Patmos. Patmos was most famous for its Cave of the Apokalyps where scholars believe the Apostle John lived out his final days writing the Book of Revelation.

After leaving the cave, we toured St. John's Monastery nearby. Of the monastery, Mary Jo wrote:

"I've seen enough skulls to last a lifetime."

Near the end of our year in Greece, we looked back on the memories with joy and relish.

We spent some of it apart, but cherished every moment together. Mary Jo put together three photo albums and a travel log of memories. The last entry in her travel log read:

"Had some Dunkin' donuts and did a bit of shopping."

We enjoyed our time in Greece, but we were eager to return home – to our country, our family and friends.

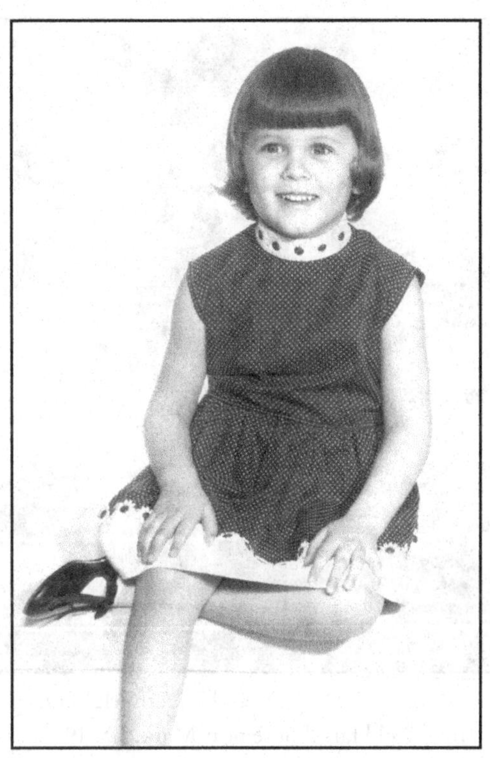

Always photogenic, five-year old Mary Jo strikes a pose in a dress made by her Grandma Archibold, April 1970.

Mary Jo feeds a lamb on her grandparents (McMains) farm, 1969.

Dressed for church, Helen and LaVern McMains pose by the old farmhouse near Mark, IA, 1972.

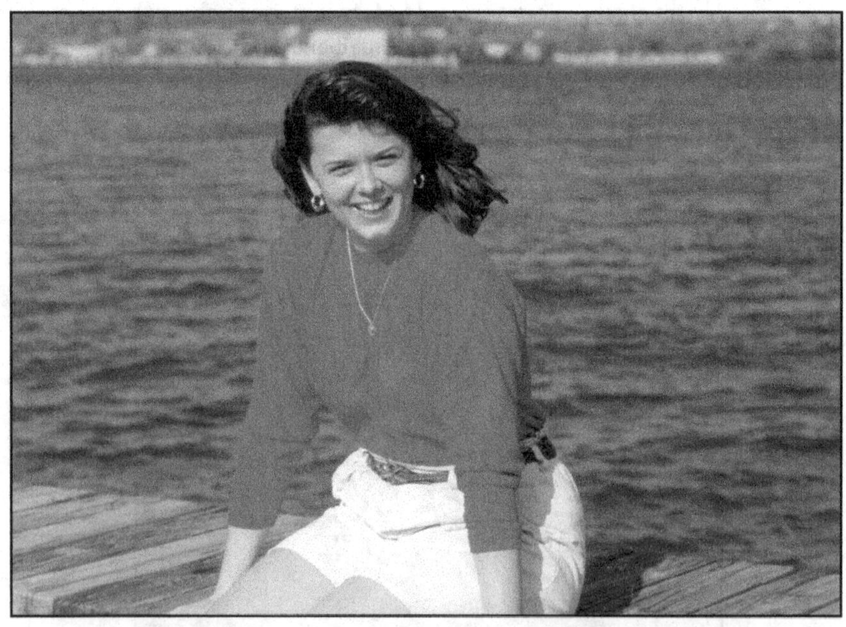

Mary Jo, as featured in *Christian Single* magazine, July 1994. Pictured on riverfront at Old Town in Alexandria, VA.

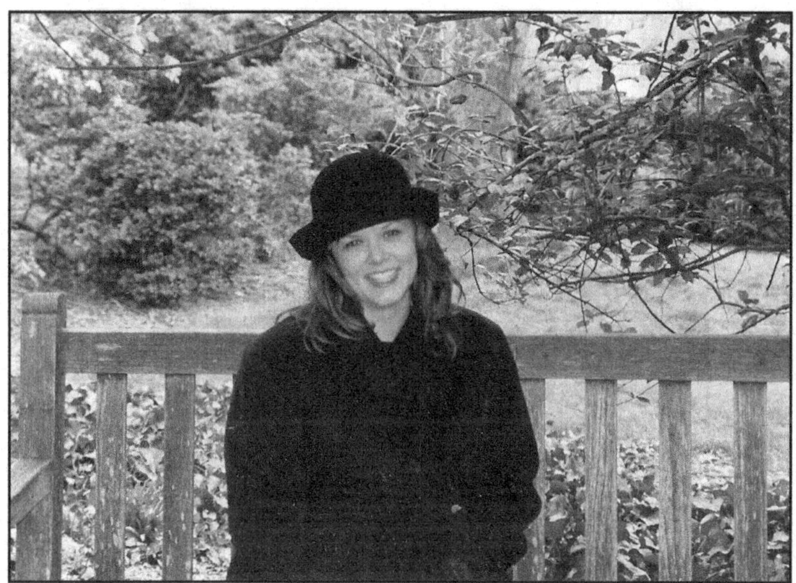

Mary Jo sits on the "engagement bench" in the gardens of the National Cathedral in Washington D.C., shortly after the author proposed marriage, March 1998.

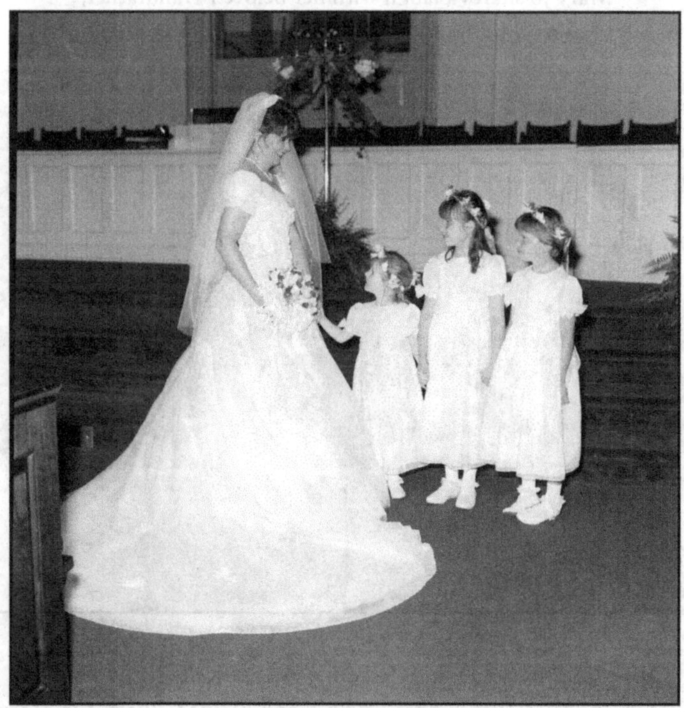

Mary Jo, on wedding day with her nieces, (L-R): Abigail Hoffmann, Amanda Hoffmann and Chelsey Greubel, June, 1998.

Mary Jo shares a laugh with her beloved grandfather, LaVern McMains, on her wedding day, June 1998.

Friends with new mother, Mary Jo. Clockwise: Mary Jo, Gill Abernathy, Becky Duke, Catherine Friend, Kelly Mine, Nancy Thompson, Alice Turner, Sara Bridwell and Elaine Gilliam. On Mary Jo's birthday, at the Fillmore House, Alexandria, VA, April 2001.

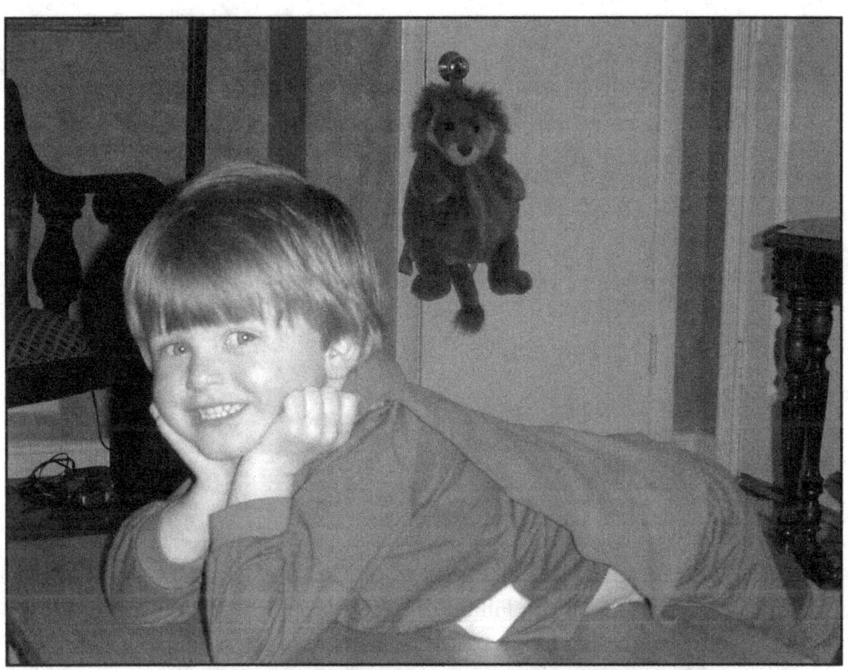

Silas poses for his mother at the house on Holmes Run Parkway in Alexandria, VA, January 2003.

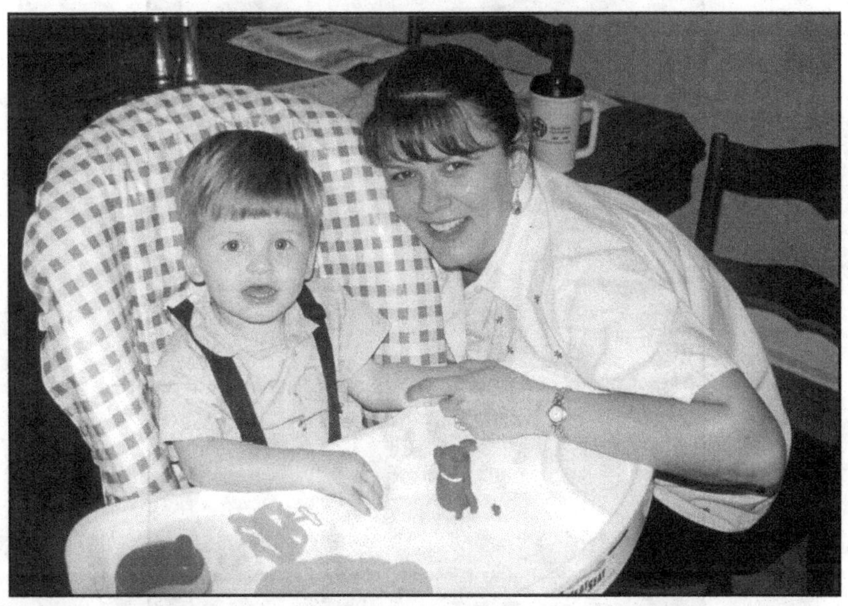

Mary Jo and Silas pose with a few of his Play-Doh creations at house on Holmes Run Parkway in Alexandria, VA, July 2003.

Mary Jo and Lydia, at house on Fillmore Street, Alexandria, VA, November 2003.

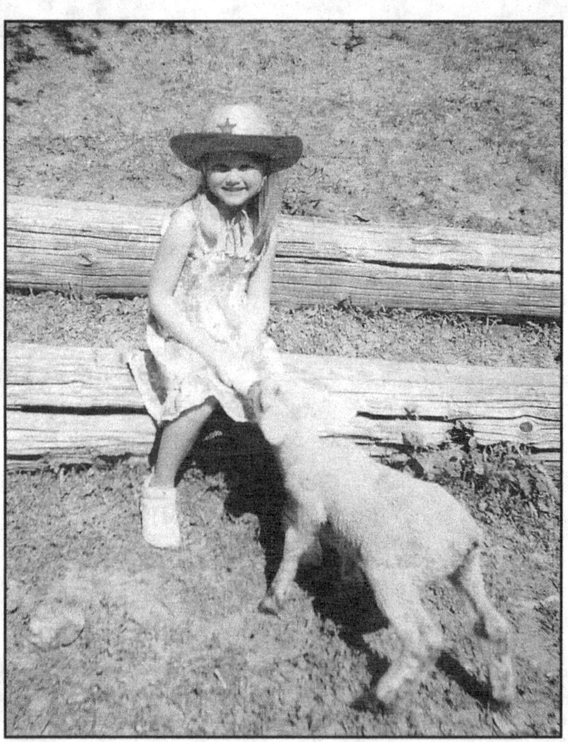

Lydia feeding the lambs, just as her mother did 40 years before. Plymouth County, IA, May 2006.

A family photo with Mary Jo – and the smile, grace and courage we will always remember, Mason City, IA, December 2006.

Mary Jo with Silas and Lydia, in our backyard on Mother's Day. Though she'd cut her hair short, her smile gives little indication she was to begin chemotherapy treatments the next day. Sioux City, IA, May 2007.

Four generations of McMains girls: Karen, Mary Jo, Lydia and Helen. At a tea party for Mary Jo's birthday, Luciano's Restaurant, Sioux City, IA, April, 2008. Photo by Tim Knight.

Mary Jo and Lydia with two of their best friends: JoLynn Handel (with Lydia on left arm) and her daughter, Halena. At Handel's house, Sioux City, IA, January 2009.

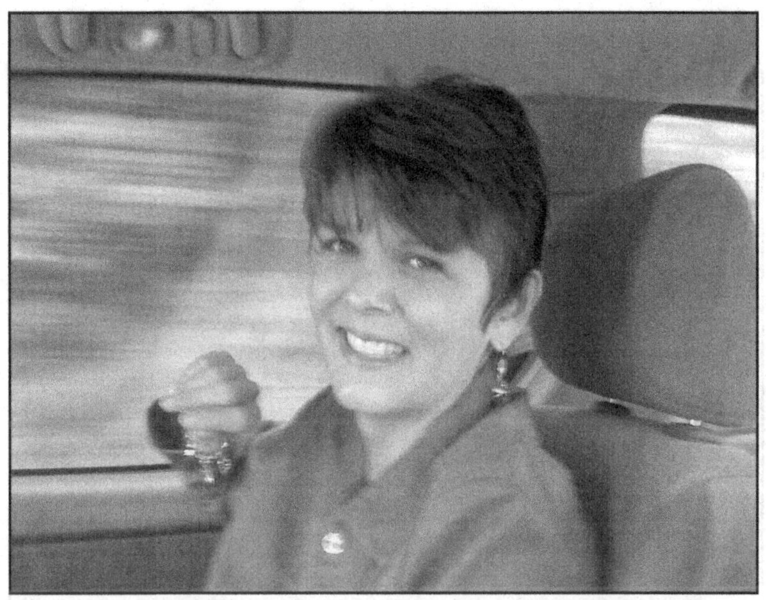

Mary Jo in Vermont in the last full year of her life. She'd had brain surgery the previous day at Mayo Clinic in Rochester, MN but insisted on getting on the plane and enjoying a long-planned vacation with family and friends. Photo taken near Stowe on October 12th, 2008.

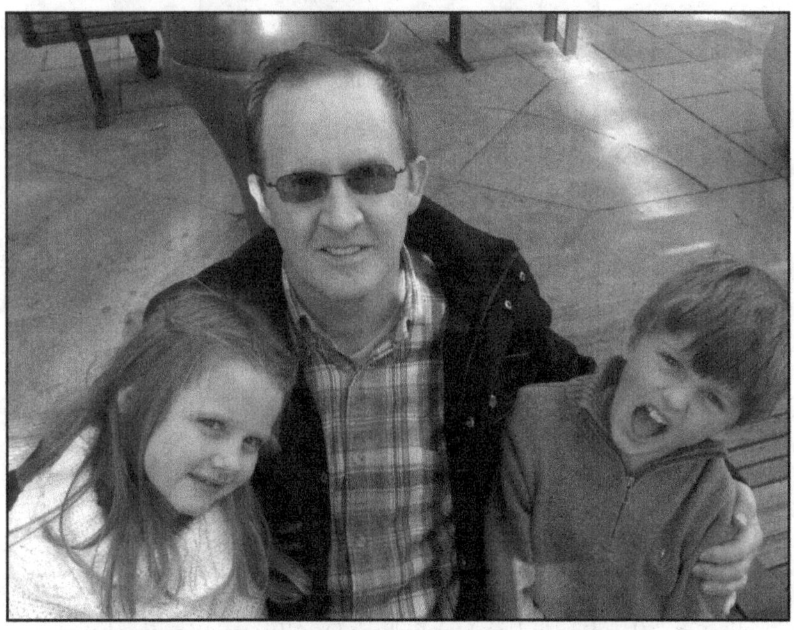

Our little family in Denver for Silas' birthday, November 2009. Photo by the author's brother, Eric Hoffmann.

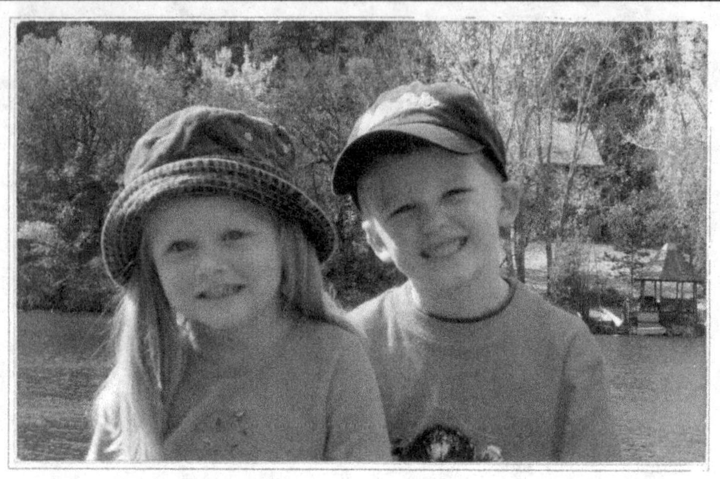

PRIORITIES

"A Hundred Years From Now It Will Not Matter What My Bank Account Was, The Sort Of House I Lived In, Or The Kind Of Car I Drove...But The World May Be Different Because I Was Important In The Life Of A *Child*."

This framed photo was on Mary Jo's desk – and now sits on the author's desk. The photo of Silas and Lydia was taken in Rapid City, SD, October 2006.

Silas, Lydia and author at a park in Monterey, CA. Nancy Martin Rouse of RRK Studio painted this original oil, which she titled "en tete avel l'amour" (Leading in Love) for Father's Day. The painting was based on a photo taken by Christina Severinghaus in January 2010.

Gingersnap Streusel Pumpkin Pie

Ingredients:
1 (15 oz) refrigerated pie crust
10 gingersnap cookies
2 Tablespoons sugar and ¾ Cup sugar
1 Tablespoon all-purpose flour
2 Tablespoons chilled butter, cut into small pieces
3/4 Cup sugar
1 1/2 teaspoons ground cinnamon
1/2 teaspoon ground ginger
1/4 teaspoon salt
1/4 teaspoon ground nutmeg
1 (15-oz) can unsweetened pumpkin
1 (12-oz) can evaporated fat free milk
1 large egg and 3 large egg whites

Directions:

1. Preheat oven to 350 degrees.
2. Roll dough into 12-inch circle; fit in a 10-inch deep-dish pie plate. Fold edges, flute and freeze for 30 mins.
3. Place cookies, 2T sugar and flour in a food processor and process until ground. Add butter and pulse until crumbly.
4. Mix 3/4C sugar with remaining ingredients. Pour into crust.
5. Bake at 350 for 35 mins. Sprinkle crumb mixture over pie, then bake an additional 20 minutes or until center is set.
6. Cool to room temperature. Serve with whipped cream and/or ice cream.

My Bulldog Snores

by Mary Jo Hoffman

My pups are the best and they love me a lot,
Whenever I cry they come at a trot.
They sleep near my crib to protect me at night,
but Zoe's so loud, she gives me a fright.
While Xenia is dreaming and Dad's fast asleep,
Zoe thrashes and snorts; she's not counting sheep.
During the day she's as quiet as can be,
but at night it's much different. Totally.
She's as loud as a chainsaw going full bore,
then she wakes herself up with one final roar.
My mom says she's alright, it's just how she's made,
but I can't help but wonder if it's something she's ate.
Do all dogs do this I'd like to know,
I hope you can answer the question below.
My dog snores, does yours?

Lydia with Zoe the bulldog, Sioux City, IA, January 2006.

A Poem for MJ

by Linda Guggenmos

I only knew you for a while
God's choice not mine to be,
He taught me well, you were my friend
The lessons I would see.
We sat in chairs, the nurse would call
We waited for so long,
The news was good for me to hear
You wished that yours was wrong.
A warrior showed thru brilliant smile
I always wondered how,
The strength of God showed all you did,
You walked that last long mile.
I won't forget our talks we had
So simple and so plain,
I prayed for you for many days
They weren't at all in vain.
Two years passed by the ups and downs
Your smile would never fade,
The joy you felt and pain that came
We never knew how brave.
I always knew that God would heal
But wished it here on earth.
I miss you friend and though you're gone
I'll see you at new birth.

A Letter

by Anonymous

THEY HAD "A SMILE THAT could light up a room" is an overused adage, and in as much as it's a nice compliment, it's one that would scarcely do justice to describe Mary Jo Hoffman. For she had a smile that lit up hearts. Her smile belied the fact that she was ill, conveyed that her faith was unwavering and was curiously disarming in that it allowed you to temporarily forget the sorrow of the situation and live in the moment of a hug or a shared memory.

Mary Jo never considered herself to be special or brave, but the truly courageous never do. She inspired all, gave hope to many and was adored mother and wife of a special few. The Bible says "pray continually." We gave it our all. Selfishly, God's answer was not the one that we wanted.

At this time, we no longer need to pray for Mary Jo, for her eternity was sealed some thirty-five years ago when she accepted Christ's blood on the cross. We now concentrate our prayers on her family, who has endured much. To Brent, who was always by her side and to Silas and Lydia, who will be the bearers of her torch.

Mary Jo is in a place where sickness and earthly burdens no longer exist, but perhaps anticipation does, as she looks forward to the day when she can be reunited with family and friends.

To Be a Mother

"A man is what his mother made him."

Ralph Waldo Emerson

MARY JO AND I WERE busy newlyweds, always on the move. In the first year of marriage, we traveled every chance we could and saw a lifetime of tourist attractions.

On weekends, we swam in the warm, turquoise waters near a picturesque, private alcove the locals called "Hidden Beach." It was on the other side of a marble cliff adjacent to Kalogria Beach, and the fractured yellowish marble was marked by graffiti and included a stark personal message. "Yankee Go Home," it said in blood-red spray paint.

During most of our travels, Mary Jo and I drove the dark, harrowing roads of the Peloponnese peninsula in a beat-up brown diesel with a busted odometer. Even at night, Greeks walked the narrow shoulder-less roads in dark clothing, resulting in a more than a few quick turns of the steering wheel.

Halfway through our assignment in Greece, we returned stateside to Maxwell Air Force Base near Montgomery, Alabama for still more military training. While there, Mary Jo made a new friend in Stacey Franklin. Stacey was a new mother and fellow "military dependent."

While in Alabama, we decided to visit Albuquerque, New Mexico, which would be our follow-on assignment. We were eager to check out the area and begin a house search.[39]

Mary Jo wasn't impressed with Montgomery or Albuquerque, and so eager to keep my wife happy, I requested a change in assignment when we returned to Greece. The assignments officer responded to my email request just five minutes later. He wrote:

"Absolutely not – we only have a few officers with your background and must keep you on assignment. Sorry."[40]

Mary Jo wasn't that disappointed to hear the news, as she understood the mission came first, and we made plans to begin the transition to Albuquerque.

But a few weeks later, I was surprised by a phone call from Brigadier General Jim Totsch. He asked me to take a position as a budget officer at the Pentagon.

When I informed General Totsch I was to report to New Mexico in less than two months and the assignment couldn't be changed, he said, "Just say 'Yes Sir,' and then I'll make a phone call."

The following day, I got an email from the same assignments officer who'd denied my request previously. The email read:

"Great news, B.R.! We've decided you're most needed at the Pentagon, and we've found someone else to fill your slot in Albuquerque."

"Wow, that's amazing," I responded. It's unfortunate the email couldn't convey my sarcasm.[41]

Anyway, that's how Mary Jo and I came to return to Alexandria, Virginia.

The return to Virginia was bittersweet.

It was sweet to be among friends, but bitter to learn Debbie's cancer had returned in full force. She asked us to stay with her at her town home in Arlington, and we couldn't say no.

We enjoyed every moment with Debbie. Though weak, she was never depressed, befitting a positive, courageous woman with the nickname, "Sunny."

The nickname suited her, as did her birthday – Christmas. Debbie's smile was radiant and her laugh was loud and distinctive.

Debbie, though, knew she was dying.

During her last weekend on earth, she and her friend Joanie Armstrong drove to the beach in a convertible. With the top down, they enjoyed the warmth of the sun while singing along to the radio loud and off-key.

At the time, Mary Jo and I were anxious for Debbie, questioning whether it was too risky, against the wishes of her doctor, or if she should even leave the house…but looking back on it now, I smile to picture my friend, Debbie, with her face to the sun and the wind in her hair.

Our sweet friend Debbie passed away on October 28th of 1999.

Before she died, Debbie said her only regret was she never got a tattoo. She also joked:

"I hope to sing like a large black woman when I get to heaven. I've always wanted to be able to sing like Della Reese."

Debbie breathed her last while surrounded by her friends, singing, *How Great Thou Art.*

Debbie's death shook her friends, yet all were inspired by her grace and courage. She imparted lasting lessons in joy and optimism, and we'd draw upon those lessons later in a way we couldn't have imagined.

A few weeks after Debbie died, Mary Jo and I closed on our new house at 5333 Fillmore Avenue in Alexandria.

The new house was just 1,200 square feet, yet it was four times the size of the hooch in Greece. It was small, but nice and comfortable.

After a year of keeping our household goods in storage, we were anxious to retrieve them, but after opening the storage units, we soon realized we didn't need much of it.

We sold some of our possessions, and sadly, my beloved 1993 Harley-Davidson Fat Boy was amongst the first to go. "Sorry to hear you sold your manhood," a buddy quipped.

With a small and welcoming front porch, the house on Fillmore Street was of the Cape Cod style Mary Jo favored, with upstairs dormers and a cute, efficient layout.

The east side was dominated by a larger porch with painted wainscoting and a white baluster railing. The backyard was large for its size, and it included a fenced vegetable garden and a Costco play land.

The house sat just off Seminary Road in Alexandria – a busy thoroughfare with an exit on/off I-395. This meant it was "inside the loop" and a short commute to Washington D.C. or the Pentagon. The location made the small house disproportionately expensive, but the short commute was priceless.

We lived on Fillmore Street for three years and they were good years – great, really.

Mary Jo showed saint-like patience with my home improvement projects, including the top-to-bottom kitchen renovation. Even my ill-fated decision to sweat copper pipes on Thanksgiving Day drew only a mild rebuke.

Our daily schedule transformed along with the house.

Instead of traveling and filling our schedule with things to see and do, we enjoyed our little home and the pleasure of one another's company. Reading a book. Home Depot for a circular saw. Dinner, followed by a movie. A game of Scrabble.

Mary Jo and I talked about our relationship – and we worked at it, even attending a Marriage Enrichment Seminar. We read scripture and shared devotionals like *Moments Together for Couples.*

But mostly, we just talked and through it I learned how little I really knew of her on our wedding day. I learned more of her selfless, Godly character, and I loved her all the more.

As a husband, I also learned to draw on lessons from my own parents and the example of my in-laws.

As a child, I remember how my dad was always the one to say, "I'm sorry" – though I understood surely mom must've been at fault from time to time. What I learned is it's usually okay to say, "I'm sorry," even if you did nothing wrong. That's because it's the relationship – not who is to blame – that really matters.

Upon our return to Alexandria, Mary Jo and I also attended a new church, settling at Glencarlyn Road Baptist Church. It was a small, struggling church led by Pastor Greg Loewer.[42]

Encouraged by Pastor Loewer, Mary Jo and I began a small group Bible study in our home. Old friends Gill Abernathy and David and Karin Reese joined us, along with new friends Wendy Wright, Caroline Tirona, Mary Barkes, Sylvia Warner and Eric and Terri Focht.

We enjoyed the fellowship and everyone raved about Caroline's Filipino eggrolls. Caroline was very appreciative of the fellowship and had great respect for Mary Jo. She wrote:

"Mary Jo taught me hospitality and how to treat people. I did not read that in a self-help book. I knew it by experience, as it was done unto me."

After we got settled in our new home, Mary Jo suggested it was time to get a dog because as she put it, "It might be good practice (emphasis added) if we are ever blessed with a child."

It made sense to me, and Mary Jo and I were both puzzled when some of our friends who had children laughed uproariously at the observation.

Mary Jo, though, was quite serious.

Over the next few weeks, she read three doggie books cover-to-cover, including *The Perfect Puppy*. She also shared her sad tale of how her previous roommates didn't let her have a dog, appealing to my sympathetic nature while regaling me with the merits of Standard Poodles and Schnauzers.

Karen had warned me about Mary Jo and her way with dogs.

Mary Jo had begged for a puppy when she was a child and so when Mary Jo was about twelve, Karen brought home a little black poodle named "Ginger."

Even then, Mary Jo had read the puppy books. When Ginger began whining through the night, Mary Jo passed on what she had learned. "The book says to put a ticking clock and an old shoe in the box," she told her mother.

After passing on her advice, Mary Jo fell asleep quick as a wink, leaving her mother to watch over a still-whining Ginger.

So, to make a long story short, we got a dog. Two of them.

First, we got a boxer and named her "Xenia."

The boxer was a compromise after I complained that Mary Jo's choice of a poodle was "too sissy." With a beautiful fawn and white coat, Xenia was a skinny, athletic dog with boundless energy.

Second, we got an English bulldog and named her "Zoe."

Our friend Elaine Gilliam helped us to choose the name, as we were determined to keep the Greek theme. Zoe was brindle-colored and had the characteristic wrinkles and short snout of an English bulldog. She had no athleticism, but was highly entertaining when she was awake.

The puppies were a delightful addition to our little home and enjoyed scampering up and down the stairs, hiding under the oak buffet and competing for Mary Jo's affection.

Looking back on it with a smile and a more than a little embarrassment, I remember the puppies seemed like the center of our small world for a while.

Mary Jo and I attended canine training classes at a city park every week for six weeks. She set up an account with *Drs. Foster and Smith* and spent a fortune on stylish collars, plush doggie beds and even a special harness that attached to the safety belt posts in our SUV.

Thankfully, the doggie Snuggie had not yet been invented. God be praised.

When we went out to dinner with Kevin and Sara Bridwell, Mary Jo showed Sara pictures of the dogs and told uninspiring stories about doggie training. "Zoe got the award for 'Best Behaved,'" Mary Jo said, excitedly. I rolled my eyes.

Then suddenly, the dogs didn't seem quite as important anymore. Not unimportant – not disliked – just not *as* important.

The cause of this transformational shift in priorities was the news that a baby was on the way.

I first learned of it when I returned to my desk at the Pentagon and found a yellow stickie on my computer screen. It said:

"Your wife called to say, 'It's Official.' I hope this means something wonderful."

It was welcome, wonderful news.

Mary Jo was radiant with joy and began reading different books like *What to Expect When You're Expecting* in earnest. The puppy books were quickly tossed aside. Mary Jo was delighted with the expectation of motherhood and the answer to prayers. She had once confided to Paula:

"All I ever wanted to be was a mom – but it would be helpful to first be a wife!"

Surprisingly, neither Paula nor her mother (or mine) was the first to know. Instead, it was Kelly Mine – her friend and fellow teacher at Northern Virginia Community College – who first learned she was pregnant. Kelly wrote:

"Mary Jo and I were walking down a corridor and she was complaining of how exhausted she was, and I asked her point-blank, 'Mary Jo, are you pregnant?' She looked down and smiled, then looked at me and said, 'Yes, I am but I haven't told anyone yet.' It was such fun to share a secret!"

Shortly thereafter, Mary Jo shared the news with her mother and then mine. Then, her best friends Paula, Kathy, Gill and Sara.

Mary Jo and I were delighted when the sonogram revealed the little baby was a boy, and we set out to design a Pottery Barn-themed baby room.

A few months later, I returned home from a canoeing trip in West Virginia to find Mary Jo – now five months pregnant – in tears on the doorstep of our home.

It was her father, DW. He had passed away at his home in Indianola, Iowa from the complications of chronic obstructive pulmonary disease.

Mary Jo and I promptly returned to Indianola, where DW's wife Sandi asked yours truly to lead the memorial service. Privately, Mary Jo shared a few stories of her childhood. Publicly, I spoke of his nicknames and love of hunting, fishing and woodworking.

In truth, it was a difficult task because I felt I hardly knew the man – but I did it for Mary Jo. She loved DW until the end and was disappointed he would never know the gifted grandson who was to come.

Returning home, Mary Jo and I resumed preparations for our son, even while hosting a few get-togethers with friends. Kevin and Sara were frequent guests. Sara praised Mary Jo as a marvelous hostess and a great cook.

Mary Jo had hosted countless baby and wedding showers over the years, and now it was her turn.

Sara hosted a shower with many of her friends from church. Caran hosted another one with friends from work. Our neighbor Adele hosted still another one for everyone else.

On Thanksgiving Day, Gill Abernathy joined us for a marvelous Thanksgiving feast. Gill wrote:

"Mary Jo took on preparing a Thanksgiving meal despite being nine months pregnant. She was always a caring friend, always a hostess, always in service, ever efficient and all the while making it look easy. She was never fussy but all was done with elegant simplicity and care for others."[43]

The following evening, Mary Jo and I merged onto George Washington Parkway for the drive to the I-495 beltway and bound for Bethesda National Naval Medical Center. With Mary Jo in labor, I volunteered, "At least we don't have to worry about a breakdown thanks to this reliable new car."

Through clenched teeth, Mary Jo responded with a common retort. "You're killing me," she said.

The Bethesda National Naval Medical Center was considered the flagship of military hospitals, sometimes called "The President's Hospital" because it provided care for the president as well as members of Congress and Supreme Court justices. The main tower was an historical landmark. President Franklin Roosevelt laid the cornerstone in 1940."[44]

At Bethesda, Mary Jo and I became intimately familiar with the hallways of Building Nine, walking for hours to move the labor along. Eventually, Mary Jo was admitted and escorted to Room 13.

Inside Room 13, I stood just inside the doorway like a door guard as the anesthesiologist fumbled with the epidural placement for Mary Jo. She was unable to properly penetrate what she called the *supraspinous ligament* or "backpad."

"I don't care what you call it – I just know it hurts," Mary Jo said. Taking my cue, I moved abruptly from my position at the door, crossed over to the anesthesiologist and said, "Please go find someone else to do it. Now."

Through the night and into the next morning and afternoon, Mary Jo labored as the staff monitored heart rates and dilation. Finally, she was prompted by a dose of *pitocin* and told to push as the obstetrician grabbed the metal forceps.

"No!" I exclaimed, again using my "command voice." "Use the suction cup instead," I ordered.

Emboldened by the staff's prompt obedience to my commands, I leaned in close as they moved the bell-shaped vacuum suction cup into position. Chimes, beeps and lights suddenly filled the room, and I was shoved to the corner.

Apparently I wasn't in charge after all. Not even a little bit.

A minute later, surprised by the speed and confused by the cacophony of lights and sounds, I noticed something was different. Or I should say – someone. <u>He</u> was there.

At first, I was puzzled by the baby's cone head, later joking our baby could land a guest spot as an alien baby on Saturday Night Live. His soft little head had taken on the bell shape of the suction cup, but it appeared to return to normal before my eyes.

The technician quickly did her thing by reading off birth weight (7 pounds, 14 ounces) and length (22 inches) while I proudly snapped photos with our new digital camera.

It was 3:25 p.m. on November 24th of 2000.

The time would be remembered because when our son turned seven, he grew curious and asked me to show him the birth certificate and exact time of his birth. Every year from then on, he'd say "Can we please light the candles at 3:25 p.m. Eastern Time?"

Standing by the baby scale, I remember looking over at Mary Jo, the new mother. She was exhausted, but I saw a little grin forming.

"Don't you leave him alone for a moment," Mary Jo commanded.

"I won't," I replied. "Ever."

The boy we named "Silas" was born with a smattering of light brown hair similar in shade to the chestnut locks of his mother. He had bright, sparkling blue eyes and a piercing cry, and he did not seem pleased to have been pulled into the world.

We soon learned Silas was a healthy boy when the technician explained the "Apgar Score." The Apgar Score was a simple evaluation of newborns given at one and five minutes to indicate general health. Ten was the highest possible score.[45]

At five minutes, the technician smiled and announced "Ten-ten – we haven't had a perfect score like that in a while."

Later, the technician politely explained the Apgar Score had "limited usefulness," but I didn't listen and proceeded to brag about it to everyone within earshot.

"Our baby boy is a Ten-Ten!" I exclaimed.

Thus began a long, prideful road of bragging about my son.

In years to come, friends would say it was "fitting" that Silas was born in The President's Hospital.

On picture day in the first grade, he wore a jacket and tie and carried himself with an easy confidence. One of his classmates said "Silas, you should run for President!"

The teacher, Mrs. Reed, chuckled with amusement, but another classmate quickly interjected: "No really, I think he'd be good."

Just three years later, Silas introduced his first presidential candidate. In fact, Silas gave the official welcome to a bus of touring presidential candidates for the Iowa Caucuses. He said:

"It's great to see you all here today in Sioux City, Iowa."

As the *Sioux City Journal* reported the following day, "Silas Hoffman looked quite comfortable with the microphone."[46]

But I'm getting ahead of myself.

In Room 13, I took Silas from the technician and passed him to his mother. He'd already stopped crying despite the probing, measuring and smearing of *tetracycline* in his eyes. Even though the little baby wore a stocking cap and was wrapped tightly in a blue fleece blanket, I swear, he nestled into Mary Jo's chest.

Mary Jo had the content, angelic look of a new mother, and she looked up at me with tired and peaceful eyes, but she did not cry. I shed enough tears for both of us.

For the first best day of our lives, Mary Jo purchased not one but three baby books. She filled them with observations and memorabilia, even framing the stocking cap with the plastic wristband.

She was her mother's daughter.

Mary Jo and I had settled on the name Silas months before, as we'd wanted something unique, biblical and interesting.

"Silas" had been my call sign while on duty in Greece. It was a nickname used instead of an officer's rank and name over the radio. I'd chosen it because Silas was a missionary companion of the Apostle Paul and traveled with him through Greece.

And, well, I just liked the sound of it. So did Mary Jo.[47]

Later, we were delighted to learn most scholars believed the name Silas was derived from the Latin or Romanized "Silvanus," meaning "Man of the Woods."[48]

As he grew, the name would suit our little boy like a well-tailored ghillie suit. He was rugged, adventurous and first explored the timbers of northwest Iowa at age seven. At age eight, he landed a largemouth bass that was just a half-inch shy of the state record. By age nine, he could stick a knife in a tree from 20 feet after only a brief demonstration from his Uncle Eric.

Man of the woods. Yeah, that's about right.

Mary Jo also appreciated the symbolism of the name. In her journal, she wrote:

I've been reading a book by Francine Rivers called *The Scribe*. It's about Silas of the New Testament. Along with it, I've been studying a Beth Moore book titled *To Live is Christ* about the life of the apostle Paul. It's been great reading them together. While the book about Silas is a fictional account of his life, it's very closely linked to scripture and the history of life at that time. It makes me smile to think of my son and his namesake.[49]

It wasn't so easy to decide on a middle name. I proposed the names of several family members, but Mary Jo wanted Silas to have her maiden name of Archibold. I didn't think it made a good match with Silas, but figured Silas would just use the initial "A" anyway, and I yielded.

Before we left the hospital, we had some visitors. Kevin and Sara were the first, and we promptly gave them the titles of "Honorary Aunt and Uncle," which they accepted with great relish.

Sara was her usual, giddy self and delighted to be called "Aunt Sara." Phillip Hurst also visited, honoring us with a prayer and blessing for little Silas.

Returning home after a twenty-minute inspection of the car seat, buckles and pads, we introduced Silas to the bassinet in our bedroom. Then later, we moved him to the baby room, outfitted with a custom crib.

Just across from our bedroom, the new baby room was a small and comfortable room at the top of the stairs with bright, yellow walls and a mix of antique furniture and Pottery Barn quilts. Brightly colored, stuffed fish hung from the ceiling, bathed in sunlight from the dormer windows.

Silas enjoyed the carousel crib mobile and the sparkling, fake fish aquarium, but his favorite possession was a small, pale blue embroidered pillow. It was a treasured gift from Charley and Theresa Niemeier.[50]

A week after Silas was born, Grandma Karen arrived to dote on him. We enjoyed her company and advice and took countless pictures by the Christmas tree.

Despite my objections, Xenia and Zoe were included in the family Christmas photo. Xenia wore a stitched set of reindeer horns held on with an elastic band, and Zoe wore a Santa hat.

Both dogs looked dejected and ashamed. If Zoe could've spoken, she would've surely said "Good grief, man."

Grandma Kathy arrived shortly after Karen departed, bringing gifts like more stuffed fish. She was so eager to help, always a joy to be around and delighted to hold her fifth grandchild. Silas posed dutifully, though he was just one month old.

My mother was certain he smiled at her. I was just as certain it was gas.

It was the first of many visits from Grandma Kathy, and we marveled at her loving example and commitment to family. She returned with my father just one month later for the Presidential Inauguration.

By the time her first grandchild Amanda turned 18, Grandma Kathy had compiled a remarkable record of never missing a single one of her grandchildren's birthdays. With seven grandchildren, that worked out to about 65 birthdays across more than 12 states.

For one of those birthdays, she drove through a blizzard, past Colorado and into New Mexico. For Silas' third birthday, she arrived in Virginia at the same time as Hurricane Isabel. The candles from Silas' birthday cake were the only lights in the house.

As new parents, Mary Jo and I embraced the joy of parenthood with unrestrained wonder. We watched mesmerized as Silas batted dangling objects above him on the gym mat. Sometimes he shared the mat with Zoe.

Every burp, roll or crawl was greeted with "Ooh" or "Look what Silas did!" like only a new parent or grandparent can. We fussed over him, hugged and loved him like there was no tonight or tomorrow.

Though we became parents a little later in life, we weren't really prepared for the emotional bond and power of it. Few parents are.

It was different than the love of or for a spouse, which evolves or deepens over time if you're lucky. For our son, it was immediately deep, untarnished and unconditional.

From the moment he was born – cone head and all – we'd have given our lives for him, without question.

Maybe because of that, we were also anxious, worrisome parents, a condition that proved amusing to our friends.

Mary Jo – the professional, Capitol Hill staffer – worried about every skin blemish, body movement or temperature. When the thermometer registered 99.5 degrees, she consulted a book and called her mother.

Yours truly – the steady nuclear weapons officer – obsessed with baby-proofing the house, including the closets. Every protruding knob was a threat. Every corner was an enemy.

Over time, we lightened up – at least, Mary Jo did. We figured every sniffle didn't warrant a trip to the hospital. We decided not to record every moment through the viewfinder, but to enjoy, cherish and remember it.

In time, Mary Jo and I learned to control our anxiousness, and we discovered that parenting is hard work. If it's not, you're not doing it right. Years later on Mother's Day, Mary Jo would put it to words. She wrote:

"If being a mother doesn't seem hard or sometimes make you feel anxious or inadequate, then you're not doing it right. Yet being a mother is also the most wonderful blessing in this life, and I thank God for calling me to it."

A few friends offered both solicited and unsolicited advice on parenting. Mrs. Grassley understood Mary Jo's academic, methodical nature. She wrote:

"Throw away the book and trust your instincts. If that fails, call your mother – or call Brent's mother. Lastly, call me!"

One casualty of the all-consuming role of parent was our *relationship* with the dogs. Don't get me wrong, the dogs were still spoiled and never ignored. But make no mistake, Xenia and Zoe had moved down on the priority list. Way down.

Mary Jo felt some guilt over it and talked with Kevin and Sara about it over dinner:

"I feel bad that Xenia and Zoe aren't getting much attention. They're adjusting to life with a newborn," Mary Jo said.

Noticing my amusement, Mary Jo asked, "What's so funny, Brent – don't you care about the dogs?"

"Oh, I'm sorry. I just forgot we had dogs," I deadpanned.

We also laughed to remember Mary Jo's comment that having dogs would be good *practice* for parenting. Sure, there are books you can read. There are experienced parents you can consult. Doctors are helpful. So are prayers.

But is anyone ever really prepared to be a parent? Not so much.

That said, Mary Jo did seem to take to it naturally. She was a gifted mother – loving, protective and nurturing. She chose family over career, family before self and modeled the essential motherly attributes of patience and selflessness.

Alice Turner felt Mary Jo would be a wonderful mother and summarized it nicely in a card. She wrote:

"Motherhood is the perfect blend of being strong-willed and gentle-hearted, of wisdom, innocence, and love."[51]

It's amazing how quickly it passes. Before long, Silas was checking off developmental milestones, dutifully recorded by his mother.

Other than his Apgar Score, Silas was about average in height, weight and other markers.

Crawled at seven months. Check. Stood at nine months. Check. Took first step at 11 months. Check. Fifty percentile. Check.

Talking was the exception.

Boy, could he talk. He started babbling by three months, then "mama" and "dog" and "dada" – in that order.

Mary Jo and I read to Silas often. Mary Jo also used her linguistics degree to great effect, impressing Silas with her wide range of dialects and imitations. By his first birthday, he was babbling in partial sentences.

Silas never lacked for encouragement and Grandma Kathy challenged him with games, play-acting and competitions. She always followed it with praise. By his third birthday, Silas and Grandma Kathy were hosting magic shows and karaoke contests:

Grandma Kathy: "Introducing, the amazing, the magnificent, Silas!"

Silas: "No, no Grandma, I'm just a regular guy."[52]

Though not as likely to brag, Mary Jo was a proud mother and she laughed or applauded on cue. She also recorded most of it, passing on Silas' latest witticisms to friends or including them in a growing scrapbook. One memorable entry reads:

Mary Jo: "Silas, I think you've got a cold. Should I get you some cold medicine?"

Silas: "No, I think I need some warm medicine."[53]

These were happy, special times, that first year as a little family.

Mary Jo loved being a mother – and I loved being a father.

It just went by too darn fast.

10

Two Years

> "Things changed, people changed, and the world went rolling along right outside the window."
>
> Nicholas Sparks
>
> *Message in a Bottle*

THE NEXT TWO YEARS WERE a roller coaster ride of heart-breaking tragedy and jaw-dropping wonder.

Life is like that sometimes.

Despite the all-consuming demands of motherhood, Mary Jo stayed in touch with friends and coworkers on Capitol Hill.

Ken Cunningham and John Maxwell called or sent emails, seeking out her advice or institutional memory. She trained others to replace her as scheduler, including Leah Shimp, a lovely young lady who would serve the senator for many years.

Mary Jo enjoyed lunch on Capitol Hill with Kurt Kovarik and Kathy Nuebel, who later got married. I'm told Senator Grassley took credit for the match.

Mary Jo also stayed abreast of the latest legislation or rumors by reading *The Hill* and *Washingtonian Magazine,* but it was only a passing interest.

That's because her time and attention belonged to our son, Silas. He owned her heart – and mine.

With the perspective of new parents, we began to think of life after the military – of stability and putting down roots.

Then 9/11 happened.

Tuesday, September 11th, 2011, began as a beautiful, late summer day in the Capitol Region. The muggy haze of July and August had passed on and left a bright blue sky.

Mary Jo sipped coffee while reading the *Washington Post* at the dining room table. I dressed in regulation Air Force blue – shirt with open collar and name tag, knit pants and shiny black shoes – before kissing my wife and sleeping child goodbye.

Glancing at my Omega watch – a treasured gift from Mary Jo – I waited for the bus at Seminary Road, marveling at the cloudless sky and low humidity.

On the bus, I noticed the weather had seemed to put even the usually jaded and surly passengers of metro D.C. in a good mood. I counted not one but two smiles on the short commute to the Pentagon.

Despite its reputation as the five-sided squirrel cage, the Pentagon was an intriguing, challenging place to work.

Ironically, the ground breaking for the Pentagon had been held exactly sixty years prior, on September 11th, 1941. The monolithic mass of reinforced concrete and limestone was built in just 16 months, probably an all-time record for a landmark government contract – and this during World War II, no less.

The Pentagon was the largest office building in the world. The entire Capitol building could fit in each one of its five wedge-shaped sections. It was a small city, really, and the workplace for about 20,000 people.

A staff of two changed 250 light bulbs daily. The hallways stretched on for more than 17.5 miles and included 691 water fountains. On the lower level, there was a shopping mall where Pentagon workers could pick up a prescription at the CVS Pharmacy or a diamond ring at David Mann Jewelers.

We called it "The Building" not as a term of endearment but as a simple, bland title for an edifice so large and plain. Though it felt like a dizzying labyrinth built to hold the Minotaur of Greek legend, architects bragged it was a marvel of efficiency.

"You can get from any one place to another in just seven minutes," it was said.

Amongst the building's occupants, however, it was well known that only an experienced action officer with a heightened sense of direction could accomplish such a feat.

As an example, I once sent the new guy in our office on an errand to pick up a classified folder in the first basement of the Pentagon.

"Access the mezzanine level via the third corridor, take the second right past the purple water fountain, then a left at the end of the hall," I told him.

We never saw him again. Actually, I made that up – but it could happen.[54]

The Pentagon was unique among the world's military headquarters in that it's open to the public for tours.

Tourists were disappointed to learn the small building in the center courtyard of the Pentagon did not house a command center or nuclear reactor, as rumored, but a hot dog stand.

We nicknamed it "Ground Zero."

My workday with Air Force Logistics, Maintenance and Installations began in Room 4A264. This room designation in the ever-practical building meant it was on the fourth floor (4) of the inner ring (A) and a little past halfway down the corridor.

I've recounted the day of September 11th so many times it seems strangely surreal and yet all-too familiar. A few later, I recounted the experience to a reporter. I said:

"The day began as just kind of an average morning, drinking coffee, checking emails, much like any other office."[55]

At about 9:00 a.m., a coworker's wife called and told him about a plane crash in New York. He turned on the TV and remarked, "It looks like somebody flew a plane into one of the World Trade Towers."

The rest of us quickly joined him and gathered around the TV, debating the size of the plane and the oddity of it all. Then suddenly, there was another plane, and we looked on in horror as the towers burned.

About that time, a Muslim terrorist banked American Airlines Flight 77 through a 180 degree turn somewhere over the tip of southern Ohio and headed back to Washington D.C.[56]

Later, some speculated the Pentagon was on high alert or preparing strike plans against some unknown enemy, but we were completely unaware there was a plane headed our direction.

In fact, we were watching TV.

At about 9:37 a.m., American Airlines Flight 77 completed a tight circling maneuver over Alexandria and Arlington and then began an aggressive dive near Arlington National Cemetery.

Diving at about 500 miles per hour, the Boeing 757-200 clipped light poles along the VA-27 roadway near the Navy Annex and slammed into the west wall of the Pentagon.

The nearly supersonic impact of the aircraft instantly snuffed out the lives of all 59 people on board as it bored through limestone, steel and reinforced concrete in milliseconds.

The horrific impact combined with 9,000 gallons of A-1 jet fuel to make for a devastating, explosive force that penetrated through three of the Pentagon's five rings.

It took the lives of an additional 125 people inside the Pentagon.[57]

From my office in Room 4A264 – about 615 feet from the point of impact – the explosion felt like the epicenter of a deep, though brief, earthquake. My coworkers and I steadied our feet, even as panic filled the air.[58]

Instantly pale and sweaty, we looked at one another with shock until a voice broke the silence:

"My God, that felt like a truck bomb," someone said.

For a moment, we debated what to do – until Buddy Truax said, Let's get the hell out of here!" Buddy was a good friend and colleague, and I followed him quickly out the door.

Other than the shock and chaos, there's little I remember about those moments, but I later described it to a reporter. I said:

"It was a confused, chaotic, zombie-like walk to the outside."[59]

By the time Buddy and I made it to the outside – a few of our coworkers trailing behind – there were already emergency response crews on-site with lights and sirens blazing. The grassy field by the west wall of the Pentagon was littered with wreckage – it would later be the site of a memorial – and a fire raged from the gaping hole left by the aircraft.

Set against a beautiful blue sky, the Pentagon burned as we watched in horror. My colleagues and I felt an overwhelming grief and unfocused anger growing within us.

For my wife and family, the experience was perhaps even more difficult and traumatic, as they didn't know what was going on or if I was alive or dead for a time.

Transportation was shut down, cell towers were overwhelmed and Mary Jo feared the worst. She heard secondary explosions, though we later learned they were the sonic booms of fighter aircraft. My father assured Mary Jo that "Brent was in another part of the building," but he knew he couldn't be certain.

I've told the story many times since at club meetings, before church groups or school assemblies. Depending on the day or my mood, it can feel both frighteningly recent or like a long-ago event from another life entirely.[60]

One thing I've noticed is that before every group, every person remembers where they were, what they were doing and who they were with when they first heard of 9/11. It is a horrific, seminal event, forever ingrained in our memory.

Ten years later, a reporter asked Silas if he remembered anything about 9/11. He said:

"Not much. The people who did this thing are called terrorists and they're not very nice people."[61]

For Mary Jo, it was an emotional time to say the least. She told friends she felt "overwhelmed and petrified," showing cracks in her stoic-like demeanor and crying as the Towers fell. Many Americans felt similar emotions.

The day after 9/11, we watched as the roof of the Pentagon continued to burn and Mary Jo took a phone call:

"Hello, this is Commander Barnes from the White House. Is Major Hoffman there?"

"Uhh...yeah, sure," Mary Jo said, mouthing "What the?!" as she handed me the phone.

"We're preparing a memo for the Air Force, requesting you to report as the Director of the President's Emergency Operations Center," the Colonel said. "Okay?"

"Uh okay, yes sir," I answered.[62]

A week later, another horrific event shook our lives – and the world – when anthrax spores were mailed to several media offices. The lethal anthrax spores eventually killed five people and infected 17 others.

In October, two more letters were sent – each containing spores far more deadly and refined than the previous letters.

A letter inside read: "09-11-01 YOU CAN NOT STOP US. WE HAVE THIS ANTHRAX. ALLAH IS GREAT."[63]

Fear swept the Capitol once news broke that the Hart Senate Office Building was contaminated and Mary Jo was fearful for her friends and coworkers. The building was closed and sealed, then meticulously decontaminated using chlorine gas.

Considering 9/11, the anthrax attacks were a forgotten footnote – but at the time, we lived in fear of our own mail.

At the Pentagon, from then on, I noticed the mail arrived discolored and crispy. I later learned the mail had been *baked* with 56 kilorays of radiation – the equivalent of 200 million chest x-rays – to kill off any anthrax or other biological threat.

In the ensuing months, Mary Jo and I tried to put the monumental events out of our minds. It was not as difficult as it seemed, with little Silas spreading joy and laughter through the house. He was a bright, happy little boy, and he was our world.

Mary Jo and I also decided it was time to make a move to another house. The decision was not based on some other tragedy or a dislike of the house on Fillmore Street. It was because of some wonderful news.

We learned that Mary Jo was pregnant again, and we were delighted.

When the results from the early pregnancy test came back, Mary Jo exclaimed, "It's blue!" and sent me out for another test kit. That one was also positive: "It's a plus sign!" she yelled.

Mary Jo was also thrilled to share the news with family and friends and not nearly so secretive about it this time.

Only Xenia and Zoe seemed less than pleased.

Unlike the first time around, we also chose not to learn the baby's sex from the ultrasound. We told friends we'd be thrilled with a baby brother for Silas – and we meant it.

But privately – in the quiet of bedtime – we admitted our hearts yearned for a little girl.

First, though, there was that move.

Our friend Britt Grouby helped us to find a nice family home near Holmes Run in Alexandria. It was a much bigger home at 5327 Holmes Run Parkway – just four blocks from The Pickett House.

The house on Holmes Run Parkway was much like other homes in the neighborhood.

It was a well-built brick house with three bedrooms, two baths and a one-car garage.

Though not much over 2,000 square feet, the house had five levels, including two below the ground floor. Built in the 1950s, it had beautiful oak floors, newly refinished with polyurethane.

One bathroom had black and pink tiles and a gray bathtub, unchanged since the 1950s.

Surprisingly, that bathroom was the only room I left unchanged.

I quickly rebuilt the kitchen for Mary Jo, eager to complete it before the baby came. Silas even helped with renovations, wearing goggles and measuring everything. Once, he put a drywall screw in an electrical outlet, but he never did it again.

I redoubled my baby-proofing efforts, installing a plastic cover over each outlet and safety gates at all four stair locations.

Silas was also pleased to help me with his own room – a much larger one on the fifth level.

His room had a large window to the west. The long walls on the north and south sides sloped downward from the attic. It also had extra storage space behind the two sidewalls, so Silas and I decided to build a secret playroom behind one wall.

The entrance to the secret room was hidden by a reinforced, pivoting bookcase, which was attached to the wall by a long hinge. The bookcase served as the door to the hidden space, and it opened by pulling on a fake book, disengaging the spring latch behind it.

Silas and I were both pleased.

The other bedroom adjoined our master bedroom, and we decided to make this the new baby room. Mary Jo chose pastel colors for the wall paint, but decided to delay the decision on trim, curtains and bedding to make it appropriately girlish or boyish.

With our little family about to expand, I again convinced Mary Jo we needed another vehicle – bigger and even safer, I argued. Finally, we were ready for the baby.

First, though, Muslim terrorists came calling again.[64]

In late October, two psychotics – an adult and his apprentice – killed ten people in a sick game of sniper. Using a Bushmaster XM-15 rifle, they took turns shooting random strangers through a peephole in a blue Chevrolet Caprice sedan.

During the attacks, people were encouraged to stay inside. One handout encouraged people to "walk briskly – in jagged, unpredictable patterns." It was strange, scary and deadly.

One of the victims was shot in the head while walking beside her husband outside a Home Depot store in Seven Corners – just west on King Street. It was a store I frequented.

Another victim was shot in the head while pumping gas at a local Shell Station. In Norbeck, Maryland, a lady was shot while sitting on a bench, reading a book.

Understandably, we started to wonder if the National Capital region was a good place to raise a family. We'd talked about staying in the area after the end of my military career – now just a year away. But, as Mary Jo said, "Then came the anthrax scare and the sniper shootings."

The second pregnancy was also more difficult for Mary Jo than the first one. She was tired, caring for an active little boy, managing a household and looking forward to the due date.

Thankfully, Grandma Karen came to the rescue and came to Virginia to stay with us.

When the labor pains began, Mary Jo and I left for the National Naval Medical Center in Bethesda, Maryland. Karen reported that Xenia stood guard by Silas' bed. As always, Zoe slept through everything and her familiar snore reverberated through all five levels of the house.

Now veteran parents, the labor was not as angst-filled or worrisome as the first one – in a way any parent understands. But this does not mean it was easy or fun – as any woman knows.

At Bethesda, we began by walking the familiar corridors of Building 9 and urging the baby along.

The ordeal with epidural insertion was all-too familiar. Despite my warnings about the last insertion, the anesthesiologist punctured the *dura* – the outermost layer of meninges that protects the spinal fluid. This resulted in a small leak of spinal fluid and what's called a "post dural puncture headache" for Mary Jo.

Drugged and exhausted, she would sleep for three days after the delivery.

The delivery itself was less traumatic than for Silas, though perhaps our perspective was tempered by experience.

There was no need for forceps or a suction cup, and I didn't get shoved to the corner this time. While Mary Jo did all the work, I held her hand, brushed the hair from her brow and took lots of pictures.

This time, though, my eyes filled with tears even before the baby came, awash with emotions of anticipation, wonder and concern for my wife. Mary Jo and the baby struggled and the heart rate monitors pinged as the stress level increased.

On December 11th, 2002 – at 6:37 p.m. – the piercing sound of a baby girl's cry filled Room 17.

Yes, a baby girl.

For whatever reason, we weren't that surprised it was a girl but we were elated. She was beautiful, even angelic, and Mary Jo could hardly wait to hold her. Mary Jo waited patiently as the technician checked vitals and wrapped our little girl in a cocoon of blue and pink cotton.

The vitals were remarkably similar to that of her big brother. She weighed 7 pounds, 13 ounces and was 21 inches long – but the statistics could hardly describe her beauty.

The little girl we named "Lydia" would have our hearts for the rest of our lives.

Before the day was over, Grandma Karen came to visit the hospital, eager to see her new granddaughter. However, we hardly noticed her because she also brought Silas. Silas was wide-eyed with excitement and stared expectantly at his little sister.

Mary Jo and I had discussed several names for the baby. If he were a boy, the choices were Andrew, Reed and Jonas. But we quickly settled on one name if she were a girl.

It was a name we'd chosen years ago.

Lydia was a name we chose from the Bible – described in the Book of Acts, Chapter 16, Verse 14 as "a woman named Lydia, a dealer in purple cloth from the city of Thyatira, who was a worshiper of God."

According to the Book of Acts, the Apostle Paul was accompanied by Timothy and *Silas* when he baptized Lydia just outside the town of Phillipi in Ancient Greece. Scholars have also described Lydia as the first European convert to Christianity.

While in Greece, Mary Jo and I had visited the legendary site of Lydia's baptism. It was about a half-mile outside Phillipi and though seldom visited by tourists, it was well kept and tranquil.

A stream snaked lazily around a small island of lush grass, bordered by flat stones, set like a sidewalk. Standing in the center of the island was a cross-topped memorial of cement and white stucco. A rock path guided pilgrims to stairs that descended into the stream.

It was a simple place of beauty and reflection, and Mary Jo and I loved it.

Mary Jo and I also loved the name Lydia, despite its pedestrian meaning of "from Lydia" – an ancient region of western Asia Minor – or what is now Turkey.[65]

We were hopeful our daughter, Lydia, would reflect credit upon the faith, grace and hospitality of her namesake. Mary Jo also loved the color purple, and so the name just made sense.

Choosing a middle name proved much easier than for her brother, Silas A. Again, I suggested family names – this time "Mary" in honor of Mary Jo and her mother, Mary Karen.

And so, Lydia Mary it was.

Lydia Mary was an easy, loving baby. She bubbled with joy, was rarely fussy and slept through the night within two weeks.

Mary Jo tracked and recorded Lydia's growth in *The Complete Book of Baby and Child Care*, pleased that she met or exceeded all milestones.

Mary Jo also made homemade baby food for Silas and Lydia, experimenting with colorful recipes of carrot, pumpkin and broccoli puree.

It was and is an inestimable treasure to be a parent. We greatly enjoyed cuddling sweet Lydia, whom Mary Jo often referred to in the third person as "my darling Lydia."

For my part, I strung together adjectives, calling her "my sweet little honey" and not really caring that it sounded stupid or sappy. Lydia was a special, beautiful baby, and we were overjoyed to be her parents.

With baby Lydia demanding most of our attention, Mary Jo and I were sensitive Silas may feel "dethroned" – in therapist-speak – from his role as the first-born king.

However, we loved them both completely and deeply, even though our love for each was different, in some ways. Silas was pleased to play big brother, yet did sometimes compete for his mother's attention.

Once, when Mary Jo was nursing Lydia, Silas said, "I can do it," pointing to his chest – and Mary Jo let him try.

At the first touch of Lydia's soft baby lips on his bare chest, he squealed with laughter, pulling away and yanking his pajama shirt back down tightly.

Like childhoods often do, Lydia's first year seemed to pass in a blur, yet we cherished every moment.

Mary Jo and I often took the kids across the street to the Holmes Run playground, enjoying the swings and rings. Sometimes Silas and Lydia played with the neighbor's kids – Richie and Nia Beane. An ice cream truck came by every day at about noon. The kids loved the bomb pops.

Silas enjoyed his toy vacuum, spending hours vacuuming in the nude for some reason.

He and I painted an acrylic on canvas after a day at the park, titling it "Funnelball Morning." Lydia and I made one too – a watercolor design we made with our fingers, called "Random Thoughts."

Mary Jo, Silas, Lydia and I walked around the neighborhood nearly every evening with the dogs in tow. Silas checked the bolts on the fire hydrants at every corner. I never understood why.

Grandma Kathy visited often, bringing more gifts, but we most prized her company. She made every trip outside like an exotic, excitement-filled adventure. Every indoor board game had the feel of a television game show, complete with colorful play-by-play announcements.

Her visits also led to entertaining conversations with Silas, worthy of passing on to friends and family:

Silas: You shouldn't call mommy "Mary Jo."
Grandma: Well, why not, that's her name.
Silas: No, you should call her mommy.
Grandma: But she's not my mom. I'm your daddy's mom.
Silas: Well, it's just not right – I don't like it.

Kathy Wise also visited shortly after Lydia's birth, and she was the second and last to be given the title of "Honorary Aunt."

Kathy loved Silas and Lydia like her own, and we loved having her around.

With a new house in a new location, we also decided to make a move to another church. Based on advice from a few friends, we decided to attend National Evangelical Free Church – later renamed Cornerstone – in nearby Annandale, Virginia.

We didn't know anyone who attended there, but we knew the senior pastor, Bill Kynes, had a reputation as a kind man and a gifted preacher.

While attending an orientation at the church, Mary Jo met a lovely woman named Christina Severinghaus.

Christina was also a new member, and like Mary Jo, she had two kids in tow. She had two boys, Lukas and Noah.

As it turned out, Mary Jo and Christina had many other things in common and quickly stuck up an easy, supportive friendship.

Christina was a doting mother, but she was also well educated, professional and attractive. Her blonde hair and blue eyes hinted at her Swedish heritage. Selfless and kind, she had the gift of hospitality and was a hugger.

She was also dedicated to ministry and relationships, always serving and helping. Among family and friends, she was never heard to say "Is there anything I can do?" Instead, she would figure out what most needed done, and she would do it.

Christina's husband Bob was a pilot in the U.S. Navy, and they graciously invited Mary Jo and I to a newly formed Marriage Accountability Group. Two other couples – Rukshan and Jody Fernando and Gregory and Jennifer Laible – also joined us every week while our kids played with a sitter in the basement.

It was a memorable time of growth, driven by transparency, accountability and encouragement. Christina cooked nearly every week while Bob led the lessons.

In July 2003, I decided to move on from the military, holding strong even when the assignments officer dangled an assignment to Hickam Air Force Base in Hawaii.

At the Pentagon, my friend Buddy Truax and a few other comrades in arms hosted a nice ceremony in my honor. It was bittersweet to say goodbye to a career that had been my life for many years – to hang up the uniform and bid adieu to many wonderful friends.

Amongst the crowd were four of my best friends from Anthon-Oto High School: Marvin Keitges, Jay Schumann, Sonia Jones and Kami Ashley-Farrington. I was delighted to see my classmates and touched by their thoughtfulness, but nervous at what they might tell my colleagues – or my wife.

Secretively, I whispered to the emcee:

"Please, for the love of God, don't let any of them near a microphone."

Not long after the ceremony, Mary Jo and I decided to take a cross-country road trip.

We visited friends we hadn't seen in years – from Pennsylvania to Iowa, New Mexico to Texas and points in between. In all, we put 4,800 miles on the new family SUV. Rather than watch DVDs in the mobile player, we entertained ourselves with games like "Animal, Vegetable or Mineral" and "I Spy."

It was a fun, memorable trip.

At Christmas, we took another trip – this one back to Iowa. It was a memorable trip, but it wasn't fun.

Before we made it to Ohio, it was obvious Silas and Lydia weren't feeling well. They took turns vomiting in a sack or the toilets at rest stops. When Silas felt the urge to vomit, he said, "I've gotta go Number 3."

By the time we got to Iowa, Silas was over it. Lydia, however, seemed to have worsened, as she was tired and lethargic.

Mary Jo and I took Lydia to the hospital in Mason City, where the doctors were puzzled by her lethargy and blood work. I camped-out in her room, spelled by Mary Jo, Ron, or Uncle Phil, who surprised me with his warmth and patience.

Ron served as the hospital chaplain, and he soon brought news that another member of the family was in the hospital: Grandma Helen.

Helen hadn't been taking her medications and had also caught pneumonia. Before she passed out, she shared a final thought with her husband LaVern. She said:

"Don't do anything extra. If it's my time, that's fine. I love you."

Thankfully, it wasn't her time. Though 89 years old, Helen recovered strongly within hours and opened her eyes to see the family at her bedside. Startled, she said:

"Good grief, I'm still here?!"

We got a good laugh out of that one.

There wasn't any laughter in Lydia's room, however, and Mary Jo and I were heartsick, cuddling our beloved daughter. Our darling Lydia was deathly sick in a hospital bed. Despite prayer, we were anxious and filled with worry.

Finally, a doctor entered the room and presented a viable diagnosis. He said:

"We think it's Type 1 Juvenile Diabetes, and we need to send you to the university hospital in Iowa City."

The diagnosis was a shock, as we had no experience with it on either side of the family. Though Type 2 diabetes is common, Type 1 is not and especially in a child so young.[66]

Mary Jo and I soon learned it was a life-changing diagnosis, but our fear was tempered with the relief of seeing Lydia recover completely and quickly with a shot of insulin.

Life would never be the same, but our daughter was smiling, even giddy, and we completed the training with rapt attention.

The next few months, Mary Jo and I obsessed over becoming experts on all things diabetic. We learned how to weigh all of Lydia's food and count carbohydrates, using books like *The Calorie King*. We learned how to balance insulin doses with food intake and activity level.

We became expert on technological advances and eventually upgraded Lydia to an insulin pump with a remote control. Unfortunately, we also learned that no diligent parent of a child with diabetes ever sleeps through the night.

Through the experience, however, we also learned Type 1 diabetes was manageable and our darling little girl could live a full, healthy life.

We pledged not to view our daughter as "Lydia – the girl with diabetes." She was Lydia – sweet, precious and special – and that would never change.

Mary Jo and I figured we could handle the finger pricks and site changes and our little family resolved to move forward with joy.

As families must, we adjusted to the changes in lifestyle and priorities and the rest of the year was as fun and memorable as any before it

.

Eric, Jennifer and the girls came to visit again – now joined by a third daughter, Amelia – and we were thrilled to show them around the new Franklin Roosevelt Memorial, taking pictures by the famous cherry trees of the tidal basin.

We also played in the creek by our house – skipping stones, building tiny dams and chasing chub fish around with remote control boats.

Heather also visited with her boys – Antonio and Adrian – and we enjoyed their company, too. Silas was pleased to have another boy around to help him check the bolts on the fire hydrants in the neighborhood.

Silas and I also had our first campout in the backyard, which he called "Camp Warm and Cozy." I made a sign.

With a little help from Silas and Lydia, I also built a play land in the backyard, complete with a rope bridge and tree house. With 16 four-by-fours set in 40 bags of cement, it could've survived a nuclear blast.

Another exciting event came to our backyard that summer when the 17-year "Brood X" cicadas burrowed up from the ground.

Silas and Lydia were amazed to see the cicadas emerge from their thin, fragile shells. The cicadas left their shells on tree bark and plant stems by the thousands. The screech of the cicadas echoed through the early evening, promising to return again in 2021.

It wasn't long before we returned to Iowa again, this time for Helen and Lavern's seventieth wedding anniversary.

Their children – Charles, Karen and Phil – and grandchildren were honored to celebrate with them. My parents also graciously made the trip to the little church in Mark to join in the celebration of a long, loving marriage.

With the return home to Virginia, we started to think it might be our last. We talked of returning to our roots – of raising our kids in Iowa.

11 Going Home

"It's always sad when someone leaves home, unless they are simply going around the corner and will return in a few minutes with ice-cream sandwiches."

Lemony Snicket
Horseradish: Bitter Truths You Can't Avoid

When Mary Jo and I decided to move west, I had a couple of places in mind.

Places like South Dakota – a state I'd called home for a number of years while in the military. I loved the freedom, wide-open plains and Black Hills of The Mount Rushmore State.

I also loved Utah and Wyoming, drawn to the ruggedly picturesque mountains and the promise of living closer to my brother and his family in New Mexico.

My wife, however, was committed to return to our Iowa roots so *we* quickly narrowed it down to two locations within The Hawkeye State.

Those two locations were Mason City in north central Iowa; and Sioux City in northwest Iowa.

By no coincidence, Mason City just so happened to be the home of Mary Jo's parents; and Sioux City, the home of my parents.

The return home to Iowa made sense and followed our family roots. Mary Jo's mother and my mother had both settled in Iowa decades earlier to be closer to their parents.

In May of 2004, we visited Mason City to learn more about the town and look at houses.

Sometimes called "River City," Mason City was a town of about 25,000 people. It was perhaps best known as the setting for *The Music Man*, a stage musical and 1962 movie adaptation.

Meredith Wilson, the creator of The *Music Man*, once called Mason City home. A statue stood in his honor, next to his boyhood home just off South Pennsylvania Avenue.

We enjoyed spending time in Mason City. Ron and Karen served as tour guides, pointing out the architecture of Frank Lloyd Wright around town.

We were more impressed, however, with the people. Coming from the all-business mindset of Washington D.C., we were at once reminded of the innate friendliness of Iowans.

It seemed Pastor Ron knew everyone in town.

Silas and Lydia frolicked in East Park with Ron's grandchildren – Nathan, Javen and Neeley. The kids chased geese, slipping and sliding on the goose poop that carpeted the grass like anti-personnel mines.

Don Swann was Ron's son-in-law, and he took us fishing for crawdads along Willow Creek, knee deep in muck and loving it. Silas exclaimed, "I've got a lobster here!"

We liked Mason City, and it seemed only an issue of finding a house to our satisfaction. Though we preferred a home with an acre or two of land, Mary Jo's best hope was for a nice kitchen. As she put it:

"If possible, I'd like to avoid another, insufferable kitchen renovation."

It didn't take long to find the home of our dreams.

On the east side of town, our realtor Brett Schoneman led us to a magnificent ranch home that had belonged to a distinguished family.

It was a home we never could've afforded in the suburbs of Washington D.C.

Towering willow trees hung gracefully near the back edge of seven well-manicured acres, beckoning visitors to shade and solace. The house had long been vacant and needed a lot of work, yet we marveled at the craftsmanship of the built-in mahogany bookshelves in the library and the ornate nickel-plated hardware on the pocket doors.

Walking through the kitchen, my heart sunk when I saw the cabinets and counters, envisioning another renovation in my future. But, to my surprise, Mary Jo was undeterred, seduced by the commercial-grade Viking stove with six burners and big red knobs.

We hoped to make it our home and promptly made a fair offer, but the owner said no. We made another, higher offer but it also proved to be for naught. The owner was too emotionally attached or greedy – or both.

Two years later, he finally sold it for much less than what we'd offered. Oh well.

Mary Jo and I were disappointed when we were unable to find another property in Mason City that we liked. We prayed about it and promptly decided to turn our sights to Sioux City.

In retrospect, it probably sounds stupid to choose a new hometown based on a failed real estate offer and a prayer – but that's what we did.

Much like Mason City and other towns in Iowa, Sioux City had been stagnant for many years, with a population hovering at about 80,000 since the 1930s.

Nonetheless, it was a city positioned for growth, twice named an "All-American City" and a "Best Place to Live."[67]

Sioux City was also known for its colorful and intriguing history. Positioned near the banks of the Missouri River, Native Americans who settled in the area marveled at the bluffs of picturesque, wind-swept soil.

During the summer of 1804, the Lewis and Clark expedition moored their 55-foot keelboat along the banks of what would become Sioux City.

The expedition left a lasting mark on the area.

Sergeant Charles Floyd was the only member to die on the expedition and was buried on the bluffs overlooking the Missouri river on August 20th of 1804.

Many years later, the Floyd Monument was built in his honor, beckoning travelers along I-29 in modern-day Sioux City. In photographs, the impressive obelisk of heavy sandstone was sometimes mistaken for the Washington Monument.

Rivers, streets and buildings were later named after Lewis, Clark and Floyd in Sioux City. Lewis and Clark Park was the home of the city's professional baseball team.

Even Captain Lewis' dog – a gentle black Newfoundland named "Seaman" – was remembered by a prominent display at the Lewis and Clark Interpretive Center.

Historians reported Theophile Bruguier was the first white settler in the area. His restored cabin still stands in Riverside Park, along the Big Sioux River in Sioux City.

An early city founder, Mr. Bruguier became friends with Chief War Eagle of the Sioux Indians. He also took two of War Eagle's daughters as wives and fathered thirteen children. A statue of War Eagle was later erected on the west side bluffs of Sioux City, looking down on the Missouri River valley.

Dr. John Cook was another colorful, fascinating character from Sioux City's history.

When he incorporated the city in 1857, Dr. Cook became the city postmaster and county judge. People say Dr. Cook carried the mail around in his hat and when he saw someone he had mail for, he would then give it to them.[68]

By the 1880s, Sioux City was the fastest growing city in America and multiplied its population five times in the decade. It became famous for its opulent Peavey Opera House, the first-ever Corn Palace and boulevards lined with grand Victorian mansions.

The city seemed destined for greatness and city leaders confidently pronounced, "Whatever the community wanted, it would and could achieve." They called it doing things *The Sioux City Way.*

Unfortunately, this period proved to be the high-water mark for Sioux City. The local economy was nearly bankrupt because of the Financial Panic of 1893 and forced many of the city's leaders into insolvency.

Then came the floods.

Each decade brought a devastating flood. The Missouri and Floyd River floods of 1952 and 1953 killed 14 people and wiped out much of the legendary stockyards.

Some say the city never recovered.

By the 1960s, visitors had given it the unflattering nickname of "Sewer City" because of the wastewater treatment plant just south of the Floyd Monument and the always smelly pork processing plant just off the interstate. The city's official airport designator of "SUX" also made it the butt of frequent jokes.

One community leader remarked, "I've never seen a city with such a low sense of self-esteem."[69]

Mary Jo and I knew little of Sioux City's history and reputation when we decided to make it our home.

We knew only that the strangers we encountered treated us as friends. We noticed the architecture and amenities rivaled nearly any small city we'd seen. We marveled at the low cost of housing and the large lots with magnificent, mature trees.

Sioux City seemed to grow on both of us. Mary Jo's only complaint was "It's a shame we don't have a Dunkin' Donuts around here. Pathetic, really," she said with a smirk.[70]

With help from my mother and sister Heather, we finally settled on a house in the Sylvian Way neighborhood on the north side of Sioux City.

The street of Sylvian Avenue curved like the Big Dipper constellation through the north side neighborhood. It was a neighborhood of expansive lots and eclectic homes, most of them built in the 1960s.

The maps, street signs and U.S. Post Office all referred to the street as Sylvian Avenue, yet some long-time residents still called it Sylvian Way.

We loved the neighborhood and closed on the house at 3905 Sylvian Avenue sight unseen thanks to Heather's detailed description and video. We were impressed with its potential as a family home.

The realtor informed us the previous owners had raised eight children in it. Even when we learned the house was outdated and needed work, we moved forward.

Like the city itself, we also discovered the house had an interesting history.

Another previous owner, P.L. "Gus" Nymann, was the vice president of IBP, Inc. when he and his family lived in the house. IPB Inc. was a well-known meat processing company that was later bought-out by Tyson Foods.

During a strike at IBP in 1970, union thugs firebombed the house on Sylvian Avenue. Thankfully, Nymann's wife and two other women in the house escaped unharmed, but the house was gutted. A year later, the house was rebuilt, from the basement to the attic.[71]

The house on Sylvian Avenue was a split-level colonial with four large white columns and too many rooms and windows to count. With seven bedrooms and four baths, it was way more house than we needed. I almost felt guilty describing the amenities and price to our big city friends. Almost.

Though outdated with 1970s wallpaper and appliances, the upstairs had a four-season room, a wall-long brick fireplace and solid six-panel pocket doors.

Outside, the landscaping also needed work, with lilacs untrimmed for decades and a row of decaying American elm trees suffering from the ubiquitous Dutch elm disease.

In contrast, the front yard beckoned beautifully with a saucer magnolia tree at the front door. Sometimes called the "tulip tree magnolia" for its magnificent pink and purple flowers, it framed the front entrance like a Claude Monet oil painting.

In the rear, a massive black walnut tree towered over the terraced back yard with apple blossoms, evergreens and fragrant, purple lilacs within reach of its expansive branches.

Upon our arrival in Sioux City, Mary Jo's first impression of the house was a shade less than positive and encouraging.

Where I saw value and potential, she saw another kitchen renovation project. Only a year later was she able to look back and laugh about it. She said:

"You couldn't walk in the kitchen if you opened the refrigerator door."

I resolved to completely renovate the home and build a custom, executive kitchen for my patient wife.

With Silas and Lydia tagging along, I visited area home improvement stores and started kicking around ideas with Mary Jo.

We also enjoyed a tour of homes sponsored by the American Red Cross. We had a great time and picked up some ideas for our kitchen project.

When I shared my idea to combine two rooms into a completely new kitchen, Mary Jo was hesitant but relented, and I began work immediately.

By the time she returned from a weekend visit to Mason City with the kids, there was already a four-inch pile of pine sawdust on the pockmarked floor.

Though she worried we had "made a huge mistake," I asked her to trust me and six months later, she had the kitchen she wanted – the kitchen she deserved. It was even featured in a fund-raising tour of kitchens by the Sioux City Art Center called "Artistry in the Kitchen."[72]

The custom kitchen was nearly twice the size of our first home ("the hooch"). It was trimmed in five complementary woods, including white and red oak floors with black walnut inserts and an interlocking pine ceiling. A large expanse of black, speckled granite stretched under the cherry cabinets and across a large, center island.

In one of two insulated cutouts in the brick fireplace, I recess-mounted a 30-gallon aquarium. I also mounted an LCD TV onto the wall adjacent to the long center island, with electronics hidden in the pantry. I'll stop there because it sounds like I'm bragging.

Mary Jo loved her new kitchen. She was delighted to place her recipe books on the custom bookcase and experiment with new recipes from *Cooking Light.* More often, she sat in the corner alcove of the kitchen, draped in sunlight and reading her Bible on a red, Laura Ashley sofa.

Eventually, I completed the other rooms and the house became a home – though not because of the renovations. It became a home because we lived and loved in it.

A few years later, Mary Jo wrote:

"Thank you Lord for giving me this life, this family and these children. Thank you for this home – the one I didn't want – which has been such a place of rest and comfort to us."

Despite the time demands of work and home improvements, we never forgot we were parents first and included our kids in nearly everything.

The kids even helped me with home improvement projects. Silas assembled chrome sink faucets and installed wood planks like a carpenter's apprentice. Lydia handed me nails and screws from her child-size John Deere apron.

Gathering supplies, we played hide and seek in the lighting aisle at Lowe's and had sword fights with dowel rods. At Home Depot, Silas developed a fascination with toilet plungers. Lydia and I joined him in sticking the plungers to the waxed linoleum floor, giggling as we popped them on and off.

Before long, we settled into a routine of playing Legos and dolls daily. Mary Jo and I cherished every moment with Silas and Lydia. We told them we loved them each morning and night – and points in between.

It was a precious time. The slower pace and family orientation of Midwest living suited us.

In the summer, we opened the swimming pool, but only after repeated safety lectures and the installation of not one, but two pool alarms and a door buzzer. Mary Jo and I watched the kids like Xenia watched squirrels – ever vigilant and ready to pounce.

Heather and her boys Antonio and Adrian were frequent guests and the boys took to the chlorinated water like hippos to an African waterhole.

While the kids played in the pool, Mary Jo enjoyed sitting in a deck chair, watching Southern Sun Tea brew in a two-quart pitcher while reading *People Magazine.* She and Heather swapped the latest celebrity gossip, wondering what Renee Zellweger and Kenny Chesney ever saw in each other.

Silas, Antonio and Adrian loved playing on the small dirt cliff up by the elm trees, struggling with all manner of tools, sticks and shovels to dig-out a cave or an old tree stump.

Mary Jo nixed our plans for a dirt fort, so I designed an 80-foot waterslide of corrugated plastic signs and garbage bags, fed by two garden hoses and an auxiliary pump. The waterslide didn't hold up for long but the cousins had a ball, especially when the brown dirt of the cliff turned to mud.

The dogs also enjoyed the backyard. Xenia galloped around the large fenced-in yard like a deer pursued by a hunter, sometimes letting out a bark just to let the kids know she was there. When she wasn't sleeping, Zoe parked it on the top inner step of the pool to cool her butt in three inches of water.

Learning my lesson from the fortress-like play land I'd built in Virginia, I purchased the next one at Sam's Club. Silas assisted me in putting it together, thrilled to see the five-foot climbing wall and cedar playhouse take shape.

We also made some modifications, including a gangplank to the upper back yard, a large sandbox and a long knotted rope used to swing from the black walnut tree. Silas and Lydia were very pleased with the result, and we spent much of that summer on the green-roofed play land under the branches.

My mother visited often. She was usually a whirlwind of activity – rearranging furniture, watering plants and putting up curtains – but sometimes she came over just to sit and chat.

She and Mary Jo became good friends, though they often conspired to force new clothes or new projects upon me. On one visit, they agreed we should have a garden and set me to work tilling spots for a vegetable and herbal garden.

Unfortunately, I didn't get much help as Mary Jo admitted she was a "virtual gardener." She enjoyed picking tomatoes and peppers in her wide-brimmed Tilley hat but saved the grunt work of planting, weeding and such for yours truly. She even sent the kids out to the herb garden with a blunt-nose scissors to snip dill, thyme or basil for dinner.

Given Mary Jo's skills as a cook and hostess, we also enjoyed having friends over to our home. Aunt Sarah and Uncle Kevin visited from Virginia, as did Aunt Kathy from Texas.

Senator Grassley also stayed with us while in the area, talking people and politics with Mary Jo while enjoying a Blizzard from Dairy Queen with Silas and Lydia.

We also renewed old friendships. Mary Jo graciously hosted a reunion of sorts with some of my favorite high school classmates. The group included Marvin and his wife, Jane; Jay and his wife, Sheryl; Sonia and her husband, Steve; and Kami Ashley-Farrington.

My classmates and I enjoyed catching up while the spouses listened patiently to our stories, though Mary Jo did roll her eyes a few times. A few of the stories were told at my expense, and we took turns poking fun at each other while enjoying the barbecue.

It was a fun time and reminded me of why we became friends in the first place.[73]

Our first two summers in Sioux City were memorable, joyous and relatively stress-free. The city felt like a small town, and we even got to know our neighbors.

Mary Jo and I walked around the neighborhood, pushing the kids along in a side-by-side stroller with big, bicycle wheels. Shaded by majestic, 50-year oak trees, we walked on the streets, rarely encountering a car.

Neighbors tended to their yards or cleaned out gutters, but they rarely failed to wave or ask "How is your day?"

Sometimes, we rode bikes around the big dipper shaped street of our neighborhood. Mary Jo rode her beloved, purple Gary Fisher bike with the padded seat while I pulled the kids in a Burley trailer, complete with an orange safety flag.

In the evenings, we often enjoyed the sights, sounds and dining of our new hometown.

Mary Jo and I were frequent guests at Luciano's Restaurant on Historic Fourth Street in Sioux City. My parents owned it, so we took care not to come on a Friday or Saturday night when it was filled with reservations.

Mary Jo also relished the Victorian Opera Company – a gift shop next door to Luciano's. My parents owned that too, so Mary Jo used her family discount to build an impressive collection of brightly colored Christopher Radko ornaments and Steiff animals – the kind with a metal button and yellow flag in the ear.

When we had an appetite for pizza, we chose El Fredo's for its original sauce or Little Caesar's for their crazy bread. Sometimes, we went to Chuck E. Cheese but not for the pizza. It was awful.

With plenty of unique dining choices in town, Mary Jo and I were amused by Sioux City's mouth-watering anticipation for the arrival of Olive Garden.

Apparently we weren't the only people who were amused, as the feature story about Olive Garden in the *Sioux City Journal* went viral and was spoofed by several websites.[74]

It was also important to both of us that we make frequent trips north to Mason City to spend time with Mary Jo's family.

While Karen, Mary Jo and Lydia went shopping at Younkers in Mason City, Silas and I visited Fleet Farm – a unique store noted for its barn silo exterior, rows of Rapala fishing lures and ammunition of every caliber.

We also went fishing on the small creek that ran through East Park, where Silas caught his first bluegill with a night crawler.

While visiting Mason City, Mary Jo was also pleased to spend time with her beloved grandparents. LaVern and Helen had moved to Mason

City to be closer to Karen. In fact, they'd moved just across the street to a condominium.

Her grandparents were delighted when Mary Jo walked over each morning to read the *Mason City Gazette* and have coffee.

Back in Sioux City, we became more active in our new church. It was called Heartland Community Baptist Church, and it was far removed from the mega-church where we'd met and married.

The church had formed in the fall of 2004, evolving from a 16-person home Bible study. After meeting in a movie theater, the group signed a lease with the school district to meet in the former Hoover Middle School building.

The building just so happened to be down the street from our home on Sylvian Avenue.

When we visited Heartland Church, it didn't take long to meet all of the members, including Bob and Karen Scott, Gary and Marilyn Derochie and Jack and Karen Taylor.

They were friendly, welcoming people. Jack was a kind, selfless man who volunteered as moderator, office administrator, prayer leader and janitor. Church friends called him "Captain Jack."

Our first impressions of the worship service weren't necessarily positive, but then, we weren't looking to be entertained or coddled.

After our first visit, Mary Foster said, "I prayed this young family would return and become part of the church."

Mary Jo and I prayed too and in March of 2005, we became members #19 and #20.

The new pastor was called a few months later.

Pastor Gene Stockton was likeable, professional and sensitive to God's calling for his future. He and I shared similar backgrounds, as we'd both served in the U.S. Air Force.

Like my own wife, Gene's wife Cheri also made him softer or "more sensitive," in Gene's words. Cheri was quiet, loving and nurturing. A model couple, Gene and Cheri were honest about their own faults while challenging and encouraging others to grow in their relationship with God.

In June 2005, Gene Stockton was called and confirmed as the first pastor of Heartland Community Baptist Church. The small church in the school building had grown a little bit, to 24 members.

According to the church bulletin, an average of about 50 souls attended worship services on any given Sunday.

Before long, Pastor Stockton and the congregation noticed Mary Jo had a beautiful voice. She sang effortlessly in praise, with a clear and confident voice that could hit even the high notes without wavering. No one commented on my singing.

Mary Jo was asked to help lead the congregation in praise and worship. Drawing on her musical background with the flute and piano, she selected music and encouraged others to join the worship team. She also taught herself to play guitar, strumming the acoustic Hohner guitar I'd bought in Greece for her birthday.

But it was her beautiful voice and smile that encouraged the congregation to join in praise.

We involved ourselves fully in the ministry of the church, with Mary Jo leading the worship team. The worship team included Craig Foster, Bruce Hamel and Ta'Mara Hanscom. Mary Jo encouraged each of them to embrace their calling in worship and praise.

I led the outreach team, working with Jo Jones and Cheri Stockton to share the Gospel through the community.

Compelled by our faith, Mary Jo and I also became active in community service.

Mary Jo had long been interested in working with underprivileged children. After she read a newspaper article about it, she and I resolved to serve as Court Appointed Special Advocates for abused and neglected children.

Working with Marla Treiber and Miki Getchell – a dear friend who later joined Heartland Church – we visited children in the home of a parent or caretaker.

We conducted scheduled and impromptu interviews and reported back to the judge. Mary Jo and I shared responsibilities, but she insisted I handle the courtroom appearances. She knew I enjoyed jousting with the lawyers.

It was gratifying to make a difference, yet the cases were often heartbreaking and it wasn't common to see a happy ending.

At this time, Mary Jo also began doing more fund-raising work for Senator Grassley – which meant a lot of time on the phone and at her computer, working with her network of associates and friends in Washington D.C.

She drew on her experience as a scheduler to organize receptions or luncheons at places like The Monocle – an unassuming, yet elegant restaurant on the senate side of the U.S. Capitol.

Mary Jo also worked closely with a new group of staffers and consultants.

While John Maxwell remained as the chief campaign strategist, Ken Cunningham had moved on to start his own firm. David Young was hired to replace Ken as the chief of staff.

David was an experienced professional, and he and Mary Jo developed a good working relationship. In other words, they became friends.

She also became friends with Cory Crowley – a bright young man with a passion for pastel, tailored shirts and silk handkerchiefs. Mary Jo teased him often, saying he could be the next host of *What Not to Wear*, but he took it as a great compliment.

Leah Shimp and Gina Noll talked on the phone with Mary Jo almost daily. They served respectively as the scheduler and accountant for Senator Grassley.

Given Mary Jo's part time work in politics, the subject was sometimes a topic of conversation around the dinner table. Even Silas occasionally offered his opinions on politicians and their failings.

While Mary Jo shared my conservative convictions, she often countered or balanced my cynicism, reminding me of a conversation she once had with a reporter:

People really can make a difference in the way our government is run. But unfortunately we are very cynical about that, and I think that we, as a nation of constituents, have bought into the notion that it's going to happen anyway – that it doesn't matter. People really need to get involved in the political process.[75]

"It does matter," she insisted.

One morning, I gathered tools and supplies to head across town to work on a rental property. Adjusting the belt on my favorite battle-scarred jeans, I poured coffee into a travel mug and kissed my wife on the cheek.

Mary Jo was reading the newspaper, but she smiled and set her Boleslawiec coffee cup on the counter. She said:

"This town seems to be run by a bunch of good ole boys. You should think about running for office – you'd be good at it," she said.

"I don't think so," I replied, and headed out the door.

Later, though, I did think about it, and Mary Jo showed me the newspaper article that had caught her attention. It was a story about how the city council members took turns appointing each other as mayor.

Mary Jo and I talked some more and soon after, I put-together a three-ring "smart book" about local issues.

Inside the cover, Mary Jo inserted a note card with a quote from Margaret Mead:

"Never doubt that a small group of thoughtful, committed citizens can change the world; indeed it's the only thing that ever has."

With no political experience, I sought advice from Bill Anderson – a talented, hard-working young man who'd first learned to knock on doors and put up yard signs when he was 14 years old.

Bill had also worked for Senator Grassley. "Sure," Bill said, "I'll run your campaign – Mary Jo already told me I have to."

A few months later, I announced my campaign for the city council, opening with my campaign theme. I said:

"Sioux City is a great place to raise a family, but it must also be a great place to start a business or find a job."

During the announcement speech, I also pointed out a few criticisms, noting the city paid a consultant about $10 grand to come up with an uninspiring new slogan. "I'd have done it myself for $10 bucks," I joked.

The primary ballot for the city council had a diverse field of ten candidates, including the incumbent mayor, a city councilman and Lamont Wright. Mr. Wright was a likeable fellow with a mobile car wash business who said his candidacy was a step toward his long-term goal to run for President.

Thanks to Mary Jo, Bill and my mother, I finished first in the primary election. A month later, I finished first again in the regular election, winning by the largest margin in city history.

Lynn Zerschling, an experienced reporter assigned to cover the city beat for the *Sioux City Journal*, reported the election results. She wrote:

"Hoffman ran an aggressive, polished campaign."[76]

Mr. Wright finished tenth and last, his hopes dashed.

The *mandate* from the election victory didn't last long.

After the swearing-in, the very first vote of the new city council was to appoint a new mayor, and I was on the losing side. From property taxes to retaining walls, it was but the first time I would be on the losing side of many 4-1 votes.

During my campaign, I'd promised not to "vote to raise property taxes, whether I am alone or unanimous in that decision."

It proved prophetic. I was. Alone.

However, many citizens seemed supportive, and Mary Jo enjoyed reading about it in the *Sioux City Journal*. With coffee cup in hand, she'd read the letters to the editor out loud, even spicing it up with a snarky accent. She read:

"For Councilman-elect Hoffman, without a day's experience behind him, to get the 'behind-the-door' politics out in the open for all of us to see, was brilliant and to me, very refreshing," wrote Mike Antonovich.

"I'm glad to see him stirring the pot," wrote Jill Flynn.[77]

Ironically, I developed a positive working relationship with the newly appointed mayor, as he was professional and understanding.

Two other colleagues, however, made each debate personal, questioned motives and never saw a microphone or a camera they didn't like. As a career military officer, I'd never encountered such unprofessionalism, and I struggled with how to respond. I turned to Mary Jo for counsel. She said:

"What you should do is be who you are. Be a leader. Be tough, but fair. Show respect even if your colleagues don't respond in kind – *especially* if they don't respond in kind. And then – when the time comes – make sure they never hold office again."

The advice was classic Mary Jo. She offered both challenge and encouragement. She was kind and respectful, yet tough and unyielding. She had an implicit understanding of the delicate conflict between grace and justice.

So as I usually did, I took Mary Jo's advice to heart – especially the justice part. It was not easy, though.

On one occasion, a fellow councilman sent an inappropriate, egotistical email to my wife. On another occasion, he pressured city inspectors to investigate the work I'd done on my kitchen.

Nonetheless, I treated him with respect, for the most part. Then, when he announced his bid for re-election, I recruited and trained his opponent.[78]

Aaron Rochester was the opponent, and he was elected in a landslide. Principled and professional, Rochester swept every precinct in the election, and he and I became good friends. He was also a man of strong faith and conviction, and I admired him greatly.

Unlike many or most elective bodies, the majority of the City Council of Sioux City didn't allow a moment of non-sectarian, spoken prayer before meetings, so Aaron and I met five minutes before each meeting to pray privately.

It was the most memorable time of my brief career in public service, and Aaron and I thanked God for the opportunity to serve.[79]

Practically, it didn't make a lot of difference to have two conservatives on the city council – it was still a minority. Instead of four to one, the votes to increase taxes and spending were three to two.

In some ways, in fact, the issues grew more divisive, the rhetoric more heated and the attacks, more personal.

The slings and arrows of criticism, however, proved to be enlightening or *good* for me. I recognized I brought some of it upon myself and learned from the experience. I learned more about my own strengths and weaknesses, and I learned to show greater patience, empathy and humility.

At least, that's what Mary Jo told me. She also gave me a new quote, this one from Reinhold Niebuhr:

"God grant me the serenity to accept the things I cannot change, the courage to change the things I can, and the wisdom to know the difference."

With the summer upon us, Mary Jo and I decided to do more sightseeing with the kids. Silas was proud to upgrade to a booster seat and the kids proved to be fun, easy travelers.

During a trip to the Black Hills of South Dakota, we tracked state license plates and played "Twenty Questions." Mary Jo also enjoyed several exchanges with the kids. She wrote:

Mary Jo: This is a thing.
Silas: Is it bigger than a breadbasket?
Mary Jo: No. It's sweet. The Swiss make it.
Silas: Is it peppermint candy?
Mary Jo: No. It's common in cakes and cookies.
Lydia: Is it chicken?[80]

We marveled at Mount Rushmore as well as Silas' ability to identify the four presidents and tell us a little about each one.

Below Rushmore, we walked around the tourist town of Keystone, stopping to watch the saltwater taffy machine. We toured the Big Thunder gold mine, peppered the tour guide with questions and tried our hand at panning for gold.

In the fall, we returned to enjoy the magnificent colors of Spearfish Canyon, with flaming red and sparkling gold leaves to rival any in Maine or Vermont.

We also took a flight to California to visit the Severinghaus family but were diverted to Las Vegas for mechanical problems.

When Silas heard Mary Jo and I talking about it, he stood up in his seat and shouted "We're going to Vegas, baby!" Seriously, he did.

It brought a hearty, welcome laugh to the cabin.

Fulfilling a promise to Kathy Wise, we also took a long, long trip to Waco, Texas.

Kathy was a gracious, entertaining hostess, first welcoming us to her restored Victorian home before taking us out for barbecued ribs and brisket. It was fantastic.

She also lived up to her reputation as "Waco's Ambassador," taking us on a tour of the Mayborn Museum, where a humpback whale skull greeted us at the entrance. Silas and Lydia were awed by the 28-foot long, prehistoric skeleton of a plesiosaur.

Kathy also made her annual, passion-filled presentation for why Silas and Lydia should attend Baylor University. Dressing them in green and gold t-shirts, she patiently taught Silas and Lydia how to do the bear claw hand signal and yell "Sic 'em Bears!"

Not long after we returned from Texas, we made another trip to Mason City, but this time it wasn't for pleasure.

LaVern McMains developed an aortic aneurism, but declined surgery and asked to be moved to hospice care. It was devastating news for Helen and the rest of the family, most of whom took turns telling LaVern they loved him and prayed by his bedside.

When LaVern saw Mary Jo and Malinda, his eyes brightened with joy and tears. In his eyes, Mary Jo was still that precious little girl who fed the lambs, and he whispered sweet words of love and affection in her ear.

LaVern was not only a grandfather to Mary Jo. He was a hero. She told him so, and she told him she loved him and promised to help Karen look after Grandma Helen. LaVern passed away a few hours later on August 21st of 2006.

LaVern and Helen had been married 72 years, 9 months.

Through church, community service and politics, Mary Jo made some new, lasting friendships in Sioux City. She stayed in touch regularly with her best friends, but was thankful for new friends Jane Keitges, Cheri Stockton and Kathy Bach.

She also made some new friendships through the local home school group, including Keri Moore, Tanya Henn and Ellen Nichols. Each was devoted to the education and nurturing of their children – a selfless bond they shared with Mary Jo.

JoLynn Handel was also a home school mom, and she and Mary Jo first met at the home school group. Mary Jo was surprised to learn she lived just four houses up on Sylvian Avenue. JoLynn's husband John had recently been transferred to Iowa to oversee construction of several ethanol plants.

In JoLynn, Mary Jo found a kindred spirit – more like a sister than a friend. Mary Jo wrote:

"God sure puts people into your lives at the right time – and I thank Him for JoLynn."

JoLynn was a lovely, striking woman with blonde hair and sea blue eyes – and her heart was as beautiful as her smile. She was warm, charming and welcoming. Even in a blue and white sweat suit, she radiated class and elegance.

It was said her love of family and friends was rivaled only by her passion for the University of Kentucky Wildcats.

More important, JoLynn was an extraordinary wife and mother, unfailingly devoted to her husband and children.

John was also a great father. He was involved, patient and nurturing, and I admired his easy-going attitude. Though John worked long hours, he acknowledged his wife's more important work in raising their children at home.

The Handel children – Hayden, Holten and Halena – were a reflection of their parents. Bright, energetic and well-behaved, they were model children and quickly became best friends with Silas and Lydia.

Together, the boys made forts, terrorized neighborhood squirrels and orchestrated all day laser gun battles while the girls practiced cartwheels and karaoke in between hosting elaborate tea parties in the dining room. Mary Jo wrote:

"When we get together with the Handel family, great fun is had by all – except when the boys chase the girls!"

With her other best friends spread out from California to Virginia, Mary Jo was very grateful for JoLynn's friendship. They shared many common interests, and it was entertaining to hear the two accomplished, college-educated women share recipes, parenting tips or the latest gossip about George Clooney.

They also shared a common faith and a love of Beth Moore Bible studies.

At Heartland Church, Linda Wheat led a women's Bible study that usually met on Tuesdays. The group frequently used books by Beth Moore – a popular Christian author and teacher.

Believing God was one of their favorite Beth Moore books, but they also studied *Daniel* and *Breaking Free*, among others. Linda was an experienced teacher – disciplined and yet loving, kind and encouraging.

The women's Bible study was a wonderful time of growth and fellowship. The core group included JoLynn, Jo Jones, Cheri Stockton, Kathy Bach, Tanya Henn, Paulette Luesebrink, Mary Foster and Frances Sweet.

As they adapted to new books and schedules, a few ladies left, but others joined, including Gia Emory, Meredith Sheffield, Eleanor Tucker, Ellen Nichols and Keri Moore.

When Linda was absent, Mary Jo led the study and the women loved her for it. Speaking for all of the women, Mary Foster remembered the Bible study at Heartland as a very special time. She wrote:

"Mary Jo had a wonderful testimony, which blessed us all. We laughed, rejoiced and cried together. Praying for each other made us very close. It was a very special time – and a gift from God."

For Mary Jo, it was a precious time of reflection. She was thankful for the fellowship and grew in her faith. She wrote:

"I desire to recognize God's Supremacy, to Serve Him, to be Humble, Be Obedient, even unto death."

She could not foresee how her faith would be challenged in the two years that lay ahead.

It would be both the best and worst of times – and the last two years of her life.

12 The Cancer Diet

> "What cancer does is, it forces you to focus, to prioritize, and you learn what's important. Don't sweat the small stuff. And when somebody says you have cancer, you realize it's all small stuff. If it weren't for the downside, everyone would want to have it. But there is a downside."
>
> Gilda Radner
>
> *It's Always Something*[81]

IT STARTED AS A DULL stabbing pain in her back. "Oww!" Mary Jo said, as she reached over her shoulder for the safety belt.

She was wearing an off-white blouse, covered by a thin pink sweater, her long, brown hair hanging loosely around her shoulders.

"I must've pulled a muscle," she said.

Mary Jo and I had just said goodbye to Sara and Kevin Bridwell at Eppley Field in Omaha, Nebraska. Sara and Kevin had spent four days with us in Sioux City, traveling from their home in Alexandria, Virginia.

While in Sioux City, Sara planted flowers, played Barbie with Lydia and sipped coffee with Mary Jo. Kevin – whom we nicknamed "Gadget" – spent most of his time setting up Mary Jo's new Apple iMac.

The pain in Mary Jo's back quickly receded, but a nagging cough she'd developed continued. Her asthma had been dormant since our time in Greece, and we wondered if it had returned with the spring weather. It was April 2007, shortly after Mary Jo's forty-second birthday. Later, Mary Jo said:

"I got sick in February with what everybody calls the 'crud.' It ran its course, but I was still coughing."

John Kissel was our family doctor, and he promptly ordered antibiotics, but the cough continued. Next, Dr. Kissel ordered an X-ray and immediately noticed *something* in the lower part of Mary Jo's right lung.

He wondered aloud if it could be *histoplasmosis* – a not-so-rare condition sometimes called "Bird Droppings Disease" – but ruled it out. We were mildly concerned, but Mary Jo said:

"It's probably just scars from asthma I had as a child."

Dr. Kissel was an experienced doctor and a friend.

With perfectly coiffed white hair and a classic white lab coat to match, he was always professional and gentlemanly. Elaine was his wife, and she also became a friend.

I pressed John on a preliminary diagnosis, but he made no assumptions and promptly referred Mary Jo to a pulmonologist at St. Luke's Medical Center.

Craig Bainbridge was the pulmonologist, and he was eminently qualified and likeable. Using a bronchoscope inserted through the nose, Dr. Bainbridge took a biopsy of the lung tissue while assisted by a nurse, Sandy Nelson.

Sandy – like other medical professionals we would meet along the journey – would also become a friend. Sweet, loyal and grounded in faith, she was always quick to offer a hug and a prayer.

Unfortunately, the bronchioscopic biopsy proved as inconclusive as the X-ray, so our next visit was with a radiologist.

The following day, the radiologist took a needle biopsy of the suspect tissue, guided by a Computed Tomography – commonly called a "CT scan."

In contrast to the other tests, the results of the CT-guided needle biopsy were conclusive. Conclusively bad.

Dr. Kissel called Mary Jo at home and said the word no person ever wants to hear: "Cancer."

Specifically, it was lung cancer. Later, the pathologist informed me it was an aggressive, fast-growing tumor, called a "Grade III adenocarcinoma."

We learned the jabbing back pain she'd experienced two weeks earlier was caused by the tumor inside her lung, pressing against nerve endings in her back. Since the lung itself has no nerve endings, a lung cancer diagnosis is often made late – unless you are very lucky.

As Mary Jo later noted, "By the time you're diagnosed, you've got it bad."

The shock of the diagnosis brought a bewildering cacophony of emotion. Mary Jo cried as I held her and tried to keep it together. It felt like the world was spinning through a fast-shifting nightmare of shock, denial and anger.

Amidst the shock, Mary Jo had questions. She said:

"At that point, I think it was general disbelief and shock. How could I have lung cancer? I never smoked."

We had other questions. Was it genetic? Second-hand smoke? Radon? Asthma? Was it just bad luck?

We ruled out radon. Second-hand smoke was a possibility, but could not be substantiated and only evoked hard feelings towards Mary Jo's father. There had been no history of lung cancer in her family.

Mary Jo and I eventually realized there would never be an easy or conclusive answer to the question of "Why?"

The cancer could be classified and dissected, but there was nowhere to direct our anger and disappointment. There was no rhyme or reason. It just was.

This *shock, denial and anger* stage lasted about two days, replaced by the reluctant acceptance of reality, and we began reading anything and everything about lung cancer treatment options.

We also began to pray. Four pastors – Gene Stockton, Ron Stein, Larry Gordon and Cary Gordon – also prayed for Mary Jo with faith and fervor.

Cary Gordon would become a loyal, unwavering friend and a courageous partner in later political battles.

Next, we scheduled appointments with Mayo Clinic, known as one of the finest hospitals in the world and peerless for its commitment to patient care.

Mary Jo and I arrived at Mayo Clinic and were surprised by the skyscrapers that dominated downtown Rochester, Minnesota. Though Rochester was roughly the size of Sioux City, its skyline of Mayo Clinic buildings made it appear like a much larger, metropolitan city.

Unfortunately, we soon learned the second opinion was the same as the first.

Mayo Clinic confirmed the diagnosis of *Stage IIIA non-small cell lung cancer* – meaning the cancer had spread to certain lymph nodes on the same side of the chest or other areas within the chest. The pathology confirmed it was a fast-growing lung cancer.[82]

We entered the Gonda building of Mayo Clinic for our next appointment and barely noticed the magnificent artwork and acres of Italian marble.

Mary Jo and I took the stainless steel elevator to the oncology department on the 10th floor for our appointment with Dr. Julian Molina.

Dr. Molina specialized in lung cancer treatments. A world-renowned oncologist, he also held a doctorate degree in molecular genetics, biochemistry and microbiology. Just as important, he had a caring, considerate manner and a hopeful worldview.

We arrived shaken by the prognosis, yet Dr. Molina quickly established an easy and comforting rapport with his new patient. Speaking gently to Mary Jo, he said:

"I understand the statistics are unsettling, but that doesn't mean you aren't going to be a survivor. Besides, this is not all in your hands – or mine."

"Amen," Mary Jo said, with tears in her eyes.

In an interview a few months later, she said:

"I was very grateful for Dr. Molina's gentle reminder that I am not a statistic to God."

After an in depth explanation, Dr. Molina recommended an aggressive, concurrent treatment of radiation and chemotherapy. As Dr. Molina put it, "Basically, we're going to have to throw everything but the kitchen sink at you." Mary Jo replied:

"Please don't feel you need to hold back on the kitchen sink. If you think it would be helpful, you can also throw the sink, the bathtub and even the toilet."

Mary Jo confronted the life-changing diagnosis as she had every other challenge in her life. She faced it with stoic determination and Christ-centered confidence, mixed with wit and humor.

Telling friends and family would prove as emotional as the diagnosis.

Mary Jo's first call was to her mother, Karen. The call began in tears, but by the end both Karen and Mary Jo were both dry-eyed and determined. The following day, Karen packed up the car and drove to Sioux City with Ron and Helen in tow.

Though Ron and Helen returned later in the week, Karen would stay for about six months.

Friends and family reacted to the news much as we had – with shock and tears. It was agonizing to think of speaking with Silas and Lydia about it.

Though sweet, precocious children, Silas was only six years old and Lydia was just four. Mary Jo and I prayed about what, when and how to tell them, putting it off for about a week.

One morning, Mary Jo decided she wanted to tell the kids herself. Pulling the kids close to her side, she embraced them on the red sofa in the sunny corner of the kitchen.

Surrounded by colorful throw pillows and with a children's book in her lap, she explained it as best she could and patiently answered Silas' questions.

Mary Jo did it all with a smile and hugs. Later, she shared it with a reporter from the *Sioux City Journal*. Mary Jo said:

"The kids know I have something called cancer. They're like the bad-guy cells in my body. They know I am getting medicine that can make me kind of sick. I tell them what they need to know when they need to know it."

Mature, thoughtful children, Silas and Lydia often took the initiative to comfort and encourage their mother. Lydia enjoyed giving Mary Jo hand and foot massages. Mary Jo said:

"Nothing is more soothing than those little hands!"

Silas enjoyed reading with Mary Jo, especially the poems from *Where the Sidewalk Ends*. He also presented her with multi-colored Playdoh animals and creative Lego designs. Sometimes, he and Lydia teamed-up and wrote a Get Well card. One read:

"Dear Mom, I hope you feel better soon. and I hope your hair doesn't fall off. but your still beutfull." [sic]

News of Mary Jo's cancer diagnosis spread quickly through her network of friends and colleagues, resulting in countless cards, letters and emails.

A naturally private person, Mary Jo was humbled by the attention, yet thankful for the prayers and encouragement. She wrote:

"It's a bit overwhelming to be the focus of so much attention. But I'm humbled and honored to have all of you praying for me and cheering me on."

My mother-in-law's presence in the household was a welcome one.

Though Karen moved in to help care for Mary Jo, she became like a second mother to the kids and me.

Karen busied herself with dishes, laundry and various housekeeping chores. She played Crazy 8's and Old Maid. She built puzzles and mastered the Easy Bake oven. Mary Jo wrote:

"Her presence and assistance makes life easy and normal for us. We'd be living in chaos and stress without her. She is in constant motion with household stuff, entertaining the kids and basically taking care of our every need."

When Karen wasn't with us, my mother filled the gap. She also filled the house with laughter and energy. Mary Jo wrote:

"Grandma Kathy has been over to help with the kids this week and they have had fun doing nature science experiments, planting flowers and to quote Silas, 'running around like crazy people.' Grandma Kathy is always so enthusiastic about everything and having her over peps us all up. Even Zoe the bulldog gets excited!"

Though Mayo Clinic oversaw Mary Jo's treatment plan, most chemotherapy and radiation took place at the June Nylen Cancer Center in Sioux City.

At the Nylen Cancer Center, I peppered Dr. Greg Naden with a hundred pointless questions. Dr. Naden served as the radiation oncologist, and he answered all my questions from the process of Intensity Modulating Radiation Therapy to the differences between a PET scan and a CAT scan.

Dr. Naden explained Mary Jo would receive about five weeks of radiation therapy using computer-controlled x-ray equipment and a multi-leaf collimator to deliver precise radiation beams to the targeted area. He said:

"It's an aggressive approach, but she's healthy, and we hope to clear the lung entirely of cancer."[83]

At the same time, Mary Jo began chemotherapy treatment under the direction of Dr. Radha Rao.

Dr. Rao was a sweet, petite lady with an Indian accent. She would serve as the primary medical oncologist for Mary Jo and consult often with Mayo Clinic.

When Dr. Rao was unavailable, one of the other medical oncologists – John Michalak, Gerry Hagin or Stephen Kahanic – sometimes directed Mary Jo's treatments.

While the radiation targeted a very specific part of the body, the chemotherapy was called a *systemic treatment*. The cell-killing medications of the chemotherapy worked to kill cancer cells anywhere in the body.

Chemotherapy drugs such as *etoposide*, *vinorelbine*, *docetaxel* and *cisplatin* (which Mary Jo called, "The Heavy Hitter") were prescribed during treatment. Sometimes the drugs were administered in combination or on a shifting schedule.[84]

Mary Jo took the kitchen sink and everything else with courage and a sense of humor, though she wrote she "hated vomiting." To address the problem, Dr. Rao tried several anti-nausea drugs, but only *aprepitant* proved effective.

Each *aprepitant* pill (trade name: Emend) cost $105 dollars.[85]

At the Nylen Cancer Center, Mary Jo and I waited alongside an intriguing cast of characters for Mary Jo's name to be called. We talked about anything but cancer while she knit a purse or shared a laugh with a fellow patient.

She and Linda Guggenmos – a friend from Heartland Church – talked about music and movies. Sometimes they talked about the "one uppers" who claimed to have the most painful or vomit-filled reaction to chemotherapy. They laughed about it in a way only another cancer patient can understand.

Mary Jo also exchanged magazines, smiles and words of encouragement with Al Bengston, Joyce Sevening, Rick Mace and Brenda Winkler. Brenda served as the patient's advocate at Nylen.

I've forgotten the names of others, but they left an imprint on Mary Jo's heart – and mine.

Dennis Benson was another fellow patient.

Undeniably colorful and unforgettable, Dennis was a former U.S. Marine – though he insisted there was no such thing as a *former* marine. Most folks called him "Gunny" as an abbreviation for Gunnery Sergeant.

Gunny Benson had a handshake that could bend crowbars, but he was gentle as a bunny with Mary Jo.

Mary Jo and Dennis visited long after their respective chemotherapy treatments were over. Mary Jo talked about church, family and politics. Dennis responded with entertaining stories (mostly embellished) of his early years in the Marine Corps.

When it was time to say goodbye, Dennis and I exchanged insults in that way military men often do.

"I still can't understand how an Air Force officer could attract a woman like that," Dennis said. "I'd explain it, jarhead, but I'd probably have to draw you a picture," I retorted.

Mary Jo seldom complained about her treatments, but she did sometimes feel "kind of weak and tired," in her words.

She cut her flowing, chestnut hair and purchased a wig but seldom wore it. After she took her wig off for the first time, clumps of hair came off with it.

That night, Malinda shaved Mary Jo's head.

Odd as it sounds, Mary Jo never lost her beauty, even through the chemotherapy treatments and surgeries that were to come. In fact, some friends observed her short hairstyle made her look even more elegant or fashionable.

Friends pointed out her striking resemblance to an actress, Katie Holmes, sending her pictures from *People* or *In Style* magazines, accompanied by notes like, "Katie's almost as pretty as you, MJ!"

Mary Jo quickly grew tired of the wig and preferred to wear a scarf. At home, she generally wore nothing on her head.

Silas and Lydia were fascinated by their mother's baldness and Silas shaved his own head as a show of solidarity.

Lydia objected to shaving her golden locks ("No way," she said), but inspired her mother in other ways:

Mary Jo: I'm going to wear my scarf today; it's too hot for the magic hair (my wig).

Lydia: Mom, don't be worried about going to church without hair. All those people there are your friends and they don't care if you have any hair or not.[86]

Mary Jo often spent time in her prized kitchen. She rarely cooked during recovery from treatments, as her mother had taken charge of cooking duties – but she loved to sit and read or write.

Mary Jo sat on the red sofa by the picture window with the sun cascading over her shoulders and onto her well-worn Bible. She wrote in her journal or made notes in her Beth Moore workbook.

She filled her journal with reflections and prayers for healing – not for herself, but for family, friends and strangers. In one entry, she made a few notes about the prophet Habakkuk. She wrote:

"He was a man who trusted God, yet was perplexed by Him. He recognized that God's ways are best even if not fully comprehensible to us."

By August, doctors told us the treatments had made great progress in shrinking or killing the cancer but it only set the stage for a more radical treatment.

The next step was a complete, surgical removal of the right lung and associated, cancerous lymph nodes. Called a *pneumonectomy*, the surgery was performed at Mayo Clinic by Dr. Dennis Wigle.

Karen, Ron, Malinda and I waited anxiously through the six-hour surgery. Ron's daughter Kim and her family also joined us in the waiting room. After recovery, Mary Jo flashed a tired grin and we noticed her cough was finally gone. Dr. Wigle said:

"It was an excellent surgery – everything went very, very well."

Mary Jo and I stayed at Mayo Clinic for seven days. I slept in a cot by her bed as she slowly regained strength and inspired other patients and even the staff. A nurse said:

"She is an amazing woman. She's like a rock star here!"

It was a slow, painful recovery, however, and there were times Mary Jo hardly felt up to the challenge. She wrote:

Life is all about the unexpected, and I'll confess this past week has been particularly difficult. This whole thing has been the most painful, trying thing I've ever gone through. I was weak and for the first time in my life, I felt very frail and vulnerable. I realized the only way to get through this was to rely on the Lord for strength.

Determined to recover completely, Mary Jo began an exercise program while still in the hospital. She started with large rubber bands and moved up to aerobics and weights. I'll admit, though, that our time wasn't always well spent. We watched a lot of television.

When we returned home, Mary Jo finally embraced my dream of building a movie theater in the basement. Envisioning the man cave it would become, I grinned from ear to ear while I worked to transform the extra bedroom.

A friend helped me hoist the 65-inch, high-definition plasma screen in position on the dark, painted wall. I gingerly wiped the glass with a special soft cloth.

Silas and I gleefully adorned the theater with banners, posters and pictures of our beloved Nebraska Cornhuskers. We struggled to move the reclining chairs, but were rewarded with the push of a button. "Look at these chairs," I exclaimed. "They're electric!"

During Mary Jo's recovery, we watched more TV than we had in years.

Mary Jo loved watching *Law and Order* and so did I – until Angie Harmon left the show. We watched all of the Pixar movies. Twice. The Food Network was a favorite channel and before long, even Silas, Lydia and I could name all five of the *Iron Chefs*.

Through the fall season, Mary Jo recovered with strength and vigor. Slowly but surely the sparkle returned to her eyes.

The color returned to her cheeks as it did to the trees. Her hair came back dull and lifeless at first – what Mary Jo called "chemo hair" – but it was a luxurious sheen of brown within months.

Mary Jo was as beautiful as ever.

With Mary Jo feeling better, our whole family felt better. Visits to Mayo Clinic became less frequent. A great weight had been lifted – not removed but lifted – and we relished a return to some normalcy. In fact, Mary Jo insisted upon it. She wrote:

"I want my kids to have as normal, fun time as they can. I don't want it to be all about me."

After I installed over 1,000 square feet of hardwood flooring upstairs, Lydia and I invented a new sport we called "Wood Skiing."

The equipment included a bike helmet, flannel pajamas, fuzzy socks and a dog collar snapped around Lydia's midsection. The objective was to attach a leash to the dog collar and pull Lydia across the high-gloss oak flooring as fast as possible.

Lydia squealed while attempting 360's and backspins. Mary Jo filmed us in action and added some narration.

Lydia also entertained us with karaoke and dance, often partnering with Halena Handel for a dizzying performance of cartwheels, handstands and shimmy shakes. Mary Jo wrote:

"All those old dance recital costumes that Aunt Heather buys for her at the second-hand shops are going to her head!"

Lacking the energy she once had – and with one lung – Mary Jo stepped down as the worship leader at Heartland Church.

It was an emotional transition for Mary Jo, but she felt Heartland Church was ready for "new blood" as she called it. One morning after worship service, Mary Jo approached Bobbie Lee Sheffield and gave him a folder of guitar music.

Bobbie was a hip, talented musician who played both guitar and drums. Bobbie wrote:

Mary Jo practically glowed as we discussed the music of David Crowder and Jeremy Camp. She encouraged me to always glorify God with the gifts He gave me. Her words that Sunday morning always come to mind as I am reminded that I do not play for myself or even for the people who are listening. I play for God.[87]

Though she no longer led worship, Mary Jo was determined to worship God with her life and voice. As she said, "I can still praise God. And I will."

On one occasion, I heard her still-beautiful voice through the closed door of her downstairs office and leaned in to listen. Mary Jo was singing *Jesus Bring the Rain,* by Mercy Me. She sang:

Bring me joy, bring me peace
Bring the chance to be free
Bring me anything that brings You glory
And I know there'll be days
When this life brings me pain
But if that's what it takes to praise You
Jesus bring the rain.[88]

It was a private moment between Mary Jo and God, and I never told her I'd heard her singing, but I marveled at her courage and faithfulness.

Even in the face of pain and anguish, Mary Jo's faith was unbreakable. Mary Jo embraced the rain. I prayed for it to stop.

With the holiday season upon us, Mary Jo continued to stress *normalcy* in our plans and activities. Kevin and Sara joined us for a wonderful, extended weekend and Mary Jo was very thankful Sara cooked a terrific Thanksgiving meal and made Silas' birthday cake.

With help from Karen, I made Mary Jo's favorite dessert – a gingersnap streusel pumpkin pie. Years earlier, Mary Jo had found the recipe in a *Cooking Light* magazine, and we made the pie every holiday thereafter.

For Christmas, Karen encouraged me to make the holiday preparations minimal, low key and stress-free. I considered it but instead decided to make it what I called "The most super-fantastic Christmas we've ever had."

Rerouting circuit breakers, I strung nearly two miles of lights around pillars, poles, windows and trees and called the family to the street to witness the lighting.

When I hit the switch, it looked as if the noonday sun had set in our front yard. "I need some sunglasses!" Silas exclaimed.

Clark Griswold would've been proud.

On Christmas morning, Silas and Lydia found a hastily scribbled note from Santa alongside a half-glass of milk and two partially eaten sugar cookies. The glass door on the fireplace was left ajar and footprints of ash were visible on the oak floor, leading to one of three Christmas trees.

Silas and Lydia took it all in with jaw-dropping wonder. Mary Jo was also very grateful. She wrote:

"We've had a fun time and the kids have enjoyed themselves. I so wanted it to all be as normal as possible and not be the sick mommy Christmas."

One afternoon after the New Year, Mary Jo and I shared a quiet lunch at Panera Bread in Sioux City.

Mary Jo ordered while I went to the bathroom. She looked great, even wrapped in a knee-length cherry red trench coat to ward off the chill of winter.

When I returned, Mary Jo told me an acquaintance had approached from behind as she eyed the "Pick Two" menu, glancing at the cashier with a smile.

Acquaintance: Well hi, it's been a long time – you look great!

Mary Jo: Thanks – it's great to see you too.

Acquaintance: Are you working out – or on a new diet?

Mary Jo: Kind of – it's called the Cancer Diet.

Through what she called the "Cancer Diet," Mary Jo's best relationships became deeper, more loving and knowing.

Some of her lesser relationships became fractured or strained, but her best friends – Paula, Kathy, Gill, Sara, Christina and JoLynn – stood faithfully beside her throughout the battle with cancer. Jo Jones wrote:

"I had never witnessed such a faithful friend as JoLynn when Mary Jo was sick"[89]

Mary Jo also developed new friendships. Strangers who learned of her story through mutual friends or the media wrote to share a story or a word of encouragement. People she knew only casually opened their hearts and shared their faith and a desire to see Mary Jo healed.

We met Gary and Linda Olsen through Heartland Church and soon learned they'd lost their beloved young son in an accident years before.

Both Gary and Linda were inspiring, faithful Christians, and Linda often wrote heartfelt letters to Mary Jo. It was never just a signed card or a brief scripture verse. Linda shared her heart, her joy and tears and even memories of her son. She wrote:

"It is either utter despair or the total acceptance of God's sovereignty. There is nothing in between."

Also from Heartland Church, Jo Jones tirelessly sent cards and letters to Mary Jo, always peppered with words of inspiration, encouragement and wisdom. In fact, Jo wrote to Mary Jo nearly ever week for a year. Every card made Mary Jo smile, and she called out Jo's husband John with a quip. She said:

"I hope you have stock in Hallmark!"

Mary Jo also developed an unlikely friendship with John Donaker. John was a farmer who lived just outside the tiny town of George, Iowa.

When the *Sioux City Journal* published a story about Mary Jo in the Sunday paper, John said he read it in his truck while sitting outside church. He said:

"I was captivated, moved and heartbroken."

John was a cancer survivor. He was also a dedicated family man and exceedingly thoughtful and generous. A big, bear-like man, he was soft-spoken, kind and affable. He also had a tender heart for those battling cancer, especially Mary Jo. John wrote:

Having cancer made me more sympathetic of others fighting this battle. I understand what it feels like to taste water that tastes like metal or experience the horror of watching your hair clog the drain. But cancer does not change who you are, Mary Jo. Your husband would marry you all over again. Your mother loves you without fail. Your friends still think you're special and great.[90]

John felt genuine empathy for Mary Jo. He loved her – and her family.

He wrote faithfully and visited us whenever he was in town to pick up tractor parts. He became Mary Jo's "cancer buddy," and I admired him as a friend and brother. Mary Jo was also very grateful for his friendship. She wrote:

I've thought a lot about why a guy who is a complete stranger would take the time to encourage me and I've come to understand that God gives a special ministry to those who have had their hearts broken. Thank you for ministering to my family and me. I know that God has special blessings for you.

With each letter, John signed off "Fight hard, Mary Jo." He was a faithful and generous friend to the end, and Mary Jo and I thanked God for John Donaker daily.

Stacie Ruth and Carrie Beth Stoelting also read the story in the *Sioux City Journal.*

Stacie Ruth and Carrie Beth were talented, vivacious young ladies and we called them "The Fabulous Stoelting Sisters."

By the age of 20, the sisters had recorded an album and written a book. Each was blessed with a soaring soprano voice and had sung for audiences from President Bush to the *700 Club.*

Like John, the girls were loyal, encouraging friends. Both girls looked up to Mary Jo as a mentor and asked permission to call us "Uncle Brent" and "Aunt Mary Jo." They often brought gifts for Silas and Lydia and filled the house with song and laughter.

For Mary Jo's forty-third birthday, my family and I decided to host a High Tea party despite Mary Jo's soft objection that "Big parties should be saved for birthdays divisible by five."

With the inflexible efficiency of a former military officer, I prepared and sent elaborate invitations to twenty-four of Mary Jo's dearest girlfriends. When I received several questions, I responded politely but firmly via email. "No, you may not bring a gift – or a guest," I wrote.

Attendees included Jane Keitges, Kathy Bach, Kay Copas, Keri Moore, Linda Olsen, Linda Guggenmos, Lynn Zerschling, Miki Getchell, Peggy Hamel and more.

Most of the guests wore Easter hats and some wore elbow-length, satin gloves. Accompanied by a harpist, Stacie Ruth and Carrie Beth led the group in a rousing rendition of "Happy Birthday" for Mary Jo.

Each of the six tables for the elaborate tea party included a color-coordinated silver and ceramic tea set with embossed cards and a factoid about tea.

Individual name cards – written in JoLynn's distinctive, flowing style – were placed next to a starched napkin shaped like a miniature tuxedo or bird of paradise. My sister, Heather – a professional chef – prepared the menu while my mother helped with decorations.

It took two days to set it up.

Silas and Lydia greeted each guest at the door, escorted them to their table and at the end, presented each with a small gift. Four generations of McMains girls – Grandma Helen, Karen, Mary Jo and Lydia – posed for photographs

Mary Jo said, "It was just wonderful to see everyone." Later, she would thank them for standing by her family and share a few "lessons-learned" for other cancer patients. Mary Jo wrote:

Things I Learned in no Particular Order

- Trust God's Word – believe God NOT my experience.
- Be grateful for everything done by others – even if it's not what you would've done – that doesn't really matter.
- Trust those that love you to make decisions for you.
- Save your energy for important stuff – time with kids, loved ones and chats with friends.
- Let your loved ones know your thoughts and fears – they have them too, and we all need to talk about it sometime.

We still had the dogs. Xenia, the boxer, ran like the wind through the backyard, chasing bunnies and barking at Silas for attention. Zoe the bulldog seldom moved unless food was offered.

When Lydia batted her eyes at the pet store, I consented to get a cat. After consulting with Mary Jo, we decided on a powerful gray tomcat that wouldn't be intimidated by the dogs. Choosing yet another Greek name, we named the cat "Xerxes" and he promptly claimed Xenia's spot on the sofa next to Mary Jo.

It was inevitable Xerxes would challenge Xenia for alpha status. Unfortunately for Xenia, the big tomcat did a ninja-like cross over and left two claws embedded in her nose before she could even get out a bark. Zoe wisely retreated to the corner.

The pecking order established, we never had another problem, but Silas and I admitted we didn't much care for the cat. Silas said:

"I guess there are dog people and cat people. We are dog people. I'm sure God had a reason for making cats. We just don't know what it was."[91]

Not long after, Zoe's heart failed and she passed away on the back porch. Zoe was just nine years old and her death was especially tough on Mary Jo. She wrote:

"I'll admit to having a hard time with Zoe's death. It seems a bit ridiculous to me to still be in mourning for 60 pounds of fur and flatulence, but alas I am."

Unfortunately, the news got worse for the family pets. Xenia died of congestive heart failure about four months later during a visit to Mason City.

Ron, Don Swann and I buried Xenia in the backyard while Mary Jo and the kids looked-on. Mary Jo was distraught and shared her disappointment with Kathy Wise. She wrote:

"I am so sad. She was my girl and I really loved her."

Despite the disappointment, Mary Jo put on a stiff upper lip and began the next day with a new smile. Always moving forward, she turned grief and disappointment to joy and purpose.

While we were still in Mason City, a group of ladies from Heartland Church in Sioux City stopped by Ron and Karen's house for a visit. The ladies were on their way to Minneapolis for a conference and knew Mary Jo hadn't been feeling well.

They wanted to encourage Mary Jo and pray with her. Kay Copas wrote:

We arrived to minister to Mary Jo, yet she ministered to us. She spoke candidly about her cancer, saying she trusted God to take care of her beloved family if she wasn't healed this side of Heaven. Arriving to pray for her, she prayed for us. Her faith and trust in God was an inspiration.

The day after we returned from Mason City, I took Mary Jo and the kids on a surprise visit to see some English bulldog puppies at a farm in Nebraska. After the first puppy we chose died in surgery ("Good grief!" Silas said), I immediately drove out to the farm and picked out a new one. His name was "Lawrence."

Mary Jo and Lydia immediately renamed the bulldog puppy, "Dunkin." I assumed it was for their love of Dunkin' Donuts coffee and chocolate munchkins, but they later told me it was due to the donut-shaped hair pattern on his butt.

Dunkin' turned-out to be the best dog we ever had. His beautiful caramel and white coat formed a wishbone pattern and he had the famous under bite of the English bulldog. He also had a not-so-welcome talent for farting and snoring, but we loved him like family.

In stark contrast to Zoe, Dunkin' also showed uncharacteristic athleticism and had a sociable personality. In between his thrice-daily naps, he entertained our family with tug-of-war, keep away and the awkward way he ran sideways. We called it his "happy trot." Dunkin' adored Mary Jo and Aunt Heather.

Halfway through my term on the city council, I spoke with the city attorney about resigning my seat so it could be filled without the need for a special election. It made sense to me, but when I spoke with Mary Jo, she was less than pleased. She said:

"I can't believe you'd even consider it. Not only do I not want you to step down, I want you to step up to run for mayor or some other higher office."[92]

Mary Jo said, "Let's not live with fear of the future" and challenged me to step forward in faith. She also noted I'd helped to change the "good ole boy" system at City Hall. The next mayor would be elected rather than appointed.

My only concern was Mary Jo's health, but she brushed such concerns aside and insisted on running my campaign.

On the day of the primary election, we learned I won the five-person primary for mayor by just three votes.[93]

Mary Jo and I, however, were not present to witness the early returns.

That's because we were at Mayo Clinic.

Once again, we received somber news from Dr. Molina. Another PET scan highlighted tumor growth in Mary Jo's chest, and it would mean more chemotherapy.

The day after the primary, I called the commissioner of elections and asked to have my name removed from the ballot. He informed me it was too late – but for me the campaign was effectively over.

Mary Jo was tired and I was fearful, yet her body seemed to respond well to the newest chemotherapy cocktail and the scan results proved promising. Over three months, she recovered quickly and strongly, vibrant and beautiful.

In the spring, Mary Jo was feeling better and we decided to take a trip to Yellowstone National Park.

I'd toured the park on a motorcycle years before and was eager to show my family the Grand Canyon of the Yellowstone, with its roaring, picture-perfect waterfalls and brilliant sun-danced hues.

Of the magnificent sights of Yellowstone, Mary Jo and the kids were most impressed with the reflecting pools. With names like "Morning Glory," the pools shimmered like precious gems, reflecting clouds and pine trees like a mirror.

It was a memorable trip. On the way home, I asked Silas, "What was your favorite part of our vacation?"

"I'd say this whole vacation rocks – except for that part in the hotel where I threw up!"

Mary Jo had been sick when Silas began first grade, so she was delighted to escort him and Lydia to Clark Elementary School for the first day of school for the following year.

Shelly Banks was Lydia's kindergarten teacher. She was a delightful dynamo of enthusiasm and the kids and parents loved her for it.

Kristin Noreen was Silas' second-grade teacher. She was also a good teacher and became a friend.

With the presidential election of 2008 just around the corner, Mrs. Noreen's class wrote essays about the candidates.

Typically, students who supported Barack Obama wrote simple and uncontroversial essays about hope and change. Those who supported John McCain wrote of lofty principles like freedom and lower taxes.

With no input from his parents, Silas took a less conventional approach to the essay assignment. He wrote:

"If Obama wins, taxes will go up and we will be living in a traler (sic)."

The essay from the "Boy who would be President" was the source of much amusement in the teacher's lounge.

"I think he gets this stuff from his mother," I said. No one seemed to buy it.

Heartland Church had been growing steadily. Doubling in size each year, about 200 people attended worship services on an average Sunday in 2008.

New members included Bob Henderson – a math teacher who took over as worship leader from Mary Jo. Everyone called him "Doc." We also welcomed a new associate pastor in Dan Barnes.

In August, Pastor Gene invited Mary Jo to speak to the congregation about prayer. She accepted the invitation with some trepidation, but delivered her words with grace, humility and humor. Quoting Oswald Chambers, Mary Jo said:

"Prayer does not fit us for the greater works; prayer is the greater work."

She also thanked our church family for their support, her voice cracking slightly.

She thanked them for the food, cards and flowers. She thanked them for mowing our lawn. She thanked them for loving her family.

After the worship service, Mary Jo embraced Cheri Stockton warmly and apologized for what she called her "poor, depressing attitude" of the previous week.

I later learned Mary Jo had told Cheri she saw an osteoporosis commercial and remarked, "Well, I won't need that because I won't live that long."

The day after the worship service, Cheri came by to visit with Mary Jo once again. She also brought an elaborate pink gift bag and a new Beth Moore Bible study workbook.

Inside the gift bag was a bottle of OstoCal supplements. Mary Jo chuckled and hugged her friend Cheri. Cheri said:

"You're going to need these, Mary Jo."

Mary Jo wrote a card to thank Cheri for the supplements, and more important, "for brightening my day." At the bottom of the card, she'd written an inscription.

They were the same words she'd shared with the congregation on Sunday. Mary Jo wrote:

"I thank God for your prayers and for all you've done for me and my family. I love you."

13

Mostly Cloudy

> "I always knew looking back on the tears would make me laugh, but I never knew looking back on the laughs would make me cry."
>
> Unknown

SPEAKING BEFORE OUR CHURCH FAMILY, Mary Jo was vibrant, beautiful and pleased to tell them, "I am *mostly* cancer free."

Just a month later, however, we returned to Mayo Clinic for more scans and analysis. It was mostly bad news.

Using a glucose tracer to highlight metabolic activity, the PET scan didn't show the frightening dark red colors that can mean an active cancerous tumor in her chest. We were relieved to see a shimmering still video of greens and yellows on the high-definition screen.

But. The PET scan detected something in her brain, and a 3D magnetic resonance image (MRI) confirmed a small, 4mm tumor (about the size of a BB) on the right side. All too common for lung cancer patients, it appeared the malignant cancer had metastasized.

As often happened with trips to the doctor, we didn't get the news we'd hoped. I was scared, but Mary Jo was fearless and unflappable and asked only one question. "I just need to know if I'll still be able to go to Vermont in three weeks?" she asked the doctor.

"Well, I suppose it's possible," the doctor answered, and we scheduled the surgery.

Returning to Mason City, Mary Jo was surprisingly upbeat, sharing some business ideas, singing along to a *Third Day* album and talking with the kids on the phone. We always enjoyed driving in the car, as it was a good time to catch-up as husband and wife.

Briefly, she also shared a few frustrations about her condition, but I remember they were preceded by a quote she'd heard from her friend John Donaker. She said:

"I hate to complain since I'm alive and all, but…"[94]

She laughed when she said it.

She often did that, laughing and joking even in the face of disappointment. Sometimes with family, sometimes with her fellow cancer patients while waiting for their names to be called.

It said a lot about who she was – a rare person of joy and faith – and friends and family were always moved by her faithfulness. Tanya Henn said:

"Mary Jo's attitude and life said, 'God, I will trust you even when it hurts and makes no sense."

Publicly, Mary Jo was ever joyful, fearless and living in the moment, but that doesn't mean she never struggled. The struggle, however, led to deeper faith and understanding. She wrote:

I am receiving medical help but know that it holds little promise for me; my only hope is in the Lord. And it always has been and will continue to be – at the end of this all, He is all that I have. I will continue to pray and trust the Lord for healing but know that sometimes He has other plans and I trust that. It is much easier to write it than to live it sometimes. Please pray for my family. Brent has been so good. I'd be utterly lost without him by my side, as he is a constant source of comfort and strength. Silas – he knows that I face cancer again and will do chemotherapy and this time, he understands more – his countenance has changed and we know he is scared. Lydia – still really doesn't get it all, but that's fine. She prays diligently – hearing those sweet heart-felt prayers every evening breaks my heart. But I shall never give up hope.

On October 1st of 2008, Mary Jo and I returned to Mayo Clinic for the scheduled surgery on the brain tumor.

Though performed by a surgeon, it was not a surgery in the traditional sense but a Gamma Knife radio-surgery that delivered precise amounts of gamma radiation directly to the tumor. It required Mary Jo to wear a special helmet with spikes embedded into her skull.

The staff applied *lidocaine* to deaden the spike locations, attached the spiked helmet and took a Polaroid photo at Mary Jo's request.

In the picture, Mary Jo is smiling pleasantly through a tortuous, boxlike titanium frame. It's her usual telltale grin – perfect white teeth, a hint of a dimple and sparkling eyes.

Later, she showed the picture to a few friends, but I never liked that picture. I have my reasons.

Shortly after the surgery, we got in the car for the five-hour drive back to Sioux City. Mary Jo took ibuprofen for the discomfort from the metal spikes, but there was little to indicate she'd just had brain surgery.

The following day, we left with the kids for Vermont. Yes, the next day. On the plane, Mary Jo quipped "I should probably sit in first class since I just had brain surgery and all."

The trip to Vermont was Kathy Wise's idea.

She and her parents, Charles and Mary Alice, invited us to stay with them at the Trapp Family Lodge. The lodge was a magnificent, rustic home with a stone fireplace the size of a small garage, set in the breathtaking, colorful mountains near Stowe.

The sprawling, mountain property was owned by the Von Trapp family of *The Sound of Music.* Silas and Lydia watched the legendary musical twice, giggling and replaying the famous scene of the two nuns holding the distributor and spark plug wires, leaving the Nazi's automobile useless.

We enjoyed the company of the Wise family even more than the local tourist attractions. Charles and Mary Alice were exceedingly thoughtful and generous, insisting we pay for nothing and doting on Mary Jo and the kids. We cherished every moment with them and Kathy.

In between naps, we went on hikes, posed for photos and toured the Ben and Jerry's ice cream factory in nearby Waterbury, Vermont. It was a wonderful vacation.

Mary Jo made little mention of the brain surgery other than to joke about it.

"I've been exposed to gamma radiation, so you'd be wise not to make me angry," she quipped, in reference to the Incredible Hulk.

In a few short weeks, the brain surgery was a distant memory, and she again insisted on normality.

It may seem odd to pretend everything is normal when you're battling cancer for your life. Cancer isn't normal or welcome. It sucks, yet it can be important to some cancer patients not to be *treated* as a cancer patient.

For Mary Jo, it was important to appreciate the simple, pleasant joys of life even amidst unspeakable trials like chemotherapy and radiation.

Every patient and person is different, but that's how she wanted it. She wanted to enjoy the time she had left, whether it was a day or a decade.

The fall passed quickly as the tulip magnolia tree in our front yard shed its oblong, deep green leaves, and I prepared the backyard and pool for the approaching, Iowa winter.

Mary Jo, the kids and I busied ourselves with work, school and church activities.

Mary Jo felt and looked good, and she and I even had a few date nights thanks to my mother or hers. We enjoyed an exquisite Japanese meal at Fuji Bay and crossed Sixth Street to see Jerry Seinfeld at the Orpheum Theatre. It was a sold-out crowd, and we laughed almost non-stop.

Also at the Orpheum Theatre, we attended a concert with Michael W. Smith and Steven Curtis Chapman – two of Mary Jo's idols. She was delighted to meet them both backstage where, left alone, the three of them talked about music, kids and church.

Michael was very warm and generous with his time, and he and I even talked some politics, though I kept glancing around, wondering "Is he really interested in talking with me, and hey, is that my wife speaking with Steven Curtis Chapman?"

Silas and Lydia enjoyed school at Clark Elementary – Silas, less so – and Mary Jo and I visited early and often.

Once, I visited in a Darth Vader costume and read a book about spiders to the class.

I was sweating like a sun-drenched pig in the heavy, black costume but was determined not to reveal my identity. I was confident my deep voice – interrupted only by exaggerated, heavy breathing – was a dead ringer for James Earl Jones.

Until one of the kids interjected, "You sound funny, Mr. Hoffman."

Mary Jo relished visiting Silas and Lydia at school, sometimes to read or assist with classroom activities and sometimes just to say "Hi – I love you" and let them know she was there.

Silas' second-grade teacher, Kristin Noreen, had a special bond with Mary Jo, as she was also a cancer survivor. Kristin wrote:

"I will always remember Mary Jo coming into my classroom to read to the kids on days that she felt good. She was sweet and nice and loved her family."

On Christmas Eve, Karen called to tell us Grandma Helen had fallen and broken her hip. Helen came through the hip surgery well but fell again and broke her leg. Facing another surgery to fix her broken leg, she never really recovered.

Near the end, Helen was ready and even anxious to join her beloved husband LaVern. She spoke of heaven with hope, courage and longing.

On March 22nd of 2009, Helen joined LaVern in the next life amongst the angels. Both were 94 at the time of their deaths, buried side-by-side in Bloomfield, Iowa.

The loss was especially tough for Karen. She'd buried each of her parents, even while helping her daughter through a life-sapping battle with cancer and confronting health problems of her own.

It was also tough to share the news with my sweet, darling Lydia since she and the beloved Great Grandmother she called "GG" shared a special bond.

After LaVern passed-away, Lydia had slept with Helen whenever we visited Mason City. I'd often listen secretively and hear them giggling and whispering through the bedroom door.

Helen and Lydia were separated by 86 years, yet they were kindred spirits. Helen often remarked how much Lydia was like Mary Jo – sweet, kind and beautiful.

For Mary Jo's 44th birthday, we planned a much less elaborate affair than the tea party of the previous year.

We invited my parents, my sister Heather and her husband Lucio to join the kids and I for a nice meal. Mary Jo insisted on doing most of the cooking herself, preparing an exquisite meal of sourdough-wrapped beef tenderloin, grilled asparagus and wedge-sliced red potatoes lightly coated with olive oil and kosher salt.

It was a lovely dinner, framed by the use of our Wedgewood wedding china – bone white with a platinum edge, set on silver-plated chargers. Silas exclaimed:

"I've never seen these plates out of the cabinet!"

As a birthday gift, I ordered a bench just like the one Mary Jo sat on when I proposed in the garden at Washington National Cathedral.

The Windsor engagement bench was built of thick, teak wood and had a low back, curved arms and solid, square legs. To Mary Jo's delight, Silas and Lydia pulled back a sheet to reveal the bench. Red satin bows were decoratively wrapped around the arms.

Uncommon but not unprecedented, there was still snow on the ground in April. The month of May, however, brought warm, cloud-free skies and red-breasted robins. May is often the best month in Iowa.

The tulip magnolia revealed its pink and purple blossoms, which soon fell to the dark, mulch-covered ground. Along the driveway, the weeping cherry trees drooped with tiny white flowers, shading the deep green Hostas below.

It was a beautiful May and our little family was eager for new beginnings.

Mary Jo said she "felt great." Her eyes were as bright as her spirit, and she busied herself in the kitchen or visited the kids at school. Silas and Lydia were excited about the end of the school year, looking forward to sleeping-in, swimming and an occasional stay-up-late contest.

For a time, it seemed all was right with the world – or at least our tiny little corner of it. Though I appreciated it at the time – the simple joy of a husband, a wife and two kids sharing laughter and grilled cheese sandwiches – I cherish that time now.

It was far too brief, and we couldn't know we didn't have much time left together.

In June, we invited Marvin and Jane Keitges over for dinner. Marvin and I had renewed our friendship from high school while Jane and Mary Jo became good friends. They were selfless, loving people who were deeply committed to their children. I'd never known better parents – or people.

That night, Mary Jo and Jane spent a lot of time talking while Marvin and I entertained the kids with a *Star Wars* version of Battleship, followed by paper football across the kitchen counter.

The next day, Mary Jo told Karen that she wasn't feeling well, and they called me home from a meeting. Karen had arrived the previous Monday for a visit, staying in the mother-in-law suite in the basement that had become her second home for the better part of a year.

At first, we thought Mary Jo was suffering from the lingering effects of chemotherapy,. However, she was also struggling to catch her breath, so I took her to the emergency room (ER) at Mercy Medical Center, in downtown Sioux City.

After an excruciating wait, Mary Jo's breathing seemed to stabilize. The oxygen mask helped. We suspected pneumonia since she had suffered through it the previous January, but the X-ray was all clear and we were released.

Mary Jo and I were back at the ER the next day. I remember the date because it was our wedding anniversary: June 27th.

The anniversary would be our 11th and last.

At first, it was difficult to know how badly Mary Jo was struggling. Even with one lung and having been hit with the kitchen sink and the bathtub, she never claimed higher than an "8" on the 1-10 pain scale but it was evident she was uncomfortable and struggling to breathe.

Shortly after she was admitted, Mary Jo slumped into my arms and I pulled the call light on the wall. The nurse quickly called a "Code Blue" and a response team was there in 15 seconds.

With my mother taking the kids, Karen arrived in time to see Mary Jo transferred to the Intensive Care Unit (ICU). It was difficult for us to see Mary Jo intubated and placed on a ventilator, but it would get worse.

When Mary Jo awoke, she had lots of questions. Scribbling furiously on a notepad, she first wrote "What happened?!" Then "Is my mom here?" and "Is your mom with the kids?" along with a few others.

I answered them all and she seemed to perk-up, even managing to smile with the tube in her mouth.

The stay in ICU at Mercy would last five days. I slept in a chair in her room or the waiting room.

Karen and Ron visited often, spelling me to spend time with the kids. My mother and sister were a tremendous help. Countless other visitors stopped-by to sit, talk, listen and pray.

Pastor Gene Stockton or his wife, Cheri, came every day. The Stoelting sisters prayed with Mary Jo, as did Don and Linda Wheat – with whom we shared an anniversary date.

After the second day, Mary Jo was extubated and breathing on her own. Her throat was irritated and voice raspy, but it was important for her to tell Karen and I that she loved us. We already knew that, but she said it every day and wanted to keep saying it. She broke down only when speaking of Silas and Lydia, yet insisted, "I want to wait until I'm feeling better to see them."

The respite from the ventilator would not last long.

After an hour, her breathing became labored and she was quickly intubated again and placed back on the ventilator. It was painfully obvious she couldn't sustain breathing on her own.

We soon learned why.

A video bronchoscopy revealed a hole – called a "fistula" – between the lower trachea (windpipe) and esophagus. The pulmonologist was forthright in his assessment.

"The hole is a big one and well beyond our capabilities to treat or repair. I'm sorry," he said.

When I shared the diagnosis with Mary Jo, she was disappointed but not dismayed. She wrote questions, and I answered them as best I could.

We soon made arrangements for Silas and Lydia to visit. Aunt Malinda and a nurse were very helpful in explaining the wires, tubes and equipment so the kids would feel more at ease.

I held our children's hands as Mary Jo wrote to them, though she purposefully didn't write anything about her condition or stay in the hospital. Instead, Mary Jo scribbled questions about Barbies, Legos and what the kids had for lunch.

With the diagnosis in-hand, I turned my attention to a solution and spent the next two hours on my phone or laptop computer.

Four hours later, a charter jet from Mayo Clinic arrived at the airport with a staff of four and enough equipment for a MASH unit.

When I told Mary Jo we were going to transfer her to Mayo Clinic, her only questions was "How much is this going to cost?"[95]

We spent nearly a month in the ICU at Mayo Clinic.

Strange as it sounds, it became like a second home of sorts. Family brought photos, plants and clothing. The staff set-up a second bed for yours truly.

Karen and Ron took turns visiting, sharing babysitting duties with my mother. Family and friends came by daily.

Together, we resolved that Mary Jo wouldn't spend a minute alone – and she didn't.

Obviously though, Mayo Clinic was not a home, and we were hopeful Mary Jo would be treated and released. For their part, the doctors – called "consultants" at Mayo Clinic – worked brilliantly to try to heal Mary Jo.

One of the first procedures the consultants tried was the installation of an esophageal covered self-expanding metal stent to cover and close the fistula.

Similar but much larger than those commonly used for coronary arteries during an angioplasty, the stent effectively closed the fistula but the pressure proved too great for the cancer-weakened wall of the adjoining trachea.

The consultants huddled together to plan additional treatments.

Much of the treatment centered on pain management. The pain management team gradually increased the dosage on the *fentanyl* patch placed on Mary Jo's abdomen, a narcotic analgesic approximately 100 times stronger than morphine.

Eventually, the consultants lowered the *fentanyl* dose and settled on *propofol* for pain management. *Propofol* was a short-acting agent administered via IV and common for ventilated patients.

Sometimes called "Milk of Amnesia" for its milky appearance and effects, Mary Jo was intrigued to learn *propofol* was the drug that killed Michael Jackson.

My brother Eric read Mary Jo the story of Michael Jackson's life and death from *People Magazine*. For Mary Jo's amusement, Eric added a biting commentary in his mountain man accent.

The consultants had some success with placing another esophageal stent and the ventilator was removed.

When Mary Jo was off the ventilator, she spoke quickly, eagerly, though her voice was hoarse and scratchy. When Mary Jo was on the ventilator, she wrote in a three-ring binder.

After the first few days of procedures, Mary Jo and I settled into a routine of sorts as I read to her every day from *Harry Potter and the Half Blood Prince*.

We'd started reading the *Harry Potter* series with Silas and fell in love with the captivating characters and their story.

In her three-ring binder, Mary Jo wrote a few reflections or advice for other cancer patients. She wrote:

Go outside and walk when you can.

You are never too old to have your mother hold your head for you while you are vomiting.

Be appreciative to everyone – be gracious.

On two occasions, Karen spent the night with Mary Jo while I returned to the kids. It was both encouraging and painful to see them playing with Grandma Kathy, Aunt Heather and cousins.

Silas and Lydia wrote cards and recorded messages for their mother. We talked and played cards.

Ron spent a lot of time at Mary Jo's bedside and was a constant source of faith and strength.

During one visit, Mary Jo told Karen and me, "I think I'll start calling Ron 'Dad.'"

It had been nine years since DW had passed-away, and in truth, Ron was more a father than Mary Jo's own father had been.

Ron wasn't surprised when Mary Jo called him "Dad," but he was touched and proud.

Pastor Gene and Cheri Stockton also visited Mary Jo at Mayo Clinic several times. Each time they brought a stack of cards and letters from our friends at Heartland Church.

Kay Copas was one of those friends. She was a great friend and prayer warrior. Kay wrote:

"May your heart sing a beautiful new song of praise…"

Over a two-week period, four of Mary Jo's six best friends were able to visit – first Paula, then Christina, Kathy and Gill.

Mary Jo and Paula Nofziger had been best friends since college. They spoke lovingly and laughed often about Iowa, recipes and children. At one point, Mary Jo explained how to use a whipped cream charger, drawing a picture in her binder for Paula.

Paula treasured the time with Mary Jo and dared not think it might be goodbye. But it was hard not to think of it, and Paula broke down in tears when I hugged her outside Mary Jo's room.

Christina Severinghaus was positive and encouraging. It came easily to her as she was naturally optimistic and friendly, but it wasn't so easy in the ICU of Mayo Clinic.

Christina and Mary Jo spoke of family and even the future. I left them alone for my daily trek to St Mary's Chapel, followed by a stop at the smoothie stand in the Domitilla Building.

Kathy Wise and Gill Abernathy's visits overlapped and Mary Jo was delighted to spend time with them both. When Gill gave me a glance that conveyed "We'd like to be alone with Mary Jo for awhile," I made myself scarce again.

Some time later, Kathy told me they had called it a "Girls Night" and even watched *Mama Mia* on the TV in Mary Jo's room.

Frankly, I was relieved not to have to sit through the movie, as the thought of Pierce Brosnan singing in a musical was more than I could bear. He'll never play James Bond again.

In between the stories and laughter, Mary Jo, Kathy and Gill also shared some deeper conversations and tears. There were some things Mary Jo hesitated to tell even her husband – of struggles with her health and even with God. Kathy said:

Mary Jo told me about the revelation she had about giving up control to God. She had been pleading with God to keep her alive for the sake of her kids, but she realized God was fully able to take care of her kids – and she had married a man who would give his life for them. She needed to release them to God – to be able to release herself to God. I can't imagine anything harder for her to say because she loved her kids and husband so much and fought to live as long as her body could hold on. We wept together.

The consultants and their patient never grew frustrated or disheartened and the staff methodically pursued other treatments.

The intravenous line in Mary Jo's hand was replaced with a peripherally inserted catheter that allowed for extended medications.

Different sizes and types of stents were placed to address the fistula but all failed.

When Mary Jo's mouth became sore and irritated, a tracheotomy was performed to allow her to breathe externally.

A gastrostomy tube was also placed in her stomach for nutrition.

Each time the ventilator was removed, she crashed more quickly than the time before.

Despite the extraordinary efforts of the best doctors in the world, Mary Jo was still in the ICU. Even with million-dollar medical equipment, Mary Jo was not getting better.

She was going downhill.

Unable to speak, her handwriting grew ever more shaky.

Sometimes she would drift off while she was writing, as the combination of *fentanyl* and *propofol* put her in a dreamlike state.

Yet her faith and confidence remained unshakeable, and she wrote in her binder in lucid moments.

On July 29th, she made eye contact with me, smiled wanly and pointed to the lined paper in her binder, where she had written something. She had written:

We gotta take it one day at a time. The big picture can be overwhelming or even scary. So stay with me today – not in the tomorrow – or in mourning the lost past. It still sucks but it's what's been given to us for some reason, and I know we can handle it with God's help. His alone. God has made a way for us to be together. It's all in His hands and we trust Him for victory.

I was amazed she could write something so profound, spiritual and courageous in the midst of such pain and longing. It broke me and I apologized for the tears. But even through the tears, she smiled and wrote again. It said:

"Now, please tell the nurse <u>not</u> to use that scented lotion again – and bring me my iPhone, please!"

Profound, then funny. Spiritual, wise and witty.

The words were perfectly Mary Jo – and they would be her last.

After a time, Mary Jo scratched out a few other words I couldn't decipher and fell asleep with the pen still in her hand.

I embraced her and wept. Ron and Karen joined me and we wept together.

The next morning, Mary Jo seemed to perk up a little bit. She opened her eyes and smiled at Karen and me. Ron led us in prayer and embraced Mary Jo warmly.

However, Mary Jo was in and out of it. When she was awake, I saw her eyes were tired but not sad.

Mary Jo couldn't speak and even writing was difficult, but she communicated as much with her eyes as with a pen.

Her eyes seemed to say she was ready to go home – and not to Sioux City. She was ready to go *home.*

John Donaker was the last friend to visit Mary Jo in the ICU at Mayo Clinic.

Dressed in a short-sleeve plaid shirt and jeans, he sat by Mary Jo's bedside and waited for her to awaken. John spoke words of kindness and encouragement. He spoke of his love and admiration for his cancer buddy and left a message in her book. It said:

Remember I told you I would always be your friend no matter what. You are a special person and you taught me a lot about life. Nobody has fought harder than you have. I love you.

After John left, I pulled in close to embrace Mary Jo and look in her tired but still-beautiful eyes. I stroked her arm and told her I loved her without end or equal.

Then I gave her a manicure while sharing memories, silly stories and the daily news. She looked peaceful. Even in a hospital bed, she looked composed and elegant.

Uncertain of what the next day would bring, I glanced at the lights and readouts of the monitor, kissed her on the cheek and told her I loved her yet again.

Pulling back to hold her gaze, I told Mary Jo I was leaving for Sioux City to get the kids. She nodded gently and looked over at Karen for affirmation.

Before I left, I pointed at Mary Jo, then gestured toward my chest, twisted my fists and opened my palms. It was sign language for "You complete me."

My sign language wasn't very good and I didn't do it quite right, but Mary Jo smiled with recognition. She knew it was something I'd learned from a movie we'd seen on a date night many years ago.

In response, Mary Jo smiled again and raised her hand, extending her thumb, index and pinkie fingers to sign "I love you." I returned it and then I left.

While I was still on the road to Sioux City, Karen called to report Mary Jo had "crashed" again and a team of consultants spent half the night trying to reposition the ventilator tube.

Two more "Code Blue" conditions followed, the second while Mary Jo was on mechanical ventilation.

Our last day with Mary Jo was a surreal blur of shared tears and heavy hearts.

I hugged Silas and Lydia and prayed for strength, yet I had none and struggled with what to say or do.

In the car, I spoke in vague terms of how their mother was "not doing well" while asking about their week with Grandma Kathy and Grandpa Ray.

When Silas, Lydia and I arrived at the ICU waiting room, my parents, sister, Ron and other family members were already there waiting. Karen, Malinda and Chelsey were with Mary Jo.

We prayed together before the family left me alone for the most difficult task any man can ever face. I hugged Silas and Lydia tightly and tried not to cry while attempting to speak. I could hardly breathe.

Gently and carefully, I explained their mother was not going to make it. I said "Mommy's spirit is going home to Heaven to be with the angels" – or something like that.

I don't remember exactly what I said, but I concentrated on hugging my kids as Silas' eyes filled with tears of understanding. Lydia joined her brother in crying into my other shoulder.

I comforted them as best I could while we walked hand-in-hand to Mary Jo's room.

It was the hardest and darkest moment of my life. It felt like carrying an unseen, soul-sapping burden through an impenetrable barrier of grief.

I'd like to say God granted me strength for the walk – that I felt the presence of Jesus lifting the weight from my shoulders – but I felt utterly alone and broken.

When we entered Mary Jo's room, we were greeted by a nurse before my sweet, beautiful children instinctively moved to either side of their mother. They each held her hand.

Both looked at me with understanding, mature eyes and Lydia said "She sure looks pretty."

She did look pretty. Her cheekbones were high and colorful and her hands were lovely and smooth. The nurse had brushed her hair and wiped her face with a washcloth.

Glancing at the monitors, I knew it wouldn't be long before she left us but drew peace and strength from the pure hearts of our beloved children.

Silas and Lydia stroked Mary Jo's arms while I adjusted her light blue gown. I spoke to them about Mary Jo's unfettered love, desire and devotion. I assured Silas and Lydia we would see her again – someday, some way – on the other side.

To tell the truth, I'm not certain what I said. It's been a few years and I don't really want to remember our last moments with Mary Jo in the ICU at Mayo Clinic.

But I do remember Silas and Lydia were as brave and composed as the mother who loved them. Silas and Lydia seemed to understand Mary Jo had really been saying goodbye for a while.

It was time for her to leave us – to go *home.*

Even though she'd encountered pain, suffering and death almost daily, the nurse cried with us as we made colored handprints of Mary Jo's hands.

We stroked her arms and kissed her cheek one last time as we fought through the tears. Silas and Lydia said:

"Goodbye mommy – I love you."

Returning to the waiting room, my parents and Ron's grandkids took turns hugging Silas and Lydia tightly.

Within a few minutes, the kids were playing board games and pitching pennies along the wall and Karen, Ron, Malinda and I left the waiting room to say goodbye to Mary Jo.

It was as heartbreaking for Karen to say goodbye to the beloved daughter who used to hug her neck on Christmas Eve and whisper "Is it Christmas yet?"

It was tough for Malinda too, who used to skip through the puddles with her big sister on the way to Dairy Queen.

Karen, Ron, Malinda and I took turns whispering in Mary Jo's ear. We told her of our unbridled love and affection.

And then – Mary Jo was gone.

The days that followed were sad yet surprisingly busy.

My attention was focused on Silas and Lydia, but the family was quickly overwhelmed with decisions about flowers, plants, jewelry and photographs.

We welcomed the busyness in a strange and distracting sort of way. Perhaps that is how Americans often deal with grief. We get busy.

Though I wrote the obituary and eulogy, most of the many other tasks were checked-off by family and friends.

My sister-in-law Jennifer was a great help as she completed a list of actions items ranging from enlarging a photograph to pulling weeds in the front yard.

Jennifer completed all of her assigned tasks with an efficiency that would've made Mary Jo proud.

It came as little surprise that Mary Jo had left instructions in a small journal. Always organized, scheduling and planning ahead, Mary Jo had written "Funeral." It read:

- Cremation – memorial service only.
- No visitation unless you (Brent) want it.
- Have JoLynn sing if she can.

Unfortunately, I didn't find the instructions until months later.

The day prior to the memorial service, a visitation was held at Meyer Brothers Colonial Chapel just off Hamilton Boulevard. It was just down Lindenwood Street from our home in Sioux City.

I was reluctant to hold the visitation but Karen and Malinda talked me into it and it proved a good decision.

It made the next day's memorial service more bearable. The line for the visitation stretched on more than three hours as neighbors, classmates and politicians graciously passed on their condolences.

The memorial service was held at Heartland Community Church. Team Heartland had transformed the old school gymnasium into a welcoming setting of bright white linens and lights that contrasted nicely with a dizzying assortment of flowers.

Three enlarged photographs of Mary Jo sat perched on easels at the center of the stage, framed by nearly a hundred magnificent, memorial bouquets of calla lilies, tulips and roses of every color.

It was very pretty, and I think Mary Jo would've liked it.

Pastor Gene, assisted by Mary Jo's second father, Pastor Ron, officiated the memorial service. Our friends from Cornerstone Church composed a wonderful, touching video of Mary Jo's life, set to a soaring score.

Ta'Mara sang *Peace in the Valley* accompanied by "Doc" Henderson on keyboard. Carrie Beth and Stacie Ruth also managed to hold it together through a moving Gospel song.

Stacie Ruth also wrote a poem about her "Aunt" Mary Jo.

I wish I could remember more of the memorial service – of people thanked and embraced and of moments poignant and important. But I can't.

It felt like a strange dream as I sat with my children and just tried to fake it through the day.

Silas and Lydia were so brave. They missed Mary Jo in ways no one else could understand, but they were handsome, beautiful and somehow understanding.

As the crowd had filed in for the service, several people noticed the exquisitely felted purses carried by some of Mary Jo's girlfriends.

Paula, Kathy, Gill, Cheri and Jane were a few of the special ladies who brought their handmade multi-colored purses to the funeral. Mary Jo had made 21 of the purses in all, often knitting furiously with wool, alpaca or mohair during chemotherapy treatments.

Jane Keitges treasured her maroon, gray and black purse and clutched the smooth wool handle like a beloved family Bible. Mary Jo had also made one for each of Jane's delightful daughters – Jen and Erin. Jane said:

"It made me smile to see the other purses. It made me feel special."

When it was my turn to speak, I told the crowd of about 500 that Mary Jo had left two simple instructions for her own memorial service. Not the instructions in the journal we'd yet to find, but what she had told me privately. She'd said:

"Absolutely no open casket – and for God's sake, no open microphone."

All who knew her said "Yeah, that's Mary Jo alright" and the chuckles from the crowd helped to temper the sadness.

For the eulogy, I briefly recounted Mary Jo's many lofty achievements.

I told the crowd of Mary Jo's education at Chariton High School, the University of Northern Iowa and George Mason University.

I told them about her experience teaching English as a second language, and working with Senator Grassley.

I shared a little bit about her service to the church as well as her worldwide travels and experiences.

Mary Jo was humble, gracious and generous. She was also gifted with many talents. Old and new friends marveled at how she excelled at nearly anything she attempted.

Mary Jo was a brilliant student and a lifelong learner. When we learned her blood type was "A plus," her mother Karen said "That makes sense – it's the only grade she ever got."

She had the smooth alto voice of a soloist and could play nearly any musical instrument. When asked to serve as a worship leader, she said, "Well, I suppose I could learn to play the guitar."

And she did.

People listened closely when Mary Jo spoke – whether a child, parent or politician.

They listened not necessarily because of what she said but because of who she was. "Her words were like thunder because her life was like lightning."

Mary Jo's interests and talents were nearly limitless and seen in even pedestrian pursuits. Stephanie Laudner said:

"I once saw her start sewing a two-piece suit on Friday night and then wear it to work Monday morning. It was beautiful. Mary Jo was so talented."

Other friends marveled at her talents in different ways. One said she was a "truly remarkable woman" while another observed she "had the heart of a lion."

A congressman said "Of course, I noticed she was beautiful, but it was her talent and personality that was so impressive."

No doubt, Mary Jo Hoffman was talented. And yes, she was also beautiful.

Yet neither adjective really says much about her.

To know Mary Jo as only as a beautiful woman is not to know her at all. Her talents, achievements and interests also shed very little light on what made Mary Jo the woman she was.

Some may think the battle with cancer showed much about the person Mary Jo was – but that's not quite right either. The long battle with cancer didn't *build* her character. The battle she called the "Cancer Diet" only served to *reveal* her character.

If there was one word that best described the essence of Mary Jo, it would not be talent or beauty or achievement.

That one word was *Faith.*

It was Mary Jo's unshakeable faith in God that gave her life purpose, meaning and direction. Faith was her *raison d'etre.*

Faith guided Mary Jo's life as it guided her relationships with other people.

Once, at a training session for Court-Appointed Special Advocates, Mary Jo was asked, "What is the one thing you're most passionate about?" "Faith and relationships, she replied.

Technically, of course, that's two things, but for Mary Jo, they were intertwined and inseparable.

Faith was reflected in her humility, graciousness, kindness and compassion. It compelled her to donate anonymously, give generously and serve selflessly. She was admired for her talent and beauty, but she was beloved for her faith and kindness.

Though supremely talented and accomplished, Mary Jo considered her role as a mother to be her highest calling and far more important than work she'd previously done for CEOs, ambassadors and senators.

At the end, she met God with a ready heart, knowing this is not really the end and without regret of things said or done.

She lived as an angel among us, yet for far too brief a time.

Good Mourning

> "The best and most beautiful things in the world cannot be seen or even touched. They must be felt with the heart."
>
> Helen Keller
>
> *The Story of My Life*[96]

THE GRAVESTONE STANDS UNREMARKABLE AMONG the storied, white-speckled grounds of Arlington National Cemetery, just across the river from Washington D.C.

Like a cotton field about to be picked – the bolls bursting with tufts of white fiber – countless gravestones stand tirelessly against the changing seasons. The white marble contrasts with fields of manicured green grass.

As specified by the U.S. government, the gravestones are nearly identical: Four inches thick, 13 inches wide and 24 inches tall (above-ground). Each weighs about 230 pounds and is carved of Danby white marble in Barre, Vermont – the self-described "Granite Capital of the World."

The number on Mary Jo's gravestone is 3895-5. It doesn't include an engraved epitaph but just eleven lines of text – also mandated by government specifications.

It doesn't feel like it matters, as there are no final, brief words to convey the extraordinary woman she was. It's surreal though, to see "Mary Jo Hoffman" engraved on white Vermont marble.

Surreal. The word resonates in my mind. Alone, I thumbed through the dictionary to make sure I understood the word correctly. "Unreal, bizarre – like a mix of fact and fantasy – dreamlike," it says.

Other adjectives come to mind – somber, melancholy and lost among them. But no, it's surreal. I'm surreal.

Walking timidly through the field of marble markers, I reflect on other times I've walked through this famous cemetery near the Pentagon – as a military officer, as a tour guide, and now as a widower.

Its beauty changes with the seasons as shadows fall with the red, flaming leaves. The crest of each well-manicured hill reveals another row of white stones stretching out the horizon like the middle of a highway. The cemetery is undeniably beautiful, yet it doesn't elicit smiles or wonder.

Looking past Mary Jo's grave, the limestone façade of the Pentagon looms large, though another shape – this one of steel, sunlight glinting – draws the eyes away and upward.

The towering shape belongs to the new Air Force Memorial, with three stainless steel spires soaring more than 200 feet into the sky. The spires bring to mind the contrails of jet fighters in a precision maneuver.

Turning my eyes back to ground, I see shadows growing longer behind trees and headstones, and I remember the shadow of an American Airlines jet passed over these grounds before it crashed into the Pentagon just eight short years ago. It's surreal.

It was early October the first time I returned to Arlington, to bury Mary Jo. Silas and Lydia didn't accompany me on the trip – the three of us would visit the following summer.

There wasn't a gravestone either. It would be added in December.

There was a graveside service, though. It lasted about 15 minutes and was led by Chaplain Charlie Stutts, a distinguished Colonel in the Air Force, dressed in blues and a chest full of colorful medals. Though the sky was cloudless, fall was in the air and gold leaves fell gently from a magnificent oak tree just off Eisenhower Drive.

The small graveside service was limited to 25 people, and the chaplain did a nice job as the small crowd gathered around the gravesite. Before and after the service, smaller groups broke off and huddled together by interest or profession, each representing a different part of Mary Jo's life and legacy.

There was a small group of dear friends from First Baptist Church: Mark Rittgers, Carol Scott, Gill Abernathy, Elaine Gilliam, Kathy Wise, Kevin Bridwell and Sara Bridwell. They shared tears and spoke of Pickett House memories.

I felt sad for Mary Jo's friends. I felt sad for my children. I felt sad for myself.

Wendy Wright was wearing a lovely blue pantsuit and the Venetian glass earrings that used to belong to Mary Jo. I'd given Wendy the earrings at the memorial service in Sioux City.

Mark Disler was one of Mary Jo's favorite lobbyists. He wore black, as did all of the men.

The Handel family – John, JoLynn, Hayden, Holten and Halena – also came to the service after driving from their new home in Pennsylvania.

There was a small group of Grassley staffers – Penne Barton, Kathy Kovarik, David Young and Jill Kozeny to name a few.

Like Senator and Mrs. Grassley, they spoke of Mary Jo but didn't smile much. I thanked Senator Grassley for the touching, personal tribute he delivered for Mary Jo on the floor of the U.S. Senate. It was entered in the Congressional Record.[97]

Looking back, I don't remember a lot about the weeks or months that followed Mary Jo's death. There were tributes, memorials and cards aplenty.

A local television station covered the memorial service and Jessica Cihacek did a marvelous job of capturing Mary Jo's legacy. She said:

"Beautiful, funny, intelligent and kind, Mary Jo was also a woman tied to her faith. She left this world a young and charismatic individual at the age of 44, but she leaves behind a legacy to last a lifetime."[98]

After the memorial service in Sioux City, Grandma Karen and Grandma Kathy took turns hugging the kids while my brother Eric helped me pass out eight pairs of Mary Jo's many earrings to her special friends, including Wendy.

We gave Christina Severinghaus a pair of sterling silver earrings shaped like a leaping King Salmon. I'd purchased the salmon earrings for Mary Jo on our honeymoon in Alaska just after she landed a 36-pounder.

Eric and I gave Paula Nofziger a pair of silver earrings shaped like an oval. A sparkling garnet stone was set in the center. Mary Jo had worn the garnet earrings as long as I'd known her – most recently for a photo with Paula.

The acorn-shaped amber earrings – purchased in Warsaw, Poland – went to Eric's wife Jennifer. She and Mary Jo shared a love of amber.

To my friend Mike Yokitis – who traveled from Virginia – I gave a pair of cuff links I'd worn at the Pentagon.

About a week after the memorial service in Sioux City, another memorial service was held at First Baptist Church in Alexandria, Virginia. It was the church where Mary Jo and I had met and married and where she made friends for a lifetime.

Many girlfriends she'd met through the singles group attended the service, including Sara Bridwell, Elaine Gilliam, Catherine Friend, Carol Mills, Donna Malarkey, Rebecca Bentley Hall and Anita Chastain.

Among others who attended were Kelly Mine, Kevin Bridwell, Ric Williamson, Eric Culbreth, Mike Yokitis, Trevor Friend and Ken Chastain. Marie Grouby attended with her brother Britt.

Sadly, Marie passed away about a year later. Jason and Malinda Mori also attended with many other friends.

There was no shortage of pastors to direct the service, including Jim Witt, who had officiated the wedding for Mary Jo and me at First Baptist Church 11 years earlier.

Mary Jo's buddy Phillip Hurst was also at the service. He'd become a pastor after his stint in the Marine Corps. Roger McGee, Wayne Jenkins and Carolyn Jenkins were three other pastors and friends who attended the service.

Gill Abernathy and Kathy Wise attended all three services, including the one in Virginia. Gill wrote:

"Mary Jo had brought her friends together once again, this time in sadness but even in that, together and knowing the presence of God."

Still surrounded by stacks of cards and a freezer full of meals, the kids and I didn't make the trip to Virginia for the second memorial service. Our home was a temporary mess of chaos and emotion, made bearable only by the selfless support of family and friends.

Though I wrote cards and even took out a newspaper ad, I never felt "Thank You" was adequate for all of the support and attention but friends understood. They were the kind of friends who seldom said "Please let me know if there's anything I can do."

They just *did*.

Though I never asked or even hinted, Shannon Stoeffler and Dennis Benson took turns mowing our lawn.

Coordinated by JoLynn Handel or Cheri Stockton, nearly every member of Heartland Community Baptist Church brought at least one meal to our house. Most of the meals didn't even include a name. They just said "From a Friend."

Aaron Rochester called and said "I'm sending a maid over to clean your house."

My mother helped every Monday with the kids – and Wednesday too. My sister Heather came over every Friday to help with laundry and dishes.

Our little family was overwhelmed with generosity and thankfulness.

In the days and weeks that followed Mary Jo's passing, the mailbox at the end of our driveway was crammed-full with cards and letters. Some were hand-written on stationery by people I'd never met. Many included money. I read them all, some of them to the kids.

"Mary Jo was such a beautiful person both inside and out. She loved well." (Jo Jones)

"I loved her dearly, from the bottom of my heart. She was truly a woman of God. Thank you for the privilege of knowing Mary Jo. She fought hard." (John Donaker)

"Silas and Lydia: It was an honor and a privilege for me to know a true hero like your Mom. She loved you unconditionally and set an example in faith and kindness. I hope you will always remember her faith in God and that He and your Mom await you in Heaven." (Monte Shaw)

"We've lost a woman of great faith and talent, a dear friend – but God has one more angel." (Don & Dora Hadden)

It was a time of grieving and remembrance, but I remember little of it now.

As I once told a reporter, "There are days it feels like another life entirely." I suspect I'm not the only one who feels that way once in a while. It's hard to explain.

Getting my mind around it took a backseat to my relationship with Silas and Lydia. They owned my heart and gave my life purpose and direction. We grieved together. We remembered together. We moved forward together.

Thankfully, we had a king-size bed to help us through it.

It was a thick, plush Simmons Beautyrest advertised as "Better Sleep for the Two of You."

There were three of us, though.

It was an adjustment to share a bed. Silas was in perpetual motion and mumbled in his sleep. His bony body thrashed about and struck yours truly with an occasional elbow to the back or more sensitive areas.

In contrast, Lydia was as soft, peaceful and cuddly as a teddy bear. She clutched her soft pale blue bunny named "Boboo" and was always the first one asleep.

Since sleeping between Silas and Lydia proved too difficult, I eventually decided to sleep perpendicular at the end of the big bed.

It wasn't ideal but it worked for us. Silas, Lydia and I just wanted to be together.

I didn't know how long the sleeping arrangements would last, but we prayed together every night and then talked about most anything.

We talked about go-carts, superheroes, soft pretzels, Scooby-Doo or a thousand other subjects. We still do that and end each night with "Good night, I love you" and a cluck sound, accompanied with a trigger finger. The "trigger cluck" was something we picked up from a cartoon.

Eventually, Silas announced "I think I'll sleep in my own room tonight." Lydia said "Me too."

It had been about five months since Mary Jo passed.

For lack of a better word, it was an *adjustment* to begin life anew as a single father. I hadn't even adjusted to the title "widower" – it just sounded so old and depressing.

The mourning process was not as I expected. I'd read a couple of books and learned more about the process of grief, but that doesn't mean I understood it.

I was told counselors can help with the process, but I didn't consult one. I also didn't consult a roadmap or checklist for the journey through grief. There isn't one.

Grief visits nearly everyone at some point in life, yet it's a very personal emotion and each person must work through it in his or her own way. Grief doesn't come without first loving and those who've lost grieve quickly or deeply, passively or passionately.

In my experience, there were no rules, traditions or tips that felt universally helpful or necessary. True, mourning was accompanied by tears. But sometimes, odd as it sounds, there were smiles.

Some who grieve feel renewed, at peace and ready to move forward in a week. Some never really stop grieving. As I once heard it said, "Your mileage may vary."

There were moments I felt Mary Jo would walk through the door with a bag of groceries and a smile. I felt I could hear her chopping carrots in the kitchen while flipping through a recipe for corn chowder. I expected her to call me for dinner.

Maybe it sounds strange, stupid or surreal – there's that word again – but that's what I felt. Counselors would call this the "denial" stage of mourning.

There came a slow, painful realization that life is not a surreal dream of memories. Mary Jo wasn't coming home.

She would never thumb through her Bible again, sitting peacefully on her favorite red sofa. She would never again kneel patiently beside Silas or Lydia, hug their tender necks and whisper "I love you."

It was gut wrenching, and I wanted to yell out, but I protested silently and sadly, faking it through most days with a painted-on smile.

Though I'd not known it then, this was the "depression" stage of mourning, and it would take some time.

With a choice to bury the grief or embrace it, I generally chose the latter. While the kids were busy with school, I read things Mary Jo had written, watched family videos and listened to sad songs.

Listening to Lionel Ritchie or Diamond Rio, I sang along badly to songs of love and loss. I wondered how life could be so unfair and fate so fickle.

Reading the Bible or a daily devotional, I paused to tell God I felt deserted and betrayed. It was a struggle of the heart between God and me – and I was alone with Him.

Glimpses of sunshine came in bits and pieces – first a few hours, then a few days of joyful comfort. But the memories and mourning would always return at unexpected times and places.

Silas, Lydia and I were surrounded by memories. Walking in the woods of our family farm, we picked berries and talked about Mary Jo's triple berry pie. "It brought $125 at the pie auction," Silas remembered.

Alone, I missed the sound of her voice. I missed her biting wit and the way she called me "pookie" or "B.R."

The former was a term of endearment and the latter usually when I'd done something wrong. I missed her infectious laugh and sparkling smile.

Mary Jo had a beautiful soul, and she left a trail of beautiful memories.[99]

It was only looking backward that I understood the stages or process of mourning.

No analogy proved edifying, though I heard Josh Graves, a pastor and author, best describe it as like learning to walk again. He wrote:

"Mourning isn't magic. Grieving isn't a formula. But it is the way we continue to walk forward, even if we walk with a limp."[100]

As Silas, Lydia and I limped along, well-intentioned acquaintances offered advice or encouragement. However, it often came in the form of clichés.

"You've got to take it one day at a time," one said.

"Time heals all wounds," said another.

And my least favorite: "Everything happens for a reason."

It was a lesson our family learned during Mary Jo's battle with cancer – that people don't quite know what to do or say.

Sometimes people will put on a happy face when what's needed is a good cry. Or vice versa.

When a well-intentioned parishioner patted Mary Jo on the back and said "God will not give you more than you can bear," I gently pulled the lady aside.

"I appreciate you and your heart," I said, "but that's not what Mary Jo needs to hear. And besides, the verse reads 'God will not let you be *tempted* beyond what you can bear.'"

In the frozen food aisle at Wal-Mart – with Lydia in the cart and Silas beside it – we turned the corner and came cart-to-cart with an acquaintance. After we exchanged pleasantries, he leaned down and spoke to Lydia.

"How's your mommy doing?" he asked. Mary Jo had passed-way about three months prior.

I wonder how many other suffering souls have had to endure such lessons. I don't think God likes it.

What I learned through the experience and imparted to my children is that people just make mistakes.

God knows I've made a few.

Words don't come out right. People are at a loss for words. They offer help in the wrong form, time or place.

But here's the thing – it's okay. Really, it's okay. It's hardly ever wrong to just say "I'm sorry," and it's okay to get it wrong sometimes.

It's okay because it's the heart that really matters, and people are just trying to show you they care.

They just want you to know they love you.

Children and adults grieve differently – different ways, different times. That's another lesson I learned.

At first, it was hard for me to understand how Silas and Lydia were so well adjusted, joyous and full of life. I monitored their emotional health closely, yet they seemed to do just fine regardless.

I learned to watch for later cues of underlying grief but also learned joy and happiness from my own children. In other words:

"While we try to teach our children all about life, our children teach us what life is all about."[101]

Silas, Lydia and I also had a lot of fun together.

Surrounded by people who loved us, we played touch football in the backyard and "follow the leader" in the pool. We held family talent contests that lacked talent but not laughter.

I treasured the smiles and hugs of my children and through it, they taught me to keep living – and to enjoy it.

Sometimes, we talked about Mary Jo.

Not often, but lying in bed, I'd share a sweet memory or a funny story and encourage Silas and Lydia to share their own.

Lydia remembered playing Barbie in her bedroom, making an angel food cake in the kitchen. She remembered the Easy Bake oven, manicures and hand massages.

Silas remembered his mom was a great cook. He remembered playing Crazy 8s and reading *Harry Potter*.

We spoke of movies, including Mary Jo's favorite, *The Princess Bride*. Lydia remembered her mom enjoyed Pixar films, especially *A Bug's Life* and *Monster's Inc*.

She and Silas also remembered the last movie we saw together.

Unlike Silas and I, Mary Jo and Lydia were not avid moviegoers but in early June, Mary Jo was feeling good and decided to join us for an afternoon matinee.

It was about three weeks before she would enter the hospital for the last time.

Hand-in-hand, we ambled into the Promenade Theater on 4th Street – a comfortable, state-of-the-art 14-screen theater in downtown Sioux City.

As was our habit, Mary Jo and Lydia found seats while Silas and I got concessions – a large buttered popcorn, two blue raspberry ICEEs and diet cokes. It was always the same.

The movie *UP* had opened the previous Friday to big crowds and stellar reviews, yet I knew little about it – something about a cantankerous, old guy with balloons, I thought. Soon after the curtain parted, we learned the movie was about a widower and had a deep message woven through the high jinx and laughter.

In *UP*, Carl the widower navigates his floating house – held aloft by a thousand colored balloons – to Victoria Falls in Southern Africa. But Carl is a reluctant participant in his own adventure.

He struggles with regret and longing. He misses his beloved wife Ellie and pauses to look through a scrapbook of pictures and memories.

During the movie, our family laughed often – the kids especially enjoyed the talking dogs. But as I held my wife's hand, I also saw tears.

"Mary Jo doesn't cry at movies – what's going through her mind?" I wondered.

Later, Mary Jo and I talked about it, but only briefly because she seemed reluctant to express her emotions.

With a heavy heart, Mary Jo said, "I just want you to remember that message Ellie left for Carl. She wrote it in that scrapbook of memories."

Yes, I remembered the message. It said:

"Thanks for a great adventure...now go make some new ones."

~ Ellie

I understood the message was for me – and for my kids.

With the summer nearly over, Silas and Lydia went back to Clark Elementary School. Lydia was an eager and hard-working student and anxious to return to school – Silas, not so much.

DeeDee Watkins served as Clark's building assistant and became a loving, supportive helper for Lydia. DeeDee stood just shy of five feet, but she was a fireplug of energy and laughter. She was a giant to the children.

Some of the exceptional mothers at Clark also helped to watch out for my kids.

Kelli Heilbuth served as the head of the Parent Teacher's Association and put in as many hours as some teachers.

Holly Hesse was the mother of Lydia's best friend Isabelle, and she frequently invited Lydia over for play dates and hugs.

For the first few months, I stopped by the school nearly every day, often just to share a hug and a smile, and to let my kids know I was around.

A few times, we even skipped school to play mini-golf, take in a movie or go shopping.

When the school secretary asked, "Is the absence for medical reasons or another appointment?" I thought I might be in trouble, but responded honestly.

"Neither," I said. "We're skipping school."

The secretary smiled with understanding. She said "That sounds like a great thing to do – enjoy it."

In the fall, we planted a tree on the school grounds, partnering with a young family who'd lost their son in an accident.

Below the mulch of the blaze maple tree, we installed a brass plate on a cement pad. It included double-sealed time capsules underneath the corners for each of our families.

We did the same at our church and planted a flowering cherry tree, though we'd later replace it.

When the holiday season came around, the loss of Mary Jo felt as acute as ever. Even surrounded by family, I felt like I was completely and utterly alone.

Not lonely, but alone. Not depressed, but mourning.

My heart ached for Silas and Lydia, and so I did what became all-too normal: I faked it.

I smiled and laughed. I joined in Christmas carols and busied myself in the kitchen. I pushed the heartache deeper.

It's not the "right" way to mourn nor would a counselor label it healthy. But anyone who's lost a loved one knows how it feels when that first holiday, birthday or Hallmark moment comes up on the calendar.

It's painful. Something is missing. Someone is missing.

Few people would label Iowa winters "pleasant" and the winter of 2009-2010 was no exception. In fact, it was one of the worst on record.

The first of two blizzards hit on Christmas Eve and dumped nearly two feet of snow on the Sioux City area. The National Weather Service reported at least five inches of snow on the ground for 83 straight days.

On Christmas Day – armed with an infinite supply of chest-high snow and corn shovels – Heather and I resolved to carve a bobsled-like run for the kids down the long slope of our front yard on Sylvian Avenue.

What began as a simple chute design evolved into an Olympian masterpiece, made more challenging by a mid-course bump and a sloping, banked right turn.

Despite the frigid temperatures, Heather and I worked until we were sweaty and exhausted, but were soon rewarded with shrieks of delight from Antonio, Adrian, Silas and Lydia, as they attempted to navigate their saucer sleds through the harrowing, half pipe course.

Before long, cousin Amelia joined the budding bobsled team and the kids exhorted one another to slide ever farther. Soon the bobsled run stretched across the neighbor's lower yard and spilled out onto the street.

The cousins were soon as sweaty as the adults. Silas described it as "superfun."

I'm not sure when it was we began to adjust to the new normal of life without Mary Jo. "Adjust" isn't the right word anyway.

But I know that it came about slowly and surely because of the encouraging love of family and friends, especially my mother and sister.

At first glance, my sister Heather would seem an unlikely partner on a journey through mourning.

Tough, demanding and fearless, she worked as a chef and could handle a knife (or an employee) like a belt-fed machine gun.

Though my father Ray was known as a no-nonsense businessman, he turned to Heather when it was time to fire someone.

By her own admission, she wasn't a good listener. Her pet peeves were Democrats, laziness and whining – in that order.

Heather was a paradox of personality. Short with fools, she was infinitely patient and kind with those in need.

A tough veneer covered a sensitive, kind heart and a nurturing, motherly nature. She was a hard worker with an unyielding spirit. She adored children and dogs.

Within a month of Mary Jo's passing, Heather selflessly restructured her own life and schedule to support our family.

Sensitive to our new life, she began by dropping off exquisite desserts like 18-carrot cake.

Later, she took Lydia shopping. She took Silas to a movie and then discussed sports cars and basketball over a waffle cone treat at Cold Stone Creamery.

Nearly every visit, Heather brought a new outfit for Lydia. Every Friday, she brought Antonio and Adrian over to play and then did my laundry or helped with the dishes.

She did my laundry for two years. Two years.

When Silas, Lydia and I spent a later winter in California, we returned to find Heather had stuffed our deep freeze with more than 60 homemade entrees and desserts. The simple sight of the aluminum foil covered dishes brought tears to my eyes, yet Heather refused to take credit or payment.

When I tried to express my love and appreciation by sending "Thank You" notes, she said "Oh stop, I enjoy it."

No man could ever be blessed with a better sister – or a better friend.

The Friday play date evolved into a new family tradition we called "Pizza and Movie Night."

It began with pizza from El Fredo's or Little Caesar's, followed by a family movie like *The Last Mimzy* or *Matilda*.

Eventually even the kids tired of pizza, so my mother, sister and I took turns preparing meals like teriyaki buffalo wings or chicken corn chowder. Many of the recipes were taken from Mary Jo's expansive recipe book.

Instead of movies, we also substituted TV shows like *River Monsters* or played Wii games but the title remained. It was always "Pizza and Movie Night."

My mother and I had always been close. She was a phenomenal grandmother, always generous with her time and affection and so much fun.

She and Heather took turns ministering to our little family in a thousand different ways, from dishes to dolls. My parents were also very generous and wrote a check for a trip to Disneyworld.

Mary Jo and I'd talked about taking the kids to Disneyworld, but it was usually followed by comments like, "When the kids get older, they'll appreciate it more."

It was Sara Bridwell's idea to go to Disneyworld, and she and Kathy Wise made all of the arrangements. Both Sara and Kathy were experienced Disney travelers, and the kids and I wanted for nothing.

With Kevin Bridwell standing beside us, we were transfixed as the Disney characters performed their first song and dance number in front of the magic castle.

Lydia actually gasped when she first saw Cinderella – resplendent in blue and white chiffon. For Silas, the highlight was staying out with Sara until closing time (2:00 a.m.). They rode the Space Mountain roller coaster through the dark again and again.

It was a magical experience, and I cherished the reflection of fireworks in the eyes of my sweet children. They were happy.

Several days after returning from the "Happiest Place on Earth," I found something unexpected in a small, cherry wood buffet in the kitchen.

More like a nightstand, the buffet had one of those small, forgotten drawers that served as a gathering place for kid's toys, rubber bands or a long-lost book.

The drawer also contained a treasure. It was Mary Jo's small, spiral journal.

The inside cover of the cork-bound journal was inscribed with a note from Paula Nofziger, who had given it to Mary Jo as a gift.

Though I didn't remember it, the journal appeared well used, and it was filled with Mary Jo's distinctive handwriting. It also included a brief letter she'd left for me. It read:

You are the best earthly thing that has ever happened to me – the best friend, husband and father to our children. I'm not certain how or why because I certainly didn't deserve it, but God was so good to me when he brought me you. Thank you for being by my side – especially through all of this because I know this has been incredibly hard. I'm so proud to be your wife and feel incredibly honored to be by your side. I know we've talked about it before, but my only regret in life is that we didn't meet and marry sooner. You were worth the wait – I've never enjoyed life more.

Mary Jo had apparently written the letter before she went in for lung surgery and when I read it, I cried. Wiping the tears, I read it again and a warm smile came over me like the noonday sun.

I didn't feel regret or sadness. I felt proud.

Surely, it was even more difficult for Mary Jo to write a letter to Silas and Lydia. But she did. I imagined her agonizing over it, wondering if or when her beloved children would read her "last words."

The page was crinkled and the light blue lines faded – faded by her tears, I'm certain. Mary Jo wrote "To Silas and Lydia,"

I never thought two people could change my life so radically but you both did. Being your mother has been the greatest joy of my life and you are both amazing. Silas, you are so intelligent, inquisitive and full of energy and ideas. You are much like your father, which is a terrific thing to be! And Lydia, you are beautiful inside and out. Your sweet, patient, sensitive spirit is a blessing to all who meet you. And funny – you are both the funniest kids I know with great senses of humor. I love to hear you both laugh.

My prayer for both of you is that you will trust Jesus with your whole heart and believe Him. Not just believe *in* Him but believe Him. God is our everything – creator, protector, provider, redeemer – and we can rely on Him to do what He says He can do. Live your life for Him and you will never be disappointed as long as you are following Him.

Signed "Your loving mother," the letter was a lasting treasure for my children.

I first read the letter to Silas and Lydia while sitting in the king-size bed. To my surprise, they didn't cry even though we spoke of how we missed Mary Jo. We spoke of how she lives on in our hearts and watches over us.

In a clear but quiet voice, I told my children "She must be pleased to know we're enjoying life – and she will love you forever."

One day, I took off my wedding ring. I'd noticed the platinum and gold band had lost its luster, so I took it off, cleaned it and put it away.

That night, I also took off the lavender colored silicon wristband I'd worn since Mary Jo first entered chemotherapy. The *Powerport* imprint on the band had worn off long ago, but I had a hard time letting go of it.

Lydia was the first to notice the ring wasn't on my finger. When she asked about it, I explained my desire for the white, faded skin on my finger "to heal, kind of like my heart – you know what I mean, honey?"

Looking up at me with a sweet, precious smile and the sparkling blue eyes of her mother, Lydia said:

"Daddy, when you get to Heaven someday, mommy is going to run to you."

I hugged her tight, but she didn't cry.

I did.

15

Life After

> "Life can only be understood backwards; but it must be lived forwards."
>
> Søren Kierkegaard

THINGS ARE DIFFERENT NOW. MY eyes no longer fill with tears when I think of Mary Jo, not because time heals all wounds, but because her memory inspires joy and peace, not sadness.

Like fragments of a forgotten dream, the memories come in bits and pieces, unexpected, struggling for color and detail. They are not memories of life-changing events, but of simple, beautiful moments or "little wonders," as I once heard it described.[102]

Mary Jo is still beautiful in my memories. Her smile is radiant.

In my memories, we're riding the Eurostar bullet train to London and Mary Jo is giddy with excitement. She's wearing a plum-colored jacket. Her long, chestnut hair is full and flowing, as she turns to me with a smile.

In my memories, she sits contently on a blue and white beach chair with a book in hand, watching the turquoise waters of the Mediterranean breaking to the shore. She seems lost in thought, yet happy. She sees me watching her, and she smiles.

In my memories, the kids are with us. We're hunting morel mushrooms in the timber as the sunlight filters through a canopy of old-growth oak trees, with a light-brown carpet of leaves underfoot. Lydia's hand is in mine, and I look back to see Mary Jo and Silas trailing, their eyes trained to the ground. Mary Jo looks up, and she smiles.

There are other memories. My mind visits them from time to time, probing and pausing like a hummingbird before a nectar-laden flower. I remember things Mary Jo said or did – things meant to guide and inspire our little family to move forward with joy and hope.

I remember the gift cards, and I think of Mary Jo when I see one at the check out stand at Wal-Mart, or displayed by the counter at Starbucks.

She'd often ask me to pick up a few of the cards.

Clutching the small stack of colorful plastic cards, she'd bow her head in prayer and then rise to write a name on the card in her familiar, cursive scrawl.

Next, she'd put a gift card in an envelope, sometimes including a Post-It note with a brief message like "From a Friend." Other times, she dropped gift cards in the offering plate as it passed, confident it would end up in the hands of a person who needed it.

Every once in a while, I'd learn of a praise report from church or overhear a conversation about a blessing passed on through an anonymous gift card.

Mary Jo said nothing – and neither did I.

Privately, I questioned the practice.

"Wouldn't it be better if we gave the gift cards to Heartland Church, recording it so we could take a tax deduction?" I asked of Mary Jo. Perhaps the question reflected my self-centered heart or my disciplined, rational nature – I don't know.

Mary Jo, however, had a different perspective and her response was selfless and edifying. She said:

I understand what you're saying – and that would be okay. But would it be *better*? No, I don't think so. That's not to say it's wrong, but I like it this way. It brings praise to God. It warms my heart. I feel God's presence and affirmation. It makes me smile. That no one else knows of it is irrelevant. God knows. That's what matters.[103]

Even when no one was looking, Mary Jo was a kind and beautiful soul. She was a rare person of faith, character and courage. She lived with joyful abandonment and without fear or concern for the expectations of other people.

Mary Jo lived only to please God, and she pleased Him not by what she said, but by what she did. She pleased God by the way she lived.

Mary Jo left a remarkable legacy not because she was famous, but because she was selfless. Mary Jo's words were like thunder because her life was like lightning.

"Just in case I don't make it," she said, once.

That's how the conversation began – or at least that's how I remember it. It was an unplanned, quiet conversation in the car between a husband and wife.

I remember her words with clarity because she poured out her heart. She shared her dreams of life after for her husband and children, and she did it with eloquence and sweetness.

Mary Jo listed a few special gifts to pass on to her friends and family. "Please give the amber to Jennifer," she said.

Her voice cracked only when she spoke of Silas and Lydia. She shared her prayerful desire for them to live with faith and courage.

She continued by sharing suggestions of places we might live and things we might do. She challenged me to embrace God's calling – to make a difference.

Passionate and pure, Mary Jo's words flowed like rain, and I interrupted her just once. It was when she said, "I'd also like you to remarry, to find love again, and for my kids to have a new mother."

She said it matter-of-factly.

I was caught off guard, but Mary Jo was poised, and I sensed she must've put some thought into it. My hunch was confirmed when she gave me a list of three women she had picked out, then explained why she felt each would make a "good match."[104]

Then, Mary Jo said:

I just want you to be happy and not sad – to live life with joy and not regret. You and the kids deserve a **life after** as beautiful as the life you've shared with me, should it come to that. I want you to know that. I need you to want that. No matter what, please promise me you'll keep moving forward, B.R. – and don't make me have to hurt you.

She said it with a smile, without tears, as she punched me on the arm.

Mary Jo was selfless and always thought of others before herself, even to the end. Perhaps more than any characteristic, that faith-borne selflessness was what made her an exceptional wife and mother, daughter and friend.

She inspired all around her to live with love and generosity.

Silas, Lydia and I miss Mary Jo, but we aren't sad about it and confined to a past of mourning.

Paradoxically, her selfless love and legacy didn't make it "harder" to move forward. Not that working through the grief was easy – it was hard, painful – but the memory of her love instilled courage and confidence.

Silas, Lydia and I relished each moment beside Mary Jo, and there have been no regrets, second guesses or thoughts of living in the past. Mary Jo inspired us to live and love with confidence. She inspired us to look to the future with joyful, ready hearts.

Her beloved son Silas doesn't often speak of his mother, but Mary Jo still dwells in his heart, as do her talents. He amazes his father daily with a brilliant mind, though unlike his mother, he's not a diligent student and easily bored with school.

With the inquisitive mind of a lawyer, his friends still think he'll be president someday, but I wouldn't wish that on anyone. He has a fun-loving, adventurous nature and enjoys football, movies and playing with Aunt Heather and his cousins at the family farm.

"Go outside and don't come back until you're good and dirty," I tell him, playfully.

Mary Jo would be proud. People tell me that often, and I know they're right.

Lydia reflects Mary Jo like a mirror – beautiful, sweet and selfless. A gifted student, she's creative, artistic and introspective.

Always helpful to her father, Lydia delights in time with family and friends or seated before a blank canvas with acrylic paint and brushes in hand.

People often remark of her beauty, as she has the lovely skin and regal presence of her mother. She also has an eye for fashion, but it's her selfless heart and spirit that shines. It's not that she *looks* beautiful. She *is* beautiful.

I'd write more, but it sounds like I'm bragging.

My relationships with friends and family have changed. Some relationships are closer or more intimate, and some are different or distant. I understand, and it's okay.

Sometimes, they ask about our plans, curious or prayerful of what the future holds for our little family. Given our situation, the question is understandable. It's also one I would've answered differently in past years, when I set three, five and seven-year goals and worked hard to achieve them.

But things are different now. I don't have a bucket list, nor do I desire to go skydiving before I'm 50.

So when asked, "Will you remarry someday?" or "Where do you see yourself in five years?" my answer is consistently non-specific.

"The next five years are in God's hands," I say. So are the next five minutes.

I'll never forget Mary Jo. She was my wife, and she taught me how to live and love. She cherished each day and gave the precious gift of life to my beloved children. She was a woman of valor.

She also challenged me to "Keep Moving Forward." She taught me to live with joy. Silas, Lydia and I have some great memories, and Mary Jo inspired us to go make some new ones.[105]

If you're reading this, I hope you'll make some memories of your own.

I think Mary Jo would smile to know of it. It was a smile that lit up hearts.

It still does.

End Notes

[1] Though the Farmall (International Harvester) tractor would later be identified by its all-red color (in contrast to the now-famous green of the John Deere), early Farmall tractors were painted gray. The company switched to "Farmall red" in late 1936.

[2] 2 Thessalonians 3:10.

[3] "Hawkeye Point" is often visited by "Highpointers," whose goal is to reach the highest point in each state. LaVern and Helen's great grandson, Silas, would later visit Hawkeye Point with the family of Timothy Scott, a Highpointer, and describe it as "pretty cool."

[4] Iowans have long taken pride in their status as the leading agricultural state. I recall the dismay and disappointment years ago when Iowans learned we'd dropped to #2 in hog production, surpassed by North Carolina.

[5] "A Brief History of Davis County," 2011.

[6] Wikipedia, Bloomfield, 2011. Sadly, Roland died in 1937 as a result of a trapeze fall in Tennessee.

[7] Though none of the early buildings of Mark remain standing, the Mark Baptist Church remains a vibrant gathering place for the area. It was moved nearer to Hwy 63 and expanded in 2003.

[8] Some early residents spell it "Centreville," but maps and other documents record it as "Centerville."

[9] DW shared this with the author when we first met. I shared it at his funeral a few years later.

[10] "The History of Appanoose County, Iowa." Western Historical Co., Chicago. Wikipedia, retrieved Dec. 13th, 2008. In 1995, Hy-Vee moved its headquarters to West Des Moines, but retained a distribution center in Chariton.

[11] Three of the last four books in the series were published posthumously. *West from Home* was published in 1974. *The Road Back* was not published until 2006.

[12] Mary Jo had a good relationship with her cousins. On the McMains side, Phil and Linda had two kids – Cree and Jennifer. Charles and Judy had two boys – Doug and Dennis. On the Archibold side, Jo Ellen and Ken Johnson had two kids – Kim and Joel. Jim and Marsha had four kids: Alan, Aaron, Andy and Anita. Mike and Bunny had two kids – Holly and Michael.

[13] The traditional definition of "kissing cousin" is any cousin who is not a first cousin.

[14] *The Chariton Leader*, "Lucas County native advises Grassley on Washington duties," by Sherrie Barber, June 18th, 1996.

[15] According to a story on CNN ("Pac Man turns 25"), Pac Man would go on to generate more than $2.5 billion in quarters by the 1990s. Please pardon the extended video game details, as the author once owned a video arcade and attempted a world record with "Asteroids." One quarter and 18 hours later, I finally realized it was a colossal waste of time.

[16] Peter "Catman" Criss, the drummer, sang lead on "Beth," backed by a string orchestra, outfitted in KISS regalia. Though KISS is probably best known for "I'm Gonna Rock and Roll all Night," this soaring love ballad was their biggest hit. Also ironic, though written as a tribute to the wives of the songwriters (Criss & Stan Penridge), their wives were named Lydia and Becky, not Beth. They first titled the song "Beck" (after Becky) but Gene Simmons of KISS convinced Criss to go with the more feminine-sounding "Beth" for this love ballad.

[17] Paraphrased from a quote attributed to Clyde Kluckhohn: "Every man is like every other man, like some other men, like no other man."

[18] Sonia Jones (Sterrett), Class of 81, Anthon-Oto High School. The "she's all that" of Anthon-Oto, Sonia was the homecoming queen and class valedictorian.

[19] Endorsement in 1980 Chariton "Charger" annual, signed Marla (Piersbacher). Another endorsement signed Rachel (Mathes). No last names given for Ken and Tammy.

[20] www.uni.edu, "History of Black Hawk County."

[21] Sadly, Rev. Thomas Hammond was killed in a car accident in Michigan in 2009.

[22] www.lighthousekc.org

[23] History of First Baptist Church of Alexandria, "Celebrating Heritage and Anticipating the Future."

[24] Interview, Pam Parry, Baptist News Service. Published in *Christian Single*, July 1994.

[25] *The Chariton Leader*, "Lucas County native advises Grassley on Washington duties," by Sherrie Barber, June 18th, 1996.

[26] Excerpt from "My friend Mary Jo, A Collection of Memories and Stories," by Elaine Gilliam.

[27] Card, Nancy Thompson, "God Be Near You," August 2009.

[28] Interview, Jim Witt, February 1st, 2012.

[29] Though Mary Jo felt hurt by Jed, he called her years later and apologized. He said he felt God encouraged him to call, and he was genuinely pleased to learn Mary Jo was a wife and mother. Mary Jo said, "I felt Jed showed some character, and it was good of him to call."

[30] Satay is a popular dish of marinated, skewered meat, usually chicken. Mary Jo kept the invitation to the Singapore Embassy, dated June 21st, 1996.

[31] Quote of "friendship caught on fire" attributed to Bruce Lee.

[32] *As Good as it Gets,* Tristar Pictures, 1997. Melvin Udall, played by Jack Nicholson.

[33] Mary Jo and I later planned to go to Hawaii for our 10th anniversary, but she got sick, and it never happened.

[34] Due to military rules, and her visa, Mary Jo could not stay on-base or at the hooch longer than 90-days at a time.

[35] There were two American commanders during my tour in Araxos. Lt Col Don Sparks was well liked and very knowledgeable when he was sober. Lt Col Salvador Egea was neither well liked nor knowledgeable. As to the report, it was titled "A Strategic Alliance – Ending the MUNSS Mission in Europe." It was not well received at senior military levels, but would later gain attention from senior military leaders when I was reassigned to the Pentagon.

[36] There were three "Corinths" in the area: Corinth, Acro Corinth and Ancient Corinth. Paul's famous sermon to the Athenians is recounted in the Book of Acts, Chapter 17.

[37] *For Your Eyes Only*, United Artists, 1981, starring Roger Moore as James Bond.

[38] We traveled to Warsaw at the invitation of Michael and Dorota Wyganowskas to deliver a "Big Wheel" to their daughter Julia. Babington's Tea House sits at the base of the Spanish Steps in Rome. *Caffe Florian* is a coffee bar on St. Mark's Square and a contender for the title of "world's oldest coffee house." The "Bridge of Sighs" (*Ponte dei Sospiri*) connects the old prisons to the Doge's Palace in Venice. It was said prisoners would sigh at the view of Venice as they were taken to their cells.

[39] Continuous training is a fact of life for a nuclear weapons officer, but this temporary duty assignment was for Squadron Officer School. I'd previously requested a permanent assignment to the southwestern U.S. and was selected to serve as an instructor in nuclear weapons maintenance at Kirtland Air Force Base in Albuquerque, NM.

[40] Phone call and email to/from Captain Geoffrey Bacon, HQ AFPC/DPASL, February 18th, 1999.

[41] The assignment back to the Pentagon proved ironic because I was able to lobby for the end of the NATO mission at Araxos. The American presence ended at Araxos in January 2001.

[42] Glencarlyn Road Baptist Church continued to struggle, eventually voting to disband and presenting the church building as a "kingdom gift" to Columbia at Crossroads in 2005.

[43] Excerpt from "My friend Mary Jo," A collection of memories and Stories," by Elaine Gilliam. Also source of quotes from Sara Bridwell and Kelly Mine.

[44] The NNMC was rechristened Walter Reed NNMC on September 14, 2011, shortly after the closing of the Walter Reed Army Medical Center.

[45] The "Apgar Score" was developed in 1952 by an anesthesiologist named Virginia Apgar, but is more commonly known as an bacronym: Appearance, Pulse, Grimace, Activity, and Respiration.

[46] *The Sioux City Journal*, by Michele Linck, August 11th, 2011.

[47] Silas is featured prominently in the Book of Acts, Chapters 15-17. The other names were considered before Silas were Andrew, Reed and Jonas.

[48] Other scholars have noted "Silas" is derived from Aramaic ("asked for") or a form of the Hebrew "Saul." "Silas" is the Greek version of the Latin or Romanized "Silvanus." Some scholars have suggested it may also be derived from pre-Roman Italian languages, such as "Asilas" – an Etruscan leader and warrior-prophet.

[49] www.myfamily.com, Mary Jo Hoffman, June 20th, 2008.

[50] Silas started sleeping with this quilted, Pottery Barn pillow around his first birthday, I think. Though it was never quite like a security blanket, he slept with it until he was nearly 10. When going through his baby stuff, I asked him what he wanted to do with it and he said, "Can you frame it?" I did just that.

[51] Card, "What is Motherhood," Alice Turner, November 2000.

[52] www.myfamily.com, Mary Jo Hoffman, December 23rd, 2003.

[53] www.myfamily.com, August 12th, 2004.

[54] Even the legendary purple water fountain – a long–time navigational landmark in the first basement – became less useful after renovations.

[55] Interview, KTIV, Matt Breen, September 11th, 2005.

[56] Based on interviews and analysis, it's believed the pilot was targeting the White House, but it's a difficult target to spot from the air and the

pilot decided on the Pentagon. It's believed the target for Flight 93 was the Capitol building.

[57] The National Transportation Safety Board estimated maximum speed during the dive at approximately 530 miles per hour (See memo, February 19th, 2002). The fuel capacity of a Boeing 757-200 is 11,489 gallons so 9,000 gallons is an estimate of fuel remaining at the time of impact. As to the number of people on board, most early accounts ignored the terrorists on board when calculating the loss of life. In fact, there were 53 passengers, 6 crew and 5 terrorists on board, for a total of 64 people. With such a large population in the Pentagon, you'd expect a much greater loss of life, but the west side (Wedge 1) had only recently completed a renovation and was nearly vacant. This was, of course, little comfort to the family and friends of the 125 people inside the Pentagon.

[58] Calculated distance from office to point of impact using Google Earth.

[59] There was a brief, panicked debate within our office, with one Major saying, "Everybody just stay in place!" Buddy's reaction seemed to make more sense, and the rest of us followed suit. He later joked, "I had Major Hoffman's footprints on my back." The latter quote is from an interview with KCAU-TV, Staci DaSilva, September 11th, 2011.

[60] Quote from interview with the *Des Moines Register*, September 11th, 2011. Other reflections previously published in a column I wrote for the *Sioux City Journa*l, titled "A Day to Remember, September 11th, 2011.

[61] Interview, KCAU-TV, Stacy DaSilva, September 11th, 2011.

[62] Letter, White House Military Office, September 12th, 2001. Later, during a security review, a liaison learned of my efforts to close Araxos AB in Greece and "Major Hoffman's history of challenging the chain of command." They didn't like my answers to the questionnaire, and as a result, the White House withdrew the request.

[63] The first letters with anthrax spores were mailed on September 18th, 2001. This is an abbreviated version of one of the letters.

[64] Though not widely reported, the terrorist snipers – Muhammed and Malvo – viewed themselves as Islamic Jihadists. See trial exhibits 65-006 – 65-117.

[65] Others have suggested "Lydia" is of Germanic origin, meaning "of noble, or of a noble sort," but the scholarship better supports a Greek origin.

[66] Type 1 diabetes is an autoimmune disorder, often brought on or revealed through a virus where the body attacks itself and destroys the ability of the pancreas to produce insulin. Insulin is required for the body to process food and convert energy. Type 1 diabetes is markedly different than the much more common Type 2 diabetes.

[67] Each year, the National Civic League honors ten cities in America with the All-American City Award. *Money Magazine* named Sioux City a Best Place to Live in its August 2010 edition.

[68] www.siouxcityhistory.org

[69] As quoted in a consultant's report for the City of Sioux City and Siouxland Chamber of Commerce in 2004.

[70] Sioux City was previously home to a Dunkin' Donuts, but it closed in the 1990s. In 2012, *The Sioux City Journal* reported, "Sioux City picked for new Dunkin' Donuts franchises," Dave Dreeszen, January 19th, 2012. Mary Jo would be pleased.

[71] *The Sioux City Journal*, "New Sioux City Councilman Brent Hoffman takes office Tuesday," by Lynn Zerschling, December 31st, 2005.

[72] *The Sioux City Journal*, "Someone's in the Kitchen With the Hoffmans," Joanne Fox, May 3rd, 2006.

[73] Email, Author, "Thoughts on High School Relationships," July 19th, 2006.

[74] The original story, "Olive Garden Arrives, by John Quinlan, ran in *The Sioux City Journal* on December 10th, 2006. It later went viral and was spoofed by the Huffington Post and Gawker, among others. Ironically, it became the most read story on www.siouxcityjournal.com

[75] *The Chariton Leader*, "Lucas County native advises Grassley on Washington duties," by Sherrie Barber, June 18th, 1996.

[76] According to Woodbury County records dating to 1972, for a six-candidate regular election. Quote, *The Sioux City Journal*, "Sioux City voters elect Hoffman, Ferris and Rixner; Van De Steeg ousted," Lynn Zerschling, November 9th, 2005.

[77] Letter to the Editor, Mike Antonovich, "Opening the Door," *The Sioux City Journal*, December 18th, 2005. Letter to the Editor, Jill Flynn, *The Sioux City Journal*, January 21st, 2006.

[78] Councilman Jason Geary sent the ill-advised email in a reply-all response to a brief email I'd sent about a pending news story (I was out of town). I was livid. Mary Jo and I were also upset when we got the letter about the kitchen, but we later got a letter of apology from city inspectors. Councilman Geary was immature and seeking attention, yet in fairness, I also became hard-hearted. After his landmark defeat, I figured Geary was done with politics, but he made a bid for the Iowa State Senate just three years later. I then encouraged Bill Anderson to run and agreed to run his campaign. Geary dropped out and Anderson went on to serve in the State Senate.

[79] *The Sioux City Journal*, "Council doesn't pray out loud, but two ask for the Lord's intercession," Lynn Zerschling, July 2nd, 2008.

[80] This conversation actually occurred later, during a trip with the kids to Mayo Clinic and back. But I just like it better here, and it's indicative of the kinds of conversations we had with the kids when traveling. Mary Jo wrote it down on www.myfamily.com on May 5th, 2007.

[81] Paraphrased by Joel Siegel, "American Morning," CNN, June 13th, 2003.

[82] Description of Stage IIA lung cancer from www.cancer.gov

[83] Radiation description from www.nylencancercenter.com Dr. Naden, as quoted in *The Sioux City Journal*, by Lynn Zerschling, June 17th, 2007.

[84] Drugs are listed with their generic rather than trade name.

[85] Cost reference from www.inspire.com lung cancer support group.

[86] www.myfamily.com, Mary Jo Hoffman, July 13th, 2007.

[87] Email, Bobbie Lee Sheffield, February 19th, 2011.

[88] "Jesus Bring the Rain," from *Coming Up to Breathe* by Mercy Me, INO Records, 2006.

[89] Email, Jo Jones, May 8th, 2012.

[90] Card, "Thinking of You," John Donaker, 10-3-07.

[91] www.myfamily.com, Brent Hoffman, August 18th, 2008.

[92] Partially quoted in *The Sioux City Journal*, by Lynn Zerschling, June 17th, 2007.

[93] *The Sioux City Journal*, "Vote Canvass Breaks Tie in Mayoral Primary," Lynn Zerschling, October 12th, 2007.

[94] www.myfamily.com, Mary Jo Hoffman, May 18th, 2008.

[95] The Mayo jet cost $10 grand, and I had to guarantee it on my credit card. However, Wellmark First Administrators reimbursed me and was courteous and professional. One later bill from Mayo Clinic was a staggering $340 thousand dollars.

[96] Letter to the Rev. Phillips Brooks, June 8, 1891, reprinted in Helen Keller's biography. It's likely this saying came from Anne Sullivan, and the quote has been modified over the years to this more well known version.

[97] Senator Chuck Grassley, *Congressional Record*, Vol. 155, No. 122, August 6th, 2009.

[98] Two stories were aired on KCAU-TV, August 2nd and August 5th, 2009. Mrs. Grassley, Pastor Stockton and Councilman Rochester were interviewed.

[99] Paraphrased, quote (author unknown): "Wherever a beautiful soul has been, there is a trail of beautiful memories."

[100] Fox News, Opinion, "Is there Such a Thing as Good Mourning?" Dr. Josh Graves, July 1st, 2012.

[101] Quote attributed to Angela Schwindt.

[102] *Little Wonders* music and lyrics by Rob Thomas for Disney's *Meet the Robinsons*, 2007.

[103] After Mary Jo passed away, I sent an email with the subject line "Life After" to friends and family. In the email, I shared some reflections about Mary Jo's life, including this story. A few of those friends encouraged me to write a book.

[104] Mary Jo also told me she was inspired by a story she'd read, though Jim Witt later filled in the details. As Jim told it, the couple was from First

Baptist Church of Alexandria and the wife was dying of cancer. As a selfless gift, the wife left her husband with a list that included three of her best friends and was hopeful he would choose to marry one of them. He did. Mary Jo thought it was a touching, even romantic, story. She also shared it with her mother and two of her girlfriends.

[105]"Keep Moving Forward" was an informal motto we adopted after watching *Meet The Robinsons.*

BIOGRAPHY - AUTOBIOGRAPHY - MEMOIR

MARY JO HOFFMAN lived an extraordinary life—not because of what she said, but because of who she was. Her words were like thunder because her life was like lightning.

Life After tells her inspiring story of faith and courage. It begins on the rolling prairie of an Iowan farm; shifts through the corridors of power in Washington, DC; and ends with what Mary Jo called the "Cancer Diet."

But it doesn't really end there.

As the author writes, Mary Jo Hoffman was admired for her beauty and talent, but she was beloved for her faith and kindness. She left a legacy of faith and relationships, and her story continues to inspire all who read it.

Life After is a story of faith, relationships, and a few lesser things. It inspires and enlightens with every turn of the page.

BRENT "B. R." HOFFMAN lives in Iowa with his children, Silas and Lydia. He served a distinguished career as a military officer and survived the 9/11 attack on the Pentagon. He holds degrees from Newman University and the University of South Dakota, among others. Brent has founded several community organizations and served in public office. *Life After* is the story of his late wife, Mary Jo.

Mr. Hoffman can be contacted through his website at
WWW.BRHOFFMAN.COM

U.S. $22.95